KU-297-314

Football and Migration

Football is an incredibly powerful case study of globalisation and an extremely useful lens through which to study and understand contemporary processes of international migration. This is the first book to focus on the increasingly complex series of migratory processes that contour the contemporary game, drawing on multi-disciplinary approaches from sociology, history, geography and anthropology to explore migration in football in established, emerging and transitional contexts.

The book examines shifting migration patterns over time and across space, and analyses the sociological dynamics that drive and influence those patterns. It presents in-depth case studies of migration in elite men's football, exploring the role of established leagues in Europe and South America as well as important emerging leagues on football's frontier in North America and Asia. The final section of the book analyses the movement of groups who have rarely been the focus of migration research before, including female professional players, elite youth players, amateur players and players' families, drawing on important new research in Ghana, England, Haiti and the Dominican Republic.

Few other sports have such a global reach and therefore few other sports are such an important location for cross-cultural research and insight across the social sciences. This book is engaging reading for any student or scholar with an interest in sport, sociology, human geography, migration, international labour flows, globalisation, development or post-colonial studies.

Richard Elliott is Associate Professor and Director of the Lawrie McMenemy Centre for Football Research at Southampton Solent University, UK. He received his PhD from Loughborough University. His expertise lies in the areas of globalisation and migration in football where he has published widely. Regularly consulted by the professional football industry, he has worked in conjunction with the Football Association, the Premier League, the Professional Footballers' Association, the League Managers Association and professional clubs. He also provides expert opinion for the media, appearing in print, on radio and television in the UK and internationally.

John Harris is Reader in International Sport and Event Management at Glasgow Caledonian UniLIVERPOOL JMU LIBRARY Sport and Identities Research Cluster. He is author of *Sport and Globalization* (Palgrave Macmillan, 2010) and has published widely on aspects of international football.

Routledge Research in Sport, Culture and Society

Football and Migration

Perspectives, places, players

Edited by
Richard Elliott and John Harris

Routledge
Taylor & Francis Group

LONDON AND NEW YORK

First published 2015
by Routledge

2 Park Square, Milton Park, Abingdon, Oxon OX14 4RN
711 Third Avenue, New York, NY 10017, USA

Routledge is an imprint of the Taylor & Francis Group, an informa business

First issued in paperback 2016

Copyright © 2015 Richard Elliott and John Harris

The right of the editors to be identified as the authors of the editorial
material, and of the authors for their individual chapters, has been asserted in
accordance with sections 77 and 78 of the Copyright, Designs and Patents
Act 1988.

All rights reserved. No part of this book may be reprinted or reproduced
or utilised in any form or by any electronic, mechanical, or other means,
now known or hereafter invented, including photocopying and recording,
or in any information storage or retrieval system, without permission
in writing from the publishers.

Notice:

Product or corporate names may be trademarks or registered trademarks,
and are used only for identification and explanation without intent to infringe.

British Library Cataloguing-in-Publication Data
A catalogue record for this book is available from the British Library

Library of Congress Cataloging-in-Publication Data
  Football and migration : perspectives, places, players / edited by Richard
  Elliott and John Harris.
    pages cm
  ISBN 978-0-415-73978-8 (hbk) — ISBN 978-1-138-69524-5 (pbk) —
  ISBN 978-1-315-81638-8 (ebk)   1. Soccer—Social aspects.
  2. Transnationalism.   I. Elliott, Richard, 1950-   II. Harris, John, 1972–
  GV943.9.S64F645 2015
  796.334—dc23
                                                        2014014638

Typeset in Times
by Keystroke, Station Road, Codsall, Wolverhampton

RE – For Isabelle and Toby
JH – For my boys Thomas Wyn and Iestyn James

Contents

Illustrations

Figures

Tables

Contributors

Editors

Richard Elliott is Associate Professor and Director of the Lawrie McMenemy Centre for Football Research at Southampton Solent University, UK. He received his PhD from Loughborough University. His expertise lies in the areas of globalisation and migration in football, where he has published widely. Regularly consulted by the professional football industry, he has worked in conjunction with the Football Association, the Premier League, the Professional Footballers' Association, the League Managers Association and professional clubs. He also provides expert opinion for the media, appearing in print, on radio and on television in the UK and internationally.

John Harris is Reader in International Sport and Event Management at Glasgow Caledonian University, UK, where he also leads the Sport and Identities Research Cluster. He is author of *Rugby Union and Globalization* (Palgrave Macmillan, 2010) and has published work on numerous aspects of international football.

Chapter authors

Sine Agergaard is a social anthropologist and an associate professor employed at Section for Sports Science, Aarhus University, Denmark (and formerly in the Department of Exercise and Sports Science, University of Copenhagen). Her research on migration issues within sports has been published in a number of articles and books. She is the co-editor of *Women, Soccer and Transnational Migration* (Routledge, 2014). She is currently the head of a collaborative research project, financed by the Nordic humanistic and social scientific research council, studying the case of women's soccer migration.

Paul Darby is Reader in the Sociology of Sport at the University of Ulster. He is author of *Gaelic Games, Nationalism and the Irish Diaspora in the United States* (University College Dublin Press, 2009) and *Africa, Football and FIFA: Politics, Colonialism and Resistance* (Frank Cass, 2002). He is co-editor of *Emigrant Players: Sport and the Irish Diaspora* (Routledge, 2008) and *Soccer and Disaster: International Perspectives* (Routledge, 2005). He sits on the

Foreword

Figuring out sport migration: old maps, new trails

Joseph Maguire

Despite the research conducted over the past 20 or more years, sport migration is still typically portrayed as something to celebrate, reflecting an individual's right to move, and is thus viewed in unproblematic terms. However, sport migration is bound up in a sports medical-industrial complex, which is itself embedded in a series of power struggles that characterise the global sports system in general. We now know that such migration is marked by figurations involving athletes, owners, administrators, agents, officials and media personnel. These interdependencies are multi-layered and incorporate not only economic, but also political, historical, geographical, social and cultural factors. Thus, in seeking to explain global labour migration, a broad approach involving an examination of wider societal processes is required, an approach that finds expression in this valuable collection by Richard Elliott and John Harris.

Part of the migration process, and requiring greater attention, are questions of globalisation, national identity and inter-cultural communication, as well as more specific matters relating to, for example, 'talent pipelines', stereotyping and the ascription of qualities to athletes from different countries and ethnic and gender groups. Concepts such as established–outsider relations can be usefully deployed to capture the dynamics involved. The migration of athletes, and others involved in the sports medical-industrial complex, occurs within nations, between nations located within the same continent and between nations located in different continents and hemispheres. Movements of athletes, from their home town to their place of initial recruitment to elite or professional sports clubs and national teams, are part of these processes. Sport migrants tend to be 'hired' by a specific club or organisation and individuals reside in the host country for a limited period. However, some migrants make the host country their 'home' through marriage to a citizen, by having stayed 'attached' for a sufficient length of time to qualify for nationality status, or by being 'fast-tracked' by nations such as Qatar. In certain sports, migration has a seasonal pattern. The northern and southern hemispheres offer in sports such as cricket what amounts to two seasons of continuous play. Other sport migrants experience a transitory form of migration: in golf, the workplace is a constantly shifting tournament venue on the global circuit. For IOC and FIFA officials, travel is expressed through the Olympic network or the so-called FIFA family. How, then, have social scientists explored these trends over the past twenty or more years – what does the current map of global sport migration look like?

Social scientific research into sport migration emerged in the 1980s (Bale & Maguire, 1994). Since then, research, confined initially to Europe and North America, has spread across the globe (Maguire & Falcous, 2011). Several research themes have developed, which find expression in the work contained in this collection. These include, first, which sports are most involved, why have they been so affected, and what structural or cultural changes have thus occurred in those sports and in the societies in which they are located? Second, what are the patterns of global movement and how and why have they developed in this manner? Third, what has been the impact of and on fans in their own migration as 'tourists' or as part of a diaspora, and their perception of the sports they consume? Fourth, what has been the impact on 'host' and 'donor' countries more broadly? Fifth, why do 'professional' athletes and others within the figuration become labour migrants, how is this process contoured and shaped, and what do they experience along their journey? Sixth, in what ways does such migration reflect the movement of highly skilled workers more generally? Seventh, what implications are there for sport policy and for the domestic and foreign policies of nation-states more broadly?

From what we already know it is clear that sport labour migration has engendered hostility in some host countries. Sport labour unions have sought to protect indigenous workers by arguing for quotas and qualification thresholds to be applied to potential migrants. This resistance was matched by those concerned with the development of national teams – focusing on the development of players. Rarely is attention given to the other members of the sports medical-industrial complex. Questions of attachment to place, notions of self-identity and allegiance to a specific country are significant in this connection. Since the early writing on sport migration, there have also been significant changes in the transnational labour market, and comparisons can be drawn between the 'highly skilled' in other occupations and elite sport migrants. Over the past three decades, 'flexibility' has been a key theme in the transnational labour market. This, in part, stems from the intensification of globalisation processes, one aspect of which is the deregulation of the financial markets – with all its recent side effects. Aligned to these changes has been a global restructuring of business practices, reinforced by developments in information technology and transport/communication systems. With this growth in chains of 'glocal' interdependencies, formal and informal translocal communities have developed, and migrants' traditional 'bridgeheads' have become enhanced and realigned. In this connection there has been, in particular countries and sectors of the employment market, a shift from traditional settler migration to the more transient migration of the highly skilled. This latter process has also been fuelled by the demands on transnational corporations to brand and market themselves as 'world firms' in an increasingly flexible and globalised service community. Sport clubs such as Barcelona and the New York Yankees and global associations such as FIFA and the MLB have adopted similar strategies.

The movement of highly skilled human capital has increased significantly in terms of scale, pattern and composition. Elite sport migrants are another example of the highly skilled whose movements reflect and reinforce the changes realigning the nation-state. The associated debate has moved on from simply a discussion of a 'brain drain' to a consideration of 'brain exchange' and 'brain circulation' as well. With elite sport migrants, both 'brawn' and 'brain' are involved. That is, the drain, exchange and circulation of sport migrants involve performers, coaches, scientists, administrators and educators – vividly evident in the Olympic movement. This broader process involves development through sport with all the attendant rhetoric of building a better world, and all the associated reality of consumption and exploitation.

In examining whether the recruitment of foreign migrants is 'good' or 'bad', questions concerning power, culture and control of sport arise. What counts as good or bad depends on who decides and by what criteria – whoever defines what counts as 'success' succeeds in the contested process of sport migration. Stakeholders in this conflict include those promoting the commercial success of clubs or the prestige of the national team; entrepreneurs striving for short-term viability and officials concerned with long-term development; those who market the spectacle to the media; and those who advocate local identity and player development. These tensions have arisen in a range of sports and, as the chapters in this collection demonstrate, are likely to intensify in the foreseeable future. In addition, by directing our attention to the study of one specific sport, namely association football, Elliott and Harris, and their fellow contributors, have captured how the dynamics of migration play out along the fault lines of different societies and wider migrant trails. In doing so, they have added further to this burgeoning area of research and fruitfully suggested some new trails to follow.

References

Bale, J. and Maguire, J. (1994) (Eds.) *The Global Sports Arena: Athletic Talent Migration in an Interdependent World.* London: Cass.

Maguire, J. and Falcous, M. (2011) (Eds.) *Sport and Migration: Borders, Boundaries and Crossings.* London: Routledge.

Perspectives, places and players

An introduction to football and migration

John Harris and Richard Elliott

The words football and migration feature prominently in the everyday discourse of nations across the globe. In a number of different places football is the national sport, and the game provides "an important organizational framework for enhancing national connectivity alongside state-sanctioned strategies of integration and legitimation" (Giulianotti & Robertson, 2009, p.102). For many people, football is more than just a game and forms an intrinsic part of their most important and valued identities. Whilst the late Liverpool manager Bill Shankly's exhortation that football is much more important than life or death may well have been overstated, it cannot be disputed that the game *is* important and that it matters to people on a number of levels. Indeed, football can provide something of a comfort blanket for many migrants as they adapt to the trials and tribulations of living in a foreign country – not least the elite professional players who may (or may not) have sound support structures in place but still find that it is only on the pitch that they really feel comfortable, or the numbers of amateur players who, for one reason or another, find themselves in an unfamiliar environment.

Discussions regarding migration continue to occupy the political sphere and a range of other sporting and media discourses. It remains a contemporary and contentious issue in many locales, with debates centring upon factors such as whether immigrants are a force for good or a drain on national economies. In football, there has long been a debate in regard to the tensions created between the impacts of outsourcing and national protectionism. These tensions have accentuated in recent years as the sport has undergone considerable change and, as many of the contributors to this collection note, the numbers of players regularly criss-crossing the globe in search of the best employment opportunities have increased.

What the various chapters in this collection show is that there is now a much more fluid and complex relationship between the local and the global, one that moves beyond an overly simplistic binary division. Scholars have discussed various aspects of sport and employed terms such as "glocalisation" (Giulianotti & Robertson, 2007) and "grobalisation" (Andrews & Ritzer, 2007) to look at the ways in which the local and the global interact with one another. The first of these, adapted from the Japanese concept of *dochakuka*, which means global localisation, highlights how global processes are always understood in a local context (Robertson, 1992). Here, for example, whilst football may be played globally, the game takes on different meanings in particular places. What is important for the discussions presented in this collection is that each recognises the points of intersection and moves beyond simple demarcations.

One of the consequences of the increased interdependence of football cultures at local, regional, national and transnational levels is that patterns of migration between host and donor countries can be more easily identified. Movement, in a targeted and specific manner, is increasingly facilitated through a series of flows where links are developed and foster a series of movements between places. The identification of talent pipelines can be used to help make sense of migration, by observing the transitory patterns in the movement of athletes. Football is particularly important here as the game encompasses a greater number of migrants than any other sport.

Much of the rhetoric, and indeed many of the discussions, relating to sport would seem to suggest that migration is largely a bad thing. In some spheres it is as if migration is a problem spiralling out of control, with a series of different discourses lamenting the inevitable 'brain drains' that emerge as a result of emigration or the moral panics that develop as a result of mass immigration. Yet it is generally noted that in total only around 3% of the world's population reside in a nation outside of that within which they were born. Of course, this figure changes markedly in different places and amongst divergent groups. A recent reflection on the position of migration scholarship noted that "we were all still guilty, to varying degrees, of using our national (and sometimes regional) frames to analyse migration in other contexts or of claiming to find general properties based on our national experiences" (Levitt, 2012, p. 493). Such an analysis highlights the importance of positioning and understanding each case within a particular cultural context. We hope that the broad selection of places and players that form the focus of this collection does this.

Contemporary research on migration has moved away from questions of assimilation and integration to focus more on the dynamic and complex processes that shape the issue (see, for example, Delanty *et al.*, 2008; Harzig *et al.*, 2009). Such a trajectory reflects the scholarship on sport that discusses how, rather than being fixed and static entities, our identities are better understood as provisional, contingent and relatively unfixed (see MacClancy, 1996; Harris & Parker, 2009). Logemann (2013, p.2) recently observed that we now see an emphasis on "multiple, shifting, and hybrid identities, on transmigrants who oscillate between countries and between national, ethnic, and cosmopolitan affiliations, and on the transnational networks and institutions they build and sustain". Giulianotti and Robertson (2009, p.104) have noted with reference to football that:

> As transnational migration processes intensify, and as players explore their complex genealogies, so greater numbers of 'dual citizenship' or 'multi-national' elite players will emerge, and football will reflect the ethno-national heterogeneity of nations.

The fluidity and complexity of life for migrants who play the game in a number of different places forms a large part of the discussion that follows within this collection. Before outlining the chapters, it is important to outline a brief overview of sport and migration as a subject of academic research.

Sport, migration and football in a global perspective

The study of sport and migration has developed exponentially in the last twenty years. This reflects both the accelerated trajectory of the study of globalisation and the continued development of sport as a subject of academic research. Bale and Maguire's (1994) edited collection the *Global Sports Arena* was a key marker in this development, and it is fitting that some twenty years on Joseph Maguire has kindly provided the foreword for this collection. For three decades he has been influential in shaping the field of research concerned with the sociology of sport and sport labour migration more specifically. His contribution to the discipline, and this particular area of it, is evidenced in a wide and varied range of publications, with the more recent co-edited collection *Sport and Migration* being one of his latest substantive contributions (Maguire & Falcous, 2011).

Described by Giulianotti (1999) as the global sport *par excellence*, football offers a particularly interesting site to further examine the subject of migration in sport. Armstrong and Giulianotti's edited collections on various aspects of football have contributed a great deal to the sociological analysis of the sport and offered erudite and wide-ranging examples of the different ways in which the game matters (e.g. Armstrong & Giulianotti, 1997, 2001). To look at the game in a global perspective, it is also important to recognise the contribution of a number of other academics that have paved the way in ensuring that football is now a rich area of academic study. The breadth and scope of the work undertaken to date means that it is impossible to recognise here all the authors who have made an important contribution to the subject area, but, given the inter-disciplinary nature of this collection, it is evident that almost all of the most influential works will be referred to at some point in the pages that follow.

These will include Lanfranchi and Taylor's (2001) overview of migration in professional football, a text that provides a comprehensive historical appraisal of the subject. Wagg's (1995) edited collection on the game across five continents is another important text that provides diverse insights into the sport within and outside of the core football nations. Sugden and Tomlinson's (1998) work on the governance of international football has capably showed the ways in which power relations shape the very heart of global governance. With the ongoing debates surrounding the staging of the 2022 World Cup in Qatar, much of what they highlighted in their research seems even more prescient now. Their book exposed some of the corruption within the sport and was one of the first studies that challenged the ways in which the game was governed in the international sphere.

Other scholars, including some of those who contribute to our text here, have made significant impacts on the research base in the wider area of international football, and their work has provided a platform to enable us to offer a collection such as this. Our book has aimed to build upon these solid foundations by including chapters from those with backgrounds in geography, history, anthropology and sociology. These individuals come from a number of different nations, and their particular areas of expertise allow us to look at cases from across the world and focus on nations and/or issues that may not always have been at the centre of sport migration research.

Our aim then is to offer a broad overview of the subject area and to explore both similarities and differences in the experiences of migrants across a range of locales. Yet this does not mean that we claim to offer the definitive and final account of this subject, for it is clear that there are numerous other nations and/or particular groups that could be included, and in work of this kind there will always be some omissions. Some of these areas will be discussed in the final chapter, where we bring together the key themes of this collection and make recommendations for the direction of future research.

It would be remiss of us not to acknowledge the great speed with which changes now take place in the game. An example to clearly illustrate this would be the increased ownership of football clubs by foreign investors in England over the past few years. As in all social science scholarship, it is important to recognise the situated limits of any views put forward, given that all knowledge is historically and contextually bound and is framed through a process of reflexive mediation where the author's experiences are central (Sparkes, 2002).

By looking at the game at a number of different levels, and in a diverse range of places, this collection adds to the extant literature on football and migration by highlighting the many ways in which players move with the ball. It also includes subjects that have received considerably less attention in the scholarship to date, such as the migration of female players, the place of recreational football amongst migrant groups, and the role of the family in the decision-making process.

In trying to create this text, we were pleased to be able to secure the services of the group of scholars that have been part of this project. We strived to put together a squad of contributors comprising experienced professionals, internationally known figures and some stars of the future. Like developing a football squad, it was about achieving the best balance and putting together the right collection of people. It should be noted that many of the contributors have themselves moved between nations and experienced life as migrant workers. This alone does not automatically lead to an authoritative knowledge of the subject, but it may well foster a certain sensitivity to, and perhaps empathy with, some of the issues touched upon within the respective studies.

Outline of the book

Perspectives

We have already referred to Pierre Lanfranchi and Matthew Taylor's (2001) work on the history of football, which has long been recognised as a key text in the development of this subject area. In outlining some of the important perspectives on football migration research, it is important that an historical appraisal of the subject is presented. In Chapter 1, Lanfranchi and Taylor offer an overview of some of the early transnational networks in the game. This highlights the ways in which such work may move beyond the confines of the nation-state to fully embrace the possibilities of transnational or transcultural perspectives. In Chapter 2, Richard Elliott provides an overview of some of the increasing migrations being made in football through a range of conceptual lenses. Informed by a sociological approach that shapes his ongoing work into various aspects of international football migration (e.g. Elliott & Weedon, 2010; Elliott & Harris, 2011; Elliott, 2013), Elliott uses three particular aspects of player migration to develop this analysis. Such an approach highlights the interdependent multiplicity of processes that encompass migration in a range of contexts.

In Chapter 3, Raffaele Poli and Roger Besson offer a brief synopsis of some of the data they collect in their annual demographic studies at the CIES Football Observatory. Their contemporary analysis offers some visible insights into the range and scale of migration within the top division leagues of Europe and is important in contextualising the scale of migration in the game. Some of the statistics they highlight, such as the number of Brazilians in many of these leagues or the movement of Irish players to particular locations, are explored further in subsequent chapters of this collection.

Places

Like many undergraduate students studying sport at British universities, John Harris first ventured to the USA as a coach during the summer months and this shaped a long-standing interest in the somewhat peculiar place of football (soccer) in a country where football means something else altogether. The description of what most of the world refer to as football by a different name (soccer) points to the somewhat marginal status of the game in the national sporting landscape and is further explored in Chapter 4, which relates to the inter-relationship of the USA with other parts of the football world. This is followed by the contribution of Carmen Rial, who, in Chapter 5, examines diverse aspects of the displacements of Brazilian football players. Brazil is the most successful football nation at international level and is the world's largest exporter of football players. Rial's research shows how many of these players experience life in something of an institutional bubble that, on occasion, serves to distance them from local cultural contexts.

In Chapter 6, Seamus Kelly focuses on the case of Ireland. This research, shaped in part by his own experiences as a goalkeeper who moved across the Irish Sea to undertake a professional contract with Cardiff City Football Club, examines the micro-cultural features of professional football dressing rooms. Kelly's work points to how young migrant players cope with chronic insecurity and deal with the deconstruction of their identity following rejection from professional football. Chapter 7, by Jung-Woo Lee, examines the socio-cultural implications of football migration in his native South Korea. Lee investigates the globalisation of South Korean football and the migration of football labour. His analysis shows that, as a semi-peripheral country within the football world system, South Korea is actively engaged with the global movement of football labour. In Chapter 8, Gyozo Molnar examines the migration of football players into the Hungarian league. Molnar has, in the last decade, researched various aspects of football in Hungary (see Molnar, 2006, 2011). His contribution here further extends this body of work and analyses the reasons why players migrate to the Hungarian leagues and the problems they face. Molnar then uncovers some of the lived experiences of those plying their trade in these leagues and frames these within and around the work of the cultural studies scholar Raymond Williams (1977).

Players

Much of the published work on football and migration, and indeed the bulk of the discussion in the chapters outlined above, focuses specifically on the experiences of elite adult male football players. Our aim in the Players section is to begin to explore the experiences of other groups and to look also at different stages and influences on the migration process. This part of the book begins with the work of Sine Agergaard, who, in Chapter 9, looks at the transnational migration of elite female football players. In some ways, a glance at the literature in this area would seem to suggest that migration refers only to the experiences of male athletes. Agergaard's (2008) work on Danish handball was one of the first studies to focus on the experiences of elite female athletic migrants. In her contribution to this collection, a study of the composition of the top national squads in women's football, Agergaard highlights the fact that top-level football is still only available to women in a small number of countries. Her research also points to the outsourcing of talent and player development to the USA.

In Chapter 10, Gavin Weedon looks at the experiences of a particular migrant youth player in the top level of the English game. Weedon traces issues of adjustment, education and contractual uncertainty in a highly competitive environment. Paul Darby has long been recognised for his ground-breaking work on football in Africa (see, for example, Darby, 2002, 2010), and in Chapter 11 his co-authored contribution, with Nienke van der Meij, considers the role of the family in the decision-making processes of young Ghanaian players. Both of these case-study discussions show some of the tensions inherent in the migration process for youth players. The rich narratives of the young football players they have spoken to offer illuminating insights into the lived experiences of this specific group of migrants and many of the challenges they face. This remains an under-researched aspect of the experiences of migrant football players and offers directions for further work in this area.

In Chapter 12, the final chapter in this section, Nick Wise and John Harris hone in on the experiences of a group of Haitian recreational football players who live and work in the Dominican Republic. This study, based on ethnographic fieldwork undertaken by Wise, moves beyond the world of elite professional football and highlights the symbolic value of the game for migrants at the everyday level (see also Wise, 2011). It addresses the importance of sense of place in shaping sport within a particular locale.

Finally, we offer some concluding comments and attempt to bring together the main arguments put forward in the text and to point the way forward for future research on football and migration. We reflect upon the material presented within this collection and try to tease out some of the most pressing issues. It is a most interesting time to be looking at this topic, as the game continues to grow and change at a remarkable speed. The legendary Liverpool and Wales striker Ian Rush is often quoted as stating that his short time playing in Italy was like living in a foreign country. Whilst Rush may never have actually uttered these words, the point is a valid one and moving between nations can be an incredibly tough experience. We hope that this collection sheds further light on aspects of the migration process and highlights how football is a very important part of the global sporting landscape.

References

Agergaard, S. (2008) Elite Athletes as Migrants in Danish Women's Handball. *International Review for the Sociology of Sport* 43(1): 5–19.

Andrews, D. and Ritzer, G. (2007) The Grobal in the Sporting Glocal. *Global Networks* 7: 135–53.

Armstrong, G. and Giulianotti, R. (1997) (Eds.) *Entering the Field: New Perspectives on World Football*. Oxford: Berg.

Armstrong, G. and Giulianotti, R. (2001) (Eds.) *Fear and Loathing in World Football*. Oxford: Berg.

Bale, J. and Maguire, J. (1994) (Eds.) *The Global Sports Arena: Athletic Talent Migration in an Interdependent World*. London: Frank Cass.

Darby, P. (2002) *Africa, Football and FIFA: Politics, Colonialism and Resistance*. London: Frank Cass.

Darby, P. (2010) 'Go Outside': The History, Economics and Geography of Ghanaian Football Labour Migration. *African Historical Review* 42(1): 19–41.

Delanty, G., Wodak, R. and Jones, P. (2008) (Eds.) *Identity, Belonging and Migration*. Liverpool: Liverpool University Press.

Elliott, R. (2013) New Europe, New Chances? The Migration of Professional Footballers to Poland's Ekstraklasa. *International Review for the Sociology of Sport* 48(6): 736–50.

Elliott, R. and Harris, J. (2011) Crossing the Atlantic from Football to Soccer: Preliminary Observations on the Migration of English Players and the Internationalization of Major League Soccer. *WorkingUSA: The Journal of Labor and Society* 14(4): 557–70.

Elliott, R. and Weedon, G. (2010) Foreign Players in the Premier Academy League: 'Feet-Drain' or 'Feet-Exchange'? *International Review for the Sociology of Sport* 46(1): 61–75.

Giulianotti, R. (1999) *Football: A Sociology of the Global Game*. Cambridge: Polity.

Giulianotti, R. and Robertson, R. (2007) Recovering the Social: Globalization, Football and Transnationalism. *Global Networks* 7: 166–86.

Giulianotti, R. and Robertson, R. (2009) *Globalization and Football*. London: Sage.

Harris, J. and Parker, A. (2009) (Eds.) *Sport and Social Identities*. Basingstoke: Palgrave Macmillan.

Harzig, C., Hoerder, D. and Gabaccia, D. (2009) *What Is Migration History?* Cambridge: Polity.

Lanfranchi, P. and Taylor, M. (2001) *Moving with the Ball: The Migration of Professional Footballers*. Oxford: Berg.

Levitt, P. (2012) What's Wrong with Migration Scholarship? A Critique and a Way Forward. *Identities: Global Studies in Culture and Power* 19(4): 493–500.

Logemann, J. (2013) Europe–Migration–Identity: Connections between Migration Experiences and Europeanness. *National Identities* 15(1): 1–8.

MacClancy, J. (1996) (Ed.) *Sport, Identity and Ethnicity*. Oxford: Berg.

Maguire, J. and Falcous, M. (2011) (Eds.) *Sport and Migration*. London: Routledge.

Molnar, G. (2006) Mapping Migrations: Hungary Related Migrations of Professional Footballers after the Collapse of Communism. *Soccer & Society* 7(4): 463–85.

Molnar, G. (2011) From the Soviet Bloc to the European Community: Migrating Professional Footballers in and out of Hungary. In J. Maguire and M. Falcous (Eds.) *Sport and Migration*. London: Routledge (56–70).

Robertson, R. (1992) *Globalization: Social Theory and Global Culture*. London: Sage.

Sparkes, A. (2002) *Telling Tales in Sport and Physical Activity*. Champaign, IL: Human Kinetics.

Sugden, J. and Tomlinson, A. (1998) *FIFA and the Contest for World Football*. Cambridge: Polity.

Wagg, S. (1995) (Ed.) *Giving the Game Away: Football, Politics and Culture on Five Continents*. London: Leicester University Press.

Williams, R. (1977) *Marxism and Literature*. Oxford: Oxford University Press.

Wise, N. (2011) Transcending Imaginations through Football Participation and Narratives of the *Other*: Haitian National Identity in the Dominican Republic. *Journal of Sport & Tourism* 16(3): 259–75.

Perspectives

1 Mobility, migration and history

Football and early transnational networks

Pierre Lanfranchi and Matthew Taylor

With some exceptions, historians have contributed relatively little to the considerable scholarship that now exists on the migration of footballers. In certain respects, this is hardly surprising. The migration of football labour on a vast scale is often regarded as a phenomenon of the late twentieth and early twenty-first centuries. The bulk of the academic research on the topic has been generated by sociologists, geographers and sports studies scholars intent on explaining the nature and implications of what has become a major feature of world sport since the 1990s, and a powerful symbol of the increasing interconnectedness of cultures and societies in a global age. Examples of player mobility from earlier periods tend to be utilised as background to, or context for, later developments. This is not to suggest that historical processes are insignificant in this work. Tracing migration over long periods of time has been an important part of the research of Bale (2004), Darby (2000, 2007), Giulianotti (1999), McGovern (2002), Magee and Sugden (2002), Maguire (1999), Maguire and Falcous (2011), Molnar (2006), Poli (2004, 2006) and many others. Yet the present-centred focus of much of the literature, and an assumption, perhaps, that there is relatively little to say about migratory movements prior to the 1970s and 1980s, seem to have dissuaded historians from entering the debate. There have been exceptions, of course. A section of chapters in Bale and Maguire's (1994) ground-breaking *The Global Sports Arena* led the way, followed by the present authors' book-length treatment of the history of international football migration and some more recent historical interventions on subjects such as Algerian players in France (Frenkiel & Bancel, 2008), Africans in Europe more generally (Dietschy, 2006; Alegi, 2010a, 2010b), foreign footballers in Austria since 1945 (Liegl & Spitaler, 2008a, 2008b), female players emigrating from Scandinavia and around Europe (Botelho & Skogvang, 2013; Williams, 2013) and Irish professionals in mainland Britain (Curran, 2013). Often published in interdisciplinary sports, or history of sport, journals, this work has engaged productively with ongoing debates, though it has had little impact on mainstream academic history.

That said, prevailing historiographical trends offer promising signs of a rise of interest in the topic. Historians generally, and those working on sport in particular, have taken some time to think and work beyond national frameworks. The nation-state has generally been considered the natural and basic unit for writing and teaching history, with identities of various sorts emerging out of the tensions within and between nations. However, since the 1990s historical perspectives that focus exclusively on the nation have increasingly been under challenge. A convergence of approaches ranging from histories of cross-cultural transfer, entangled or connected history, *histoire croisée* and the overarching and increasingly popular transnational history has meant that historians of all stripes are now more likely to interrogate the nation as an analytical category. These overlapping approaches share "a common interest in the crossing of borders between nations, regions, continents or other spaces, in all kinds of encounters, perceptions, movements, relations and interactions between them, and in the way they perceived, influenced, stamped, and constituted one another" (Kocka & Haupt, 2009, pp.19–20). They have meshed with related developments, such as new imperial histories, with their focus on networks, webs of connection and vantage points away from the metropolitan centre, and the growth of writing on global history (Ballantyne, 2003; Lester, 2006; Sachsenmaier, 2011). Migration, not surprisingly, has been a central theme in all of these approaches. As the eminent migration historian Dirk Hoerder (2009) has argued, it is only relatively recently that scholars have moved beyond nation-centred readings of migration to fully embrace the possibilities of transnational or transcultural perspectives. In this view, overlapping social spaces, urban spheres, connected cities, contact zones and meeting places can be equally as important as political and territorial borders. Historical studies of migration have thus become increasingly nuanced in dealing with multiple layers "of individuals and families, of groups and classes . . . of state structures and civic societies" and in identifying and examining "transnational circuits and communities" (Hoerder, 2009, p.257).

Historical perspectives of this type, informed by new transnational, global and 'connected' approaches, have much to add to the literature on sports migration, and that of football in particular. They can provide historical depth to our understandings of determinants and patterns of migration, and the rise and fall of athletic migration systems, as well as recognition of the contradictions and complexities of migrant experiences and attitudes. They can allow us to see more clearly how football was effectively 'networked' from its beginnings, with transnational linkages preceding and subsequently complementing, though often complicating, the construction of national football cultures. More than this, however, detailed research on the mobility and migration of athletes from the late nineteenth century onwards can help to thicken scholarly understanding of the cultural aspects of early stages of globalisation, of late Victorian 'imperial globalisation', and of the increasing global interaction and interconnectedness of the pre-1914 and interwar periods (Rosenberg, 2012b; Kidambi, 2013). Ground-breaking studies of the global circuits of boxers and the outward travel of American athletes are suggestive of what can be achieved (Keys, 2006; Runstedtler, 2012). In the rest of this chapter, we outline how research into the history of football migration might enrich the fields of both sports migration research and transnational and global history.

Table 1.2 Number of career moves between clubs among FA Cup final players, 1889–1914*

No. of moves between clubs	All players	%
0	10	7.7
1	15	11.5
2	18	13.9
3	15	11.5
4	33	25.4
5	15	11.5
More than 5	24	18.5
	130	100

Source: As for Table 1.1 above.

Note: * Cup final years selected were 1889, 1894, 1899, 1904, 1909 and 1914.

130 players who appeared in selected FA Cup finals between 1889 and 1914 served at least three clubs in the Football League in the course of their careers, with considerably greater mobility registered if we include moves to clubs in the Scottish League, Southern League and other professional and semi-professional competitions. Moreover, nearly 70% of the sample moved clubs at least three times – and 30% at least five times – during their careers (see Table 1.2). Mobility was commonplace in the birthplace of the professional game, and the assumption that clubs were historically characterised by stable, locally based workforces therefore has little foundation (Lanfranchi & Taylor, 2001; Roderick, 2012).

It is generally accepted that itinerant workers and migrants were vital to the spread of organised football in continental Europe, South America and many other parts of the world. Whereas in Britain football had become a predominantly working-class game by the First World War, it was characterised by its middle class and elite profile in Europe and South America. For a particular class of young, urban, middle class men in the late nineteenth and early twentieth centuries, football was "the embodiment of a modern lifestyle" (Eisenberg, 2003, p.13). For these men, many of whom travelled for their schooling and were engaged in professions characterised by mobility, football was particularly attractive for what it came to represent, for its associations with the technological achievements and advancements of Britain and the British, and for its symbolism as a form of cosmopolitan sophistication. Some of this group could be regarded as the first 'cosmopolitan footballers', and they became instrumental in founding clubs and promoting the game within and across various territories. Men like Hans Gamper in Barcelona, Henry Monnier in Nîmes, Vittorio Pozzo in Turin, Oscar Cox in Rio and Walter Bensemann in various towns in Germany and Switzerland, all of whom lived or were educated for a time in Switzerland, the chief 'connecting point' in the dissemination of early football, played key roles not just in setting up clubs and associations but also in ensuring that football's earliest connections across Europe and South America were transnational rather than inter-national (Lanfranchi & Taylor, 2001). National units of analysis often hamper our understanding of the movement of people and ideas and the links between individuals, clubs and organisations. Mobile from its beginnings, football was circulated to localities, towns and cities and regions rather than to nations as such. Only later, particularly after the First World War, did the game become more obviously nationally orientated and framed by national interests and perspectives.

Even later, however, the mobility of players continued to shape the development of European and South American football. The personnel of the first professional leagues in mainland Europe tended to be restricted on the basis of nationality, but some were mixed and reflective of well-established touring itineraries and migratory routes. Founded in 1932, for instance, the French league included 113 foreigners among 387 professionals in its first season, a percentage of 29.2. This increased to 35% the following year, before settling down to an average foreign-player percentage of 31.7 between the 1934–5 and 1937–8 seasons (Wahl & Lanfranchi, 1995). If we focus only on these players as 'imports' and 'foreigners', moving from one nation-state to another, we are in danger of overlooking the labour circuits within which they were travelling as part of an emerging cross-national employment market. From the 1930s onwards, the recruitment policies of French clubs varied, reacting to wider local and regional labour markets and particular cultural influences: Poles and Austrians were prominent at RC Lens in the north, for example, and Hungarians and Yugoslavs, as well as British players, part of a migratory tradition at FC Sète on the Mediterranean coast (Lanfranchi, 1994). Even the British, often regarded as isolated from Europe's earliest football networks, were plugged into the transnational labour circuits of the interwar years. Forty-three British professionals joined French clubs for the 1932–3 season. For those such as Peter Dougal, who played 16 times for FC Sète that year in between spells at Burnley, Clyde, Southampton and then Arsenal, Everton and Bury, the move to France was simply one phase of an itinerant sporting career.

Networks

Networks have become central to the interconnected scholarship of migration, transnational and global history. It is a term which has been used casually to refer to social connections of any type but has also been thoroughly examined and defined by those seeking to place it at the centre of their understanding of how people, goods, capital and knowledge travelled the world and how empires and migration systems functioned. Together with the related notions of 'circuits' and 'webs', networks have been employed imaginatively by imperial historians to make sense of the connections that bound the British World together. A "complex web of family, cultural, commercial, and professional networks linked the British in Britain with the British overseas", two leading advocates of the British World perspective have argued (Buckner & Francis, 2005, p.16); this "plethora of networks", constituted the "cultural glue" of empire (Bridge & Fedorowich, 2003, p.6). With their focus on the interlocking economic and cultural links that spanned the empire, Gary B. Magee and Andrew S. Thompson have utilised the idea of networks to examine how "private, unofficial and provincial interests" in Britain were connected "with their overseas contacts and communities". A networked approach, they argue, allows historians to see the empire "for what it really was", that is, "an interconnected zone constituted by multiple points of contact and complex circuits of exchange" (Magee & Thompson, 2010, p.16). It is indicative of new ways of mapping continents, for instance, with an emphasis not on territorial units but on a representation of space akin to "a satellite picture taken at night . . . shaped by brightly illuminated nodes of cultural exchange and the lines of communication between them" (Ther, 2009, p.219). The emphasis here, in imperial, transnational and global settings, is on networks as personal, social and informal alliances, which often operated alongside or complemented formal institutions but could run counter to them. Networks have opened up particularly rich opportunities for migration historians precisely because of their fit with a growing tendency to study personal experiences and informal and open relationships that operated beneath, around and across structural and institutional forces (Delaney & MacRaild, 2005).

The emerging networks of the nascent football world nested within larger migration systems. Hoerder, a leading advocate of the approach, has argued that migration systems "link regions of different cultures . . . with interconnected patterns of mobility that continue over time" (Hoerder, 2009, p.255). He has outlined four major migration systems across the world in the nineteenth and twentieth centuries: an Atlantic system connecting Europe and the Americas, as well as Europe with its colonies; an Asian system of both free and indentured labour developed under the rule of European powers, and extending across the Pacific to the Americas; a Russo-Siberian system; and a North China to Manchuria system (Hoerder, 2012). Football's initial dissemination and subsequent networking developed primarily within the Atlantic system. As we have noted, the game spread on the back of the mobility of people, both temporary and permanent, and, as it became more organised, recurrent patterns of mobility started to develop. As players moved around the British Isles, across Europe to the earliest organised and professional leagues, between cities and regions in South America and southern Europe and from various parts of Africa to the clubs and leagues of the European colonial powers, they established routes of mobility and migration that over time became deeply entrenched but yet were never static or mutually exclusive. Both state controls and the regulations of football's own administrative bodies could limit certain aspects of the movement of footballers, but the game's networks, some of which, we should remember, preceded the emergence of FIFA and of many nation-states, tended to exist outside these formal structures.

We can get a snapshot of how football migration changed over time by briefly examining two transcontinental football networks, the first linking parts of South America and southern Europe, and the second connecting Africa with imperial cities and nations in Europe. Mass migration between Europe and South America laid the basis for the later mobility of professional athletes. More than six million Europeans, for example, arrived in Argentina between 1869 and 1914, and 58% of the population were, by 1914, either born outside the country or the children of immigrants. Italian migrants were the most numerous by far – two million between 1876 and the First World War – most from the north of the country (Hoerder, 2012; Belich, 2009). Return migration was high, and many Italian emigrants moved abroad for a couple of years, adopting what has been called a 'straddling' strategy, "somewhere between settling and sojourning", through which they maintained "footholds both home and abroad" (Belich, 2009, pp. 128, 532). This, alongside the very low take-up by Italian immigrants of Argentine citizenship, was the backdrop for the migration of large numbers of Argentinians (60 in total), as well as smaller numbers of Uruguayans and Brazilians, to the Italian league between 1929 and 1943. These athletes were moving, in a certain sense, as part of an established transnational migration network, and many displayed dual identities reflecting the linked cultures of two societies. A number, such as Julio Libonatti, Raimundo Orsi and Renato Cesarini, represented both Argentina and Italy in international competition. Their movement was facilitated by a number of the 'information flows' identified by Magee and Thompson (2010) in their analysis of migrant networks (see also Lanfranchi & Taylor, 2001). Information from friends and colleagues was crucial in many cases: Cesarini followed his friend Orsi from Buenos Aires to Juventus in Turin, while Guillermo Stabile, who arrived in Genoa in 1930, encouraged a cluster of friends and team-mates to follow him to the port club. Elsewhere, employers recruited players after watching them play in Europe or during trips to South America or made use of informal or formal agents acting as intermediaries operating between two societies. For Raffaele Sansone, personal connections and external intermediaries combined to convince him to move from Peñarol in Montevideo to Bologna (Lanfranchi & Taylor, 2001, p.85):

> At the time my friend [Francisco] Fedullo played for Bologna. He mentioned my name to the Bologna directors who were looking for new Uruguayan signings and had a kind of agent who lived in Montevideo. He came to offer me a contract. I accepted immediately and arrived a month later via Genoa.

The connections between South America and parts of southern Europe continued to be significant after the Second World War, though the migration of South American footballers diversified and shifted according to wider economic trends as well as the policies of sports federations. Buenos Aires, in particular, emerged as a hub for the best players on the continent. Over a quarter of the 625 Uruguayan professionals who left the country between 1958 and 1983, for instance, went to Argentina, a higher proportion than those who went to Europe. Intra-continental mobility, in multiple directions, was a feature of Latin American football migration that has certainly been underplayed. At different times, leagues in Mexico, Peru, Colombia and even Guatemala, some of them operating outside FIFA, were able to attract players from across the continent. Indeed, of the 32 Brazilians working in the top divisions of South and Central American leagues in 1963, eleven were in Argentina, ten in Mexico, four in Colombia and three in Peru (Lanfranchi & Taylor, 2001). Increased regulation of the import of non-nationals in the Italian league from 1947, meanwhile, and restrictions on foreign players in France and Spain from 1962, and in Italy in 1966, led to a significant reduction in transatlantic migration. Nonetheless, the migrant and sporting networks linking the River Plate and southern Europe continued to be important. Thus in the 1966/7 season there were still 11 Argentinians, three Brazilians and three Paraguayans out of a total of 46 foreign players in the French league, and five Argentinians, ten Brazilians and one Peruvian and Uruguayan (out of 30 foreigners) in Italy's Serie A (Lanfranchi, 1996).

Transnational networks, often regarded as a central component in the contemporary migration of footballers from Africa to Europe, existed in different, and less institutionalised, forms from at least the 1930s. The top-down recruitment networks of the leading European clubs today were preceded by more informal, loosely knit social networks based predominantly on colonial relations and interactions (Poli, 2005). The movement of players from francophone Africa (from the 1930s) and the Portuguese territories (after the Second World War) to clubs in the metropolitan centre was facilitated by the particular status of many of these places as overseas provinces as well as by prevailing policies of assimilation. For large numbers of young post-war Algerian footballers, for example, who read French newspapers, watched French films and followed the careers of earlier north African sports stars in Europe such as the Moroccan Larbi Ben Barek, a 'desire for France' was a key factor in explaining why so many wished to migrate. While playing for wealthy Algerian clubs, players like Mohamed Maouche and his team-mates regularly encountered European life and football, travelling every August to France and Switzerland between 1951 and 1954. Various channels of migration were in operation during the 1950s; recruitment agents were important in some cases, as was the existence of family and friends, and large Algerian communities, in France. Hamid Kermali's passage and settlement were aided by two Algerian friends who worked at a local factory: "I slept at their place, I ate at their place until I did a trial at Mulhouse" (Frenkiel & Bancel, 2008, pp.1035–6). Portuguese club sides regularly toured Mozambique and Angola during the 1940s and 1950s, and Benfica, Sporting Lisbon and Porto even set up feeder clubs in Luanda and Lourenço Marques (now Maputo) (Darby, 2007; Alegi, 2010a).

Not all migrants followed colonial paths to the metropolitan centre; neither were they always recruited through established and formalised systems. The mobility of football players, like other forms of migration, was often the product of complex structural and messy personal circumstances. The case of Darius Dhlomo, a black teacher and midfielder from Durban, demonstrates that football in apartheid South Africa was connected to wider transnational networks. But it also confirms the importance of personal connections and informal social networks. Inspired by the successes of a handful of black South African football emigrants, Dhlomo wrote in 1957 to clubs in England and Sweden to offer his services. In January 1958 he was contacted by the Dutch club Hercules Almelmo, possibly as a result of a recommendation from a board member who had seen him play while on a business trip to Natal, or perhaps due to a tip-off from Steve Mokono, a black South African already playing for the club. As black Africans, Dhlomo and

Mokone were unusual in Dutch football and Dutch society, which was far from cosmopolitan at the time. Dhlomo enjoyed short careers in both professional football and boxing but stayed in the Netherlands, marrying a Dutch woman, starting a family, working as a social worker in Arnhem and integrating fully into Dutch society (Alegi, 2010b).

For all its advantages, we need to be aware of some of the potential pitfalls and limitations of networked approaches to the history of transnational mobility and migration. First of all, as Simon Potter and others have shown, it can be argued that the expansion of transnational networks led not to the broadening but rather to the contracting of existing connections. In the case of the mass media, commercial, technological and institutional changes "worked to limit participation and narrow the range of discussion" across the British Empire. This may well be applicable to the organisation of international football, with the arrival and expansion of FIFA, dominated as it was for decades by Europe and South America, and the increasing influence of national and regional federations, limiting existing connections between different parts of the world and "at times rendering such links less fluid and reciprocal" (Potter, 2007, pp.638–9). There is also a danger, as a number of scholars have pointed out, that the language of 'networks', 'flows', 'connectivity' and 'circuits' fails to acknowledge fundamental inequalities of power and influence, the limits of interconnection and the unevenness of relationships across borders, continents and empires. "Real historical space", as one historian has observed, "was not flat or smoothly liquid but deeply grooved; persons and things moved on long but carefully defined circuits" (Rodgers, 2013, p.9). Following on from this, it is important to remember that networks could help to circulate colonial discourses and ideas about racial and gender inequality that contributed to discrimination and exploitation. In the case of the movement of both South American and African footballers to and within Europe, there are numerous cases of racial discrimination and stereotyping, many of which obstructed the careers of migrants and defined their personal experiences (Lanfranchi & Taylor, 2001; Lester, 2006; Alegi, 2010a). Historians have yet to fully explore the extent to which racism and discrimination in football constituted a transnational phenomenon carried via global debates and migration networks (Lake & Reynolds, 2008).

Hubs and contact zones

At the centre of football's early cross-national networks were particular nodes and meeting places where players, teams and officials congregated, stopped off or crossed paths. A number of key football cities acted in this sense as migratory hubs. Paris was one example, as Julien Sorez has recently outlined. From the initial diffusion of the sport in France, Paris became significant as an international centre for the emerging game (Sorez, 2012). Parisian sports leaders such as André Espir and Robert Guérin were instrumental in the creation of FIFA in 1904, and later in the formulation of the organisation's particular brand of "sporting internationalism" (Dietschy, 2011, p.513). Paris also hosted the 1900 and 1924

Olympic Games and became 'world football capital' when it spearheaded France's World Cup finals tournament in 1938. In the 1890s and 1900s it acted as an "interface with the British sports world", with the tours of British teams centred on the capital and British émigrés influential in the committee rooms of the earliest French football organisations (Sorez, 2012, p.1129). Later, reflecting the city's position as an accommodation centre for migrants from the French provinces and beyond, some of its clubs, such as Racing Club de Paris, prioritised the recruitment of Central European stars; they also focused on international fixtures but failed to attract a strong local following or to maintain a fixed location. Between the wars, Sorez argues, the influence of Paris in French football declined with the rise of provincial clubs and competitions, although it continued to be significant as an international meeting place and a key connecting point between football networks encompassing Britain, Central and Eastern Europe, Africa and South America (Sorez, 2012).

Vienna, similarly, became a hub for sporting contacts and exchanges in Central Europe, playing a vital role in the movement of football talent across the continent and beyond. The Austrian capital was closely connected to the emerging football cultures of Prague and Budapest through shared sporting traditions and styles of play and between the wars became instrumental in the construction of a network of cross-national competition, out of which the club-based Mitropa Cup and the International Cup for national sides emerged (Horak & Maderthaner, 1996; Marschik, 2001). Football in Vienna was a 'sport for migrants' from its beginnings, benefiting from the involvement of local Czechs such as Matthias Sindelar and Josef 'Pepi' Bican, who played for both Rapid Vienna and Slavia Prague, as well as Hungarian imports such as Alfréd Schaffer, Jenö and Kalman Konrad, Imre Schlosser, Béla Guttmann and József Eisenhoffer (Liegl & Spitaler, 2008b, 2008c). The city's clubs toured widely and continuously, bringing them into contact with institutions, administrators and players across the continent. Numerous players and trainers from Vienna were also transferred to foreign clubs, internationalising the 'Vienna School' at a time when, it has been argued, the city "had largely lost its significance within Europe" (Marschik, 1999, p.218). Sixty-one Austrians, 59 Hungarians and 43 Czechs were registered with French clubs between 1932 and 1939, while in Italy a considerable number of playing positions (before a ban on foreigners in 1926) and coaching roles were taken by Central Europeans, many of whom had passed through Vienna or Viennese clubs (Lanfranchi & Taylor, 2001; Foot, 2007).

Transnational and global histories have placed considerable emphasis on the specific sites where networks were forged and reinforced, as well as rejected and broken. These sites, whether large regions, towns and cities or particular venues and buildings, it has been argued, "provide a rewarding observation post for the historian" (Saunier, 2013, p.40). International matches and tournaments are good examples. World Cups, as well as Olympic and regional competitions, were catalysts for the increased mobility and migration of footballers and the extension of existing networks. From 1930 to 1970, for example, an average of just over 11 players migrated to France per tournament after representing another nation at the World Cup, with the figure reaching 14 in 1934 and 1950 and 19 in 1962 (Lanfranchi, 1994). Touring likewise facilitated further mobility, as players were offered contracts in the places they played, or were scouted on their travels. This was true of numerous members of touring teams from Europe to the professional American Soccer League during the 1920s and had worked in the opposite direction in 1917, when the trainer and a full-back of the touring All-American Soccer Football Club in Sweden and Norway were offered coaching positions in Sweden when the tour was over. In other circumstances, such as the Basque representative team who were touring Latin America in 1937 when their homeland was occupied by nationalist troops, travelling offered the opportunity of permanent relocation for those members of the team who refused to return to Franco's Spain (Dietschy, 2006; Taylor, 2011).

Conclusion

This chapter has surveyed the history and historiography of the mobility and migration of footballers and offered suggestions for new approaches and areas of focus. Its main arguments – that football was a mobile cultural form from its earliest development, and that transnational perspectives open up connections across borders and boundaries that tend to be overlooked within national frames of analysis – are in some respects not particularly contentious. They would certainly not surprise those scholars of the nineteenth and early twentieth centuries whose focus is increasingly on how "transnational social and cultural currents circulated across and beyond national states and drew the world together in new ways" (Rosenberg, 2012b, p.816). As is becoming widely acknowledged, the "dense and varied social networks and cultural entanglements" of the twenty-first century had significant forerunners in earlier periods: historians understand more now than they ever have, for instance, about the flows of information, ideas, people and goods across the globe that helped to produce multiple and varied attachments and connections from the 1850s onwards (Rosenberg, 2012b, p.816). Networks were central to this, and the period up to 1945 was, as Emily S. Rosenberg has recently suggested, "an era of transnational networks" (Rosenberg, 2012a, p.25). Given that football developed and spread with the movement of people, it is hardly surprising that the game should have advanced a culture of mobility that brought it into tension with national bodies, nationalist ideologies and international governing structures. The evidence and examples provided in this chapter should remind us that football connected people and places, though rarely uniformly or smoothly, across the world right from its beginnings and that the mobility of players and coaches was central to this, making links as well as highlighting differences in an increasingly global game.

References

Alegi, P. (2010a) *African Soccerscapes: How a Continent Changed the World's Game.* London: C. Hurst & Co.

Alegi, P. (2010b) A Biography of Darius Dhlomo: Transnational Footballer in the Era of Apartheid. *Soccer & Society* 11(1–2): 46–62.

Bale, J. (2004) Three Geographies of African Footballer Migration: Patterns, Problems and Postcoloniality. In G. Armstrong and R. Giulianotti (Eds.) *Football in Africa: Conflict, Conciliation and Community*. Basingstoke: Palgrave Macmillan (247–66).

Bale, J. and Maguire, J. (1994) (Eds.) *The Global Sports Arena: Athletic Talent Migration in an Interdependent World*. London: Frank Cass.

Ballantyne, T. (2003) Rereading the Archive and Opening up the Nation-State: Colonial Knowledge in South Asia (and Beyond). In A. Burton (Ed.) *After the Imperial Turn: Thinking with and through the Nation*. Durham, NC: Duke University Press (102–21).

Bantman, C., David-Guillou, A. and Thomas, A. (2002) The French in England (1880–1914): Anonymous Travellers and Migrants. In C. Geoffrey and R. Sibley (Eds.) *Going Abroad: Travel, Tourism and Migration*. Newcastle: Cambridge Scholars Publishing (2–12).

Belich, J. (2009) *Replenishing the Earth: The Settler Revolution and the Rise of the Anglo-World, 1783–1939*. Oxford: Oxford University Press.

Birley, D. (1999) *A Social History of English Cricket*. London: Aurum.

Botelho, V. and Skogvang, B.-O. (2013) The Pioneers: Early Years of the Scandinavian Emigration of Women Footballers. *Soccer & Society*. Published online 16 October 2013: DOI: 10.1080/14660970.2013.843909.

Bridge, C. and Federowich, K. (2003) Mapping the British World. *Journal of Commonwealth and Imperial History* 31(2): 1–15.

Buckner, P. and Francis, R.D. (2005) Introduction. In Philip Buckner and R. Douglas Francis (Eds.) *Rediscovering the British World*. Calgary: University of Calgary Press (9–20).

Cook, J.W. (2008) The Return of the Culture Industry. In J.W. Cook, L.B. Glickman and M. O'Malley (Eds.) *The Cultural Turn in US History: Past, Present and Future*. Chicago, IL: University of Chicago Press (291–318).

Curran, C. (2013) The Migration of Irish-Born Footballers to Britain, 1945–2010. Unpublished paper delivered at the 'FA 150' Conference, National Football Museum, Manchester, 2–4 September.

Darby, P. (2000) The New Scramble for Africa: African Football Labour Migration to Europe. *European Sports History Review* 3: 217–44.

Darby, P. (2007) African Football Labour Migration to Portugal: Colonial and Neo-colonial Resource. *Soccer & Society* 8(4): 495–509.

Davis, T.C. (2000) *The Economics of the British Stage, 1800–1914*. Cambridge: Cambridge University Press.

Delaney, E. and MacRaild, D.M. (2005) Irish Migration, Networks and Ethnic Identities since 1750: An Introduction. *Immigrants & Minorities* 23: 2–3.

Dietschy, P. (2006) Football Players' Migrations: A Political Stake. *Historical Social Research* 31(1): 31–41.

Dietschy, P. (2011) French Sport: Caught between Universalism and Exceptionalism. *European Review* 19(4): 509–25.

Eisenberg, C. (2003) From England to the World: The Spread of Modern Football. *Moving Bodies* 1(1): 7–22.

Foot, J. (2007) *Calcio: A History of Italian Football*. London: Harper Perennial.

Frenkiel, S. and Bancel, N. (2008) The Migration of Professional Algerian Footballers to the French Championship, 1956–82: The 'Desire for France' and the Prevailing National Contexts. *International Journal of the History of Sport* 25(8): 1031–50.

Giulianotti, R. (1999) *Football: A Sociology of the Global Game*. Cambridge: Polity Press.

Hoerder, D. (2009) Losing National Identity and Gaining Transcultural Competence: Changing Approaches to Migration History. In H.-G. Haupt and J. Kocka (Eds.) *Comparative and Transnational History: Central European Approaches and New Perspectives*. Oxford: Berghahn (247–71).

Hoerder, D. (2012) Migrations and Belongings. In E. Rosenberg (Ed.) *A World Connecting, 1870–1945*. Cambridge, MA: Harvard University Press (435–589).

Horak, R. and Maderthaner, W. (1996) A Culture of Urban Cosmopolitanism: Uridil and Sindelar as Viennese Coffee-House Heroes. *International Journal of the History of Sport* 13(1): 139–55.

Huggins, M. (2004) *The Victorians and Sport*. London: Hambledon.

Kelly, V. (2005) A Complementary Economy? National Markets and International Product in Early Australian Theatre Managements. *National Theatre Quarterly* 21(1): 77–95.

Keys, B. (2006) *Globalizing Sport: National Rivalry and International Community in the 1930s*. Cambridge, MA: Harvard University Press.

Kidambi, P. (2013) Sport and the Imperial Bond: The 1911 'All-India' Cricket Tour of Great Britain. *Hague Journal of Diplomacy* 8: 261–85.

Kocka, J. and Haupt, H.-G. (2009) Comparison and Beyond: Traditions, Scope, and Perspectives of Comparative History. In H.-G. Haupt and J. Kocka (Eds.) *Comparative and Transnational History: Central European Approaches and New Perspectives*. Oxford: Berghahn (1–30).

Lake, M. and Reynolds, H. (2008) *Drawing the Global Colour Line: White Men's Countries and the International Challenge of Racial Equality*. Cambridge: Cambridge University Press.

Lanfranchi, P. (1994) The Migration of Footballers: The Case of France, 1932–1982. In J. Bale and J. Maguire (Eds.) *The Global Sports Arena: Athletic Talent Migration in an Interdependent World*. London: Frank Cass (63–77).

Lanfranchi, P. (1996) *On Y Va! European Footballers on the Move*. London: European Movement UK.

Lanfranchi, P. and Taylor, M. (2001) *Moving with the Ball: The Migration of Professional Footballers*. Oxford: Berg.

Lester, A. (2006) Imperial Circuits and Networks: Geographies of the British Empire. *History Compass* 4(1): 124–41.

Liegl, B. and Spitaler, G. (2008a) *Legionäre am Ball: Migration im österreichischen Fußball nach 1945*. Vienna: Braumüller.

Liegl, B. and Spitaler, G. (2008b) Refugees, Guest Workers and Foreign Players, wieninternational. Retrieved 30 November 2013 from: http://wieninternational. at/en/print/node/7151.

Liegl, B. and Spitaler, G. (2008c) Viennese Czechs and Czech Viennese, wieninternational. Retrieved 30 November 2013 from: http://wieninternational.at/en/print/node/7661.

McDowell, M.L. (2012) Football, Migration and Industrial Patronage in the West of Scotland, c.1870–1900, *Sport in History* 32(3): 405–25.

McDowell, M.L. (2013) *A Cultural History of Association Football in Scotland, 1865–1902*. Lampeter: Edwin Mellen.

McGovern, P. (2002) Globalization or Internationalization? Foreign Footballers in the English League. *Sociology* 36(1): 23–42.

MacRaild, D.M. and Martin, D.E. (2000) *Labour in British Society, 1830–1914*. Basingstoke: Macmillan.

Magee, G.B. and Thompson, A.S. (2010) *Empire and Globalisation: Networks of People, Goods and Capital in the British World, c. 1850–1914*. Cambridge: Cambridge University Press.

Magee, J. and Sugden, J. (2002) 'The World at Their Feet': Professional Football and Labour Migration. *Journal of Sport and Social Issues* 26(4): 421–37.

Maguire, J. (1999) *Global Sport: Identities, Societies, Civilizations*. Cambridge: Polity Press.

Maguire, J. and Falcous, M. (2011) (Eds.) *Sport and Migration: Borders, Boundaries and Crossings*. London: Routledge.

Marschik, M. (1999) Between Manipulation and Resistance: Viennese Football in the Nazi Era. *Journal of Contemporary History* 34(2): 215–29.

Marschik, M. (2001) Mitropa: Representations of 'Central Europe' in Football. *International Review for the Sociology of Sport* 36(1): 7–23.

Molnar, G. (2006) Mapping Migrations: Hungary Related Migrations of Professional Footballers after the Collapse of Communism. *Soccer & Society* 7(4): 463–85.

Poli, R. (2004) *Les migrations internationals des footballeurs: Trajectories de joueurs camerounais en Suisse*. Neuchâtel: CIES.

Poli, R. (2005) Football Players' Migration in Europe: A Geo-economic Approach to Africans' Mobility. In J. Magee, A. Bairner and A. Tomlinson (Eds.) *The Bountiful Game? Football Identities and Finances*. Oxford: Meyer & Meyer Sport (217–33).

Poli, R. (2006) Migrations and Trade of African Football Players: Historic, Geographical and Cultural Aspects. *Africa Spectrum* 41(3): 393–414.

Potter, S.J. (2007) Webs, Networks and Systems: Globalization and the Mass Media in the Nineteenth and Twentieth-Century British Empire. *Journal of British Studies* 46: 621–46.

Richards, J. (2001) *Imperialism and Music: Britain, 1876–1953*. Manchester: Manchester University Press.

Roderick, M. (2012) Domestic Moves: An Exploration of Intra-national Labour Mobility in the Working Lives of Professional Footballers. *International Review for the Sociology of Sport* 48(4): 387–404.

Rodgers, D.T. (2013) Cultures in Motion: An Introduction. In D.T. Rodgers, B. Raman and H. Reimitz (Eds.) *Cultures in Motion*. Princeton, NJ: Princeton University Press (1–19).

Rosenberg, E.S. (2012a) Introduction. In E.S. Rosenberg (Ed.) *A World Connecting, 1870–1945*. Cambridge, MA: Harvard University Press (3–25).

Rosenberg, E.S. (2012b) Transnational Currents in a Shrinking World. In E.S. Rosenberg (Ed.) *A World Connecting, 1870–1945*. Cambridge, MA: Harvard University Press (815–996).

Runstedtler, T. (2012) *Jack Johnson, Rebel Sojourner: Boxing in the Shadow of the Global Color Line*. Berkeley, CA: University of California Press.

Sachsenmaier, D. (2011) *Global Perspectives on Global History: Theories and Approaches in a Connected World*. Cambridge: Cambridge University Press.

Saunier, P.-Y. (2013) *Transnational History*. Basingstoke: Palgrave Macmillan.

Sorez, J. (2012) A History of Football in Paris: Challenges Faced by Sport Practised within a Capital City (1890–1940). *International Journal of the History of Sport* 29(8): 1125–40.

Taylor, M. (1997) Proud Preston: A History of the Football League, 1900–1939. Unpublished PhD thesis, De Montfort University.

Taylor, M. (2011) Transatlantic Football: Rethinking the Transfer of Football from Europe to the USA, c.1880–c.1930s. *Ethnologie française* 2011/4: 645–54.

Taylor, M. (2013) The Global Ring? Boxing, Mobility, and Transnational Networks in the Anglophone World, 1890–1914. *Journal of Global History* 8: 231–55.

Ther, P. (2009) Comparisons, Cultural Transfers and the Study of Networks: Towards a Transnational History of Europe. In H.-G. Haupt and J. Kocka (Eds.) *Comparative and Transnational History: Central European Approaches and New Perspectives*. Oxford: Berghahn (204–25).

Tischler, S. (1981) *Footballers and Businessmen: The Origins of Professional Soccer in England*. New York: Holmes & Meier.

Vamplew, W. (1988) *Pay Up and Play the Game: Professional Sport in Britain, 1875–1914*. Cambridge: Cambridge University Press.

Vamplew, W. (2008) Successful Workers or Exploited Labour? Golf Professionals and Professional Golfers in Britain, 1888–1914. *Economic History Review* 61(1): 54–79.

Wahl, A. and Lanfranchi, P. (1995) *Les footballeurs professionnels: Des années trente à nos jours*. Paris: Hachette.

Williams, J. (2013) *Globalising Women's Football: Europe, Migration and Pro-fessionalization*. Bern: Peter Lang.

Wittmann, M.W. (2010) Empire of Culture: US Entertainers and the Making of the Pacific Circuit, 1850–1890. Unpublished PhD thesis, University of Michigan.

Woollacott, A. (2011) *Race and the Modern Exotic: Three 'Australian' Women on Global Display*. Clayton, Victoria: Monash University Publishing.

2 Chasing the ball

The motivations, experiences and effects of migrant professional footballers

Richard Elliott

When the English Premier League's then 22 teams engaged in their first weekend of matches in August 1992, only 13 non-British players made appearances. John Jensen, Jan Stejskal, Anders Limpar, Craig Forrest, Peter Schmeichel, Andrei Kanchelskis, Robert Warzycha, Eric Cantona, Ronnie Rosenthal, Michel Vonk, Gunnar Halle, Roland Nilsson and Hans Segers formed a distinct group of relative outsiders who were selected to play in the league's first games. English football was transformed after 1992, however, and the new money, glamour and media exposure that quickly enveloped the league soon attracted an increasing number of foreign players to ply their skills within it. Indeed, by the Premier League's 2001/02 season, foreign player appearances outnumbered those being made by their indigenous counterparts (Elliott, 2009), and by the conclusion of the 2012/13 season foreign players accounted for over 60% of the overall playing personnel (Poli *et al.*, 2013). In a little over 20 years, the English Premier League had become one of the most cosmopolitan sports leagues in the world.

The involvement of foreign players in England's Premier League has inexorably altered both that competition and the game in England more broadly. However, the transformation that occurred in England is only one example of the developing globalisation of professional football and the increasing cosmopolitanism of its workforce. With increasing regularity, players and other workers connected to the sport are criss-crossing the globe in search of the best employment opportunities. The result is an increasingly complex series of interdependent processes that reflect a range of social, cultural, economic and political issues.

The intention of this chapter is to examine some of these issues through the lens of three particular aspects of player migration that have been captured in a range of, largely, sociological analyses. The first part of the chapter examines the motivations of migrants and seeks to question the commonly misappropriated monocausal assumption that those professional footballers who migrate from one country to another to ply their trade are singularly motivated to do so by financial gain. Whilst this part of the chapter will identify that the desire, or indeed the need, to earn a salary can be a significant motivator for many players, the importance of financial gain should, in fact, be juxtaposed within a more complex series of processes that influence the migrants' decisions to either stay in one place or leave for another. The second part of the chapter explores the lived experiences of migrants and draws attention to the multifarious range of problems they can face when living and working in a foreign environment. In this part of the chapter, issues relating to detachment and assimilation will be examined. The final part of the chapter is concerned with the effects of foreign players on indigenous football cultures. The migrations of increasing numbers of professional players between nations and the clubs and leagues situated within them are not without consequence. In this respect, this final part of the chapter will include discussions of the deskilling of donor nations and the marginalisation of local labour.

The overall intention of the chapter is to highlight the interdependent multiplicity of processes that encompass the migrations of players in a range of sporting and cultural contexts and to explore the complexity of these movements as they are occurring in the contemporary professional football environment. To begin to do this, the first part of this chapter examines what it is that motivates players to migrate from one country to another to secure their employment in the game.

Should I stay or should I go? The motivations of migrant professional footballers

There can be little doubt that one of the most ubiquitous markers of the contemporary globalisation of professional football has been the increase in the numbers of players who now migrate from one country to another in search of employment opportunities and to ply their athletic labour. The majority, if not all, of the world's elite professional football leagues now host players (and other associated workers including owners, managers, coaches, medical and sports science staff) from a broad cross-section of places. These movements have increased significantly in the last 20 years or so. Therefore, whilst there is a certain amount of truth in the argument that migration in football is as old as the game itself (see Taylor's chapter in this collection and Taylor, 2006), it has been during the game's more recent history that an intensification of the globalisation of the game's labour force has really become evident (see Poli *et al.*, 2013).

The reasons for the intensification in migratory movements are reflective of a series of interdependent processes, some that are specific to the game and others that are manifest in broader processes of globalisation. For example, at a general level, the ability to traverse the globe with relative ease has made places that, until recently, seemed distant appear close. Moreover, technological advancement, in recent times driven by internet-based technologies, has made global communication cheaper and easier. More specifically, in football the increasing commercialisation of the game at the elite level, driven, in part, by the developing symbiosis that is observable between sponsors, advertisers and the media, has resulted in the exponential growth in salaries for elite players plying their trade in one of Europe's core leagues (Deloitte, 2012). The 1995 Bosman case also significantly impacted the mobility of players (Taylor, 2006) and influenced the salaries they are able to command.

An analysis of the changing financial structure of professional football, particularly in Europe's 'big-five' leagues (English Premier League, German

Bundesliga, Spanish La Liga, Italian Serie A, French Ligue 1), highlights the significant growth in club and league revenues, media rights sales, player valuations and salary costs (see, for example, the annually produced Deloitte Review of Football Finance and Football Money League). The rise in salary costs is particularly significant, given that some European leagues have witnessed enormous salary growth in the last 20 years. The increase in salaries has led some scholars to argue that the major influencing factor in determining a player's decision to migrate is the desire to secure the greatest financial reward that can be offered by a club (Andreff, 2009). Outside of professional sport, such contentions would seem sensible, given that migration often occurs to take advantage of positive wage disparities (Fischer *et al.*, 1997).

Whilst the desire to command the highest salary may influence a player's decision to migrate, it is rarely the only antecedent to a player's move. As Maguire and Pearton (2000) have identified, the practice of "following the money" (p.761) is often interconnected with a broader series of processes that reflect political, historical, cultural and geographical patterns. In this respect, research that has examined the motives behind the movements of professional footballers has identified that a range of processes contour the decision to migrate.

For example, research has shown that among these processes the need to seek out a 'professional sporting experience' is of great importance for some migrant groups, particularly those for whom obtaining employment in one of Europe's established elite leagues is a prerequisite to be considered 'professional' in the football context (Maguire & Stead, 1998; Stead & Maguire, 2000). Additionally, some players are motivated by the search for an intensity of commitment or by the desire to test their abilities at the highest level (Molnar & Maguire, 2008). These examples show that the significance of ambition should never be underestimated when considering what it is that motivates professional footballers to leave one country for another (Elliott, 2013a, 2014a, 2014b).

Indeed, ambition, it would seem, often permeates the decisions that players make when deciding whether or not to move to a particular club or league. Whilst there have been several high-profile examples of players who have rejected transfers that may have represented (financial) advancement in their career's (consider Brazilian Kaka's rejection of a reported £500,000 per week wage to transfer from AC Milan in Italy to Manchester City in England, for example), the career trajectories of most professional footballers are targeted towards securing what they perceive to be the 'best' employment opportunity available to them at that time. Best, as the Kaka example shows, doesn't always necessarily mean the one that pays the most, however. For some players ambition is marked by their desire to secure employment at a club where they feel they may be granted increased exposure, perhaps by playing in one of Europe's prestigious competitions such as the UEFA Champions League or UEFA Europa League (Magee & Sugden, 2002; Elliott, 2013a, 2014a). On other occasions players may move to a club that they perceive to be commensurate with their abilities but situated in a league that they think may act as a 'springboard' or 'stepping-stone' to somewhere else – somewhere better (Elliott, 2013a). For other migrants it may simply be about being given the opportunity to play the game. What might be described as peripheral 'squad' players whose playing time has been restricted at 'big' clubs in established leagues may choose to migrate to smaller clubs in more peripheral leagues because they have been promised the opportunity of increased playing time (Elliott, 2014a). Whilst the club and the league may be less prestigious, for some players the simple desire to actually play the game is what motivates them to migrate from one place to another. As long as these players are able to support themselves financially, the salary offered is, on occasion, inconsequential.

It is all too easy to get carried away when discussing professional football and to focus one's attentions exclusively on the small minority of superstars who migrate seamlessly between the biggest clubs of Europe's most prestigious leagues. Outside of football's established core a network of more and less peripheral leagues exists which, whilst still professional, are a world away from the Premier League, Primera Division, Serie A, Ligue 1 or Bundesliga. In this respect, whilst some players may be able to actively select from a range of employment opportunities within Europe's elite leagues, for the majority of migrants the choices are considerably more limited. In some cases, the player may have little or no choice at all in where they ultimately migrate to. Magee and Sugden (2002) have shown, for example, that sometimes players can be pushed from a particular location. This is an interesting point because push factors are often overlooked in favour of a focus on those things that pull players to particular locations.

The development of professional football's contemporary global political economy means that it is not always the case that a player will be presented with a full range of choices from which to actively select their migration destination. Outside of the games established leagues, a player's range of options may be significantly more limited for one reason or another. Indeed, it should be borne in mind that not all professional athletes are part of a "free moving cosmopolitan population who strategically engage in migration to further careers and earn significant wealth" (Carter, 2011, p.5). For many professional footballers the decision to migrate will be shaped by a range of issues comprising a number of push and pull factors.

These issues can include, for example, the overproduction of athletic labour and the resultant flooding of leagues in different parts of the world. This has certainly presented a problem for Brazilian players. Brazil produces huge numbers of professional footballers every year, exporting those who don't remain in the country to leagues across the globe (see Rial's chapter in this collection and Rial, 2008; Poli *et al.*, 2013). Whilst the most talented players are able to secure employment in the game's established European leagues, other Brazilian migrants of lesser ability have to secure playing opportunities where they can, sometimes in what might be described as the game's semi-core locations, and some in the game's more peripheral regions.

Many Brazilian professional footballers seek employment outside of their homeland because the sheer number of players is exacerbated by the lack of professional playing opportunities that exist in Brazil. Other than a minority of clubs such as Corinthians, São Paulo and Flemengo, for example, opportunities to play at the highest levels in Brazil are limited, given the relative inferiority of the Brazilian Serie A when compared to the financially dominant leagues in Europe. In this respect, the overproduction of indigenous athletic labour coupled with the lack of opportunities for domestic career development in Brazil push many of Brazil's most talented players to leagues outside of the country – mostly in Western Europe. Less talented Brazilian players can be found in a range of other places, including North America, Scandinavia, Eastern Europe, Asia, the Middle East, Africa and Australasia (see Rial's chapter in this collection and Poli *et al*., 2013).

Lack of opportunity has also been seen to push North American football (soccer) players out of the American sporting space (see Harris' chapter in this collection and Elliott & Harris, 2011). Whilst American professional players are produced in far fewer numbers than their Brazilian counterparts, the lack of professional playing opportunities in North America for players of greater ability means that the best players are nearly always forced to secure employment outside of the USA. This has been the case for some time. After the collapse of the North American Soccer League (NASL) in 1984, there was no professional league at all in the USA until the formation of Major League Soccer (MLS) in 1996. During this period, the best players in the United States had no choice but to look abroad for professional playing opportunities. Since 1996 Major League Soccer has grown. However, the league still fails to offer a level of competition commensurate with the abilities of America's top professional footballers. To demonstrate this, consider that the USA squad that competed in the World Cup Finals in Germany in 2006 included players employed by clubs in England, Germany, Holland and Belgium, whilst the 2010 World Cup squad included a number of players registered with English Premier League clubs, including all three of the goalkeepers (Elliott & Harris, 2011).

A similar pattern has emerged in Africa in recent years, where the increasingly commonplace migrations of African players to leagues in Europe and other parts of the world can be identified as the result of a lack of opportunities in the various leagues located on the continent (see Van der Meij and Darby's chapter; Darby, 2007; Darby *et al*., 2007). Whilst some clubs (predominantly those located in North Africa, including Al-Alhy in Egypt and Esperance in Tunisia) have professionalised to a point where they are able to retain some of their local players for longer, the majority of African clubs lack the financial, football or infrastructural conditions to match the level of ability or ambition of an increasing number of highly talented African players. The result is that with increasing regularity African players are seeking or being sought by teams in Europe's more established leagues and in a range of other places.

These examples can be used to capture some sense of the complexity of migrant motivation. What they show is that the motivations of professional football's increasingly cosmopolitan workforce cannot be reduced to any single causal factor – and certainly not financial gain alone. A player's decision to migrate should not simply be reduced to a series of intrinsic and largely personal influences. To be truly meaningful, a range of structural concerns, or push factors, should also be taken into consideration. Only when considered alongside the mix of more personal determinants of the motivation to migrate can any realistic observations be made with respect to what it is that really motivates professional footballers to move from one place to another to ply their trade. This is important, because understanding something about the player's motivation to migrate may well help to indicate, in part, how the migrant will likely cope with the demands of migration as they experience their period of foreign sojourn – something that the next part of this chapter explores in greater detail.

Living on the edge: the precarious nature of foreign sojourn

A player's decision to leave one country for another to secure their athletic employment is nearly always a difficult one. As the previous section of this chapter has shown, outside of a small band of elite players who may possess more control over the decision to work in one place or another, for the most part professional footballers will be subjected to a range of push and pull factors that will influence whether they migrate or not, and where to.

Arguably, the manner in which a player is pushed from one location and pulled to another will, in part, help to shape how the migrant initially experiences that particular movement. Concomitantly, however, a range of other interdependent processes also contour how successfully the migrant might be assimilated and how, ultimately, they might experience that particular period of migrant employment. The experience will be shaped by a mix of the personal and social circumstances of the migrant: for example, whether they are married, in a relationship, or have children; their age; their level of ability; the point in their career at which the migration occurs; how they are recruited; and any previous experiences in other places. Arguably, each of these factors, or a combination of them, can influence the migrant's aptitude for assimilation and affect their overall capability to cope with a particular movement.

An absolute priority, however, for successful adjustment is the migrant's ability to learn and speak the language in the host nation (Weedon, 2011). Whilst migration to a foreign place will always present a range of challenges for migrants, if the migrant is able to speak the language of the host nation, particularly understanding the specifics of the football vernacular, and to comprehend aspects of local culture more broadly, the ability to traverse through the day's routine tasks both at work and away from it can be eased significantly. The studies that have traced the experiences of migrating professional footballers have shown how these workers place great value on the ability to communicate and understand cultural cues effectively in the host environment. Migrants have argued that the ability to speak the language (or potentially learn it more quickly if it is similar to their own) not only permeates decisions in respect of potential destinations, but also inevitably helps migrants to integrate in the new environment and cope more effectively (Stead & Maguire, 2000; Elliott, 2013a).

On many occasions, however, the migrant will (initially at least) not be able to communicate effectively. They may also struggle to adapt culturally in the host environment. When this happens, the player may be exposed to a range of issues. For some players these issues may be as simple as not being able to manage day-to-day tasks such as paying bills or purchasing goods and services. For others, a misunderstanding or misinterpretation of certain aspects of the host culture or laws may occur. These types of issues can further exacerbate the sense of dislocation that migrants sometimes feel when first encountering what, to them, is an alien environment. When the player is dislocated from their support network, what might seem like minor issues for local workers can be significant obstacles for migrants.

Transfers from a team in one country to another team in a different country can often happen quickly and unexpectedly for players (Roderick, 2006). Because of this, players are rarely given much opportunity to prepare or to research their new employer or the city, region or even the country in which it is located. Moreover, they frequently move alone initially, leaving, for varying periods of time, their partners, children, other family members and friends. Indeed, migration to a foreign country often requires a player to detach themselves from their social and familial support network for at least a short period (Elliott, 2014a).

This period of detachment can be very difficult for players as they come to terms with their new migrant status, removed from their primary social networks and those people and things that are familiar to them. Many professional footballers grow accustomed to the support they receive from their families and friends as their careers develop. This support often begins in the family during the player's childhood, but intensifies if it becomes apparent that the ability exists to build a career in the game. Rarely, if ever, will a career in professional football emerge in isolation. Professional footballers will always be enmeshed in a network of interdependent social and familial relationships developed over a number of years and framed within the broader political economy of the game.

When detached from these networks, often many miles from home, in a foreign place where the player may not speak the language or understand the local culture, loneliness and isolation (sometimes bundled together with other emotions and referred to simply as 'homesickness') can be a significant problem (Weedon, 2011). Players often spend significant amounts of money and much of their free time attempting to communicate with their friends and family. Migrant players have, in the past, been seen to refer to "massive phone bills" (Stead & Maguire, 2000, p.47) as they try to maintain the important links that now extend beyond national borders. More recently, internet-based technologies, such as Skype, have revolutionised the way in which players can communicate with their support networks, providing cheaper media through which they can develop a series of ongoing, but ultimately 'virtual', relationships (Elliott, 2013a).

Detachment can be a significant problem, however, and one that places an enormous strain on relationships – particularly between players and their partners. It is unrealistic to conceive of the migrations of professional footballers as not contaminating the lives of significant others (Roderick, 2012). However, whilst professional footballers continue to migrate with increasing regularity, many partners, it is argued, are becoming less likely to surrender their own employment prospects and identities (Roderick, 2012). This can mean that some partners may be less likely to migrate with the player, preferring instead to remain at home. Whether the player's partner chooses to remain in one place or migrate to another, the period in which separation occurs can be particularly difficult for migrant players, one in which relationships can be tested, and, in some cases, break down (Stead & Maguire, 2000).

The loneliness that some migrants feel can be particularly problematic for professional footballers, who will often find themselves under the specific sorts of scrutiny that a career in professional sport engenders. In some cases, the loneliness felt by migrant players may not only influence their overall mood state off the pitch, but also their ability to perform on it. Inevitably, if a player is not able to perform to the best of their abilities (or, more likely, to a level that reflects the amount of money the club paid for them), coaching staff and fans will quickly become frustrated. This sense of frustration will often be fuelled by the inevitable criticism that will be levied by the local, national or, in some cases, global media, which will rarely consider the complex range of issues that can ultimately affect a migrant's capacity to perform to the best of their abilities in a foreign and sometimes alien environment.

One player for whom these problems have been apparent is Vincent Pericard. Having played in the French Ligue 1 with St Etienne, Italian Serie A with Juventus, the English Premier League with Stoke City and Portsmouth, and also represented France at under-21 level, Pericard was described as the man who would be 'worth billions' in a French documentary that was made about him when he was 17. However, the Cameroonian-born striker was forced to retire by the age of 29, having never realised his full potential. He attributed his failure to both culture shock and the loneliness that he felt defined his career as a migrant in a number of different places. Pericard argued that this loneliness was born of being detached from his family and friends, but also arose because he didn't speak the host language in some cases and in others was unfamiliar with local culture. During his period of migration in England, Pericard was jailed for lying in court in respect of a driving conviction. He was subsequently prescribed anti-depressant medication to counter the increasingly deteriorating mood state that ultimately forced him out of the game at the point when he should have been performing at the peak of his abilities.

After ending his playing career in English non-league football, and as a direct result of the difficulties he faced during his career, in 2012 Pericard established a not-for-profit organisation to address the issues of dislocation, adjustment and loneliness among migrant professional footballers moving to England. The organisation offers a range of support services to migrant players and their families in an attempt to enhance the process of social and cultural assimilation – issues sometimes overlooked by clubs. These services are focused on those elements of the migration process that have been seen to cause the most significant problems for players and include, among others, foreign language courses and cultural awareness training.

Raising awareness of the problems that migrant professional footballers can face is important, particularly when considering that each migration is always in flux and bound within a series of dynamic processes that change as the period of sojourn progresses. For example, players often arrive at new foreign clubs with a great sense of optimism, as transfers are normally considered to be positive moves (Roderick, 2006). This means that, in the early weeks of a migration, players often feel settled and perform well. However, over time, and after what can sometimes feel like an extended holiday, players can become exposed to a heightening sense of dislocation that intensifies as they spend more time separated from family, friends and familiarity. This period ultimately leads to a realisation of what it means to be a migrant worker in a foreign country and whether or not the migrant has the capacity to cope in their new environment (Elliott, 2014a). Irrespective of whether the migrant stays in one location or makes a number of subsequent transfers within or beyond national borders, the point here is that the migrant's experience will be a dynamic and constantly changing one. This should be borne in mind when considering what it means to assume the role of outsider in an established community, where migrations cannot be seen to occur without effect. The next part of the chapter explores this area in greater detail.

Overpaid and over here: the effects of migration in football

The involvement of increasing numbers of migrant professional footballers in leagues located in various parts of the world cannot occur without consequence. Indeed, the rising number of foreign players in some leagues has become the source of considerable debate among the game's key stakeholders and the media in recent years. Predominantly these debates have centred on the perceived negative effects of foreign player involvement, where it is argued that the apparent 'feet-drain' (Elliott & Weedon, 2010) that is occurring exists on two levels. Firstly, at the donor level, a 'deskilling' (Maguire *et al.*, 2002, p.37) of football talent occurs in the leagues that are seen to be economically less powerful relative to those located in the professional game's economic core. Secondly, in host nations, the recruitment of foreign players stifles the development of indigenous talent, taking its place and squeezing it out to the margins of the professional game.

Debates surrounding the deskilling of donor nations have, to this point, most commonly focused on those African nations that consistently lose their most talented footballers to teams located in the richer Western European leagues. For example, in 2003 Sepp Blatter, President of the Fédération Internationale de Football Association (FIFA), vilified those European clubs that had benefited from the recruitment of African players, describing them as "neo-colonialists who don't give a damn about heritage and culture, but engage in social and economic rape by robbing the developing world of its best players" (Darby *et al.*, 2007, p.143). Academic research that has sought to trace the recruitments of African players to various leagues outside of the continent have continued, in part, to support the idea that the movements of these players represent a form of neo-colonial exploitation (see Darby, 2002, 2007, 2011; Poli, 2006; Darby *et al.*, 2007).

The commercial supremacy of the established Western European leagues and the teams located within them means that the transcontinental transfer of African players to European leagues has become an increasingly common characteristic of world football (Cornelissen & Solberg, 2007). Whilst the individual players themselves benefit from these transfers in terms of an improvement of living and working conditions and the often astronomical remuneration they are able to command relative to average wages in their home nations, the teams and leagues from which they have been recruited find themselves in a state of perpetual underdevelopment (Darby, 2011).

Arguably the foundations for the processes that result in many African players leaving their respective nations for Europe's core leagues are laid in the academy system that ultimately prepares them to migrate (see Van der Meij and Darby's chapter). Whilst some clubs, predominantly located in North Africa, are able to train and retain some of their most talented players for longer (Darby *et al.*, 2007), for many young African footballers the academy is merely the stepping stone to a career abroad if they possess sufficient talent.

This is not to say that the system in operation is all bad, however. Whilst there are a number of examples of unscrupulous agents and 'informal' academies that prey on the vulnerability of young Africans, arguably the development of players in the more established and formal academy system has a number of benefits for African football. For example, it has been argued that the development of players in well-organised academies has contributed to the improvement of African national teams comprising players who have received superior training as part of their academy education (Darby *et al.*, 2007). These teams are increasingly made up of players who have subsequently migrated to play in Europe's established leagues. Thus, they are exposed to some of the world's best facilities, training and technology. They are also regularly training and playing against the world's best players, constantly testing, at the highest levels, the skills and abilities that subsequently benefit their national teams (see Elliott & Weedon, 2010, for a broader discussion of the concept of 'feet-exchange').

Arguably, the exodus of Africa's best playing talent results in both positive and negative consequences. Whilst the improved performances of some African nations in major tournaments since the early 1990s might, in part, be reflective of the increasing numbers of African internationals plying their trade outside of their respective home nations, African football still resides very much at the periphery of the game's global world order. This might be expected as long as African teams continue to be unable to retain more of their talented players for longer. It should be borne in mind, however, that migration alone cannot explain the persistent underdevelopment of professional football in Africa; broader structural factors, such as poor administration, government interference and corruption, also continue to hamper the development of the game in the region (Darby *et al.*, 2007).

The deskilling of donor nations is one consequence of the increasingly complex enmeshment of migrations in professional football's global configuration of leagues. The contemporary game's global political economy is one where labour flows can be seen to travel largely from east to west and from south to north, mimicking the flows observable in a range of other spheres of highly skilled employment (see Lee's chapter). These flows are largely based on the professional game's power geometry – one that means that by and large the world's most talented players will gravitate towards Europe's more established, and significantly wealthier, leagues. If deskilling is the consequence for those nations that traditionally assume the role of donor within this global figuration, for host nations the consequence is the marginalisation of local labour and the associated ramifications for youth and national team development.

In the last 20 years an increasing number of the world's best professional footballers have migrated into and between Europe's established leagues. These migrations are a signifier of the broader processes of globalisation that really began to influence the development of professional football at the end of the twentieth century (Elliott & Weedon, 2010). They are also a signifier of the commercialisation that occurred and provided new revenue streams for clubs, allowing them to lure foreign imports with the promise of higher salaries and greater levels of exposure in Europe's prestigious league and cup competitions. During this period, the numbers of foreign players making appearances in some European leagues exceeded those of their indigenous counterparts (Elliott, 2013b). In England and Germany, where this was the case, the effects on youth and national team development were argued to be disastrous.

In England's Premier League, for example, the number of foreign players employed by clubs continues to be a source of considerable debate, perennially within the English media, but also among some of the game's most prominent figures, including FIFA President Sepp Blatter, Union des Associations Européennes de Football (UEFA) President Michel Platini, and English Professional Footballers' Association (PFA) Chief Executive Gordon Taylor. Indeed, in a 2007 PFA-commissioned report entitled "Meltdown: The Nationality of Premier League Players and the Future of English Football", Gordon Taylor concluded that English football was in 'crisis' as a consequence of the numbers of foreign players recruited to ply their trade in the English Premier League (Elliott & Weedon, 2010).

Similar arguments had been made in respect of German football, where the influx of foreign-born players was argued to have diluted the base of German talent from which the national team could be selected (Merkel, 2007). For example, in 2004 Gerhard Mayer-Vorfelder, the then President of the Deutscher Fußball Bund (DFB), the national governing body for the sport in Germany, commented: "How can we expect young German forwards to develop in the Bundesliga, if seventy per cent of all forwards are foreign-born?" (Brand & Niemann, 2006, p.131).

The increases in foreign player numbers observable in the Premier League and the German Bundesliga have created similar problems and drawn parallel criticisms. These criticisms are largely focused on the ways in which the recruitment of 'ready-made' foreign imports stifles opportunities for indigenous talent, thus blocking the developmental path of local players and subsequently affecting national team development. The response in England and Germany to these problems has been somewhat different. Indeed, the German response has been to completely restructure the sport, placing a much greater emphasis on the development of local players who can qualify to play for the German national team (Elliott, 2013b). Part of this restructure included a new requirement for all 36 professional clubs in the top two Bundesliga divisions to build youth academies. Crucially, of the intake that was to be trained within each academy, it was stipulated that 12 players had to be eligible to play for the German national team.

Additionally, and somewhat serendipitously, the German football system also benefited from the collapse of the KirchMedia TV Company. KirchMedia held the rights to broadcast the Bundesliga, and it was the money that had flowed into the league from KirchMedia that had bankrolled it since the early 1990s (Mikos, 2006). When the company collapsed in 2002, Bundesliga clubs were left in severe financial difficulty. Faced with huge, and totally unsustainable, wage bills, the clubs had no choice but to release many of their foreign players, replacing them with younger, and much cheaper, recruits from their own youth teams. This enforced policy not only injected new home-grown talent into the German football system, but also, when combined with the infrastructural legacies of hosting the 2006 World Cup, resulted in increased attendances, as fans who had been put off by the lack of local players in Bundesliga teams suddenly returned to support a new generation of German players in new or renovated stadia.

In England the response to increasing numbers of foreign players has been far less defined. Within the country's academies there is no stipulation that the players being recruited should be eligible to play for the national team. Instead, the Premier League introduced a variant of UEFA's home-grown player rule for the start of the 2010/11 season which dictates that clubs cannot name more than 17 non-home-grown players aged over 21 in a squad of 25. As in the case of UEFA's broader principle regarding home-grown players, the crucial difference that exists between the English and German systems is that whilst a percentage of the players recruited into German academies must be eligible to play for the German national team, no such stipulation exists in England because home-grown players are not necessarily English. Home-grown players are defined, irrespective of nationality, as those who have been trained by a club of the same national association for a period of three years between the ages of 16 and 21. Whilst the home-grown player rule may assist young players in gaining more experience in Premier League senior teams, it is less likely to significantly enhance the numbers of players eligible to play for the England national team. This further underlines the complexity of the effects of foreign-player involvement on indigenous football cultures and the policies that are designed to manage youth and national team development effectively.

The examples used here show that the migrations of professional footballers affect donor and host nations in different ways. It should, of course, be borne in mind that few leagues can be described solely as a host or a donor as many will adopt a dual role in both the exporting and the importing of football labour. Whilst it is more likely that those clubs located on the periphery of the world football system will act as donors, at the game's core the two-way movement of players is much more likely to be visible. Within each individual league, and therefore social, cultural, economic and political context, the specific nuances of that particular place will largely dictate the migratory flows observable.

Conclusion

Professional football has changed enormously in the last 20 years. The mediatisation and subsequent commercialisation of the game that occurred in a number of Western European leagues during the 1990s and which further intensified and spread during the late twentieth and early twenty-first century period, coupled with a number of changes to employment law, have resulted in increasing numbers of players migrating from one country to another to secure their athletic employment in the game.

The interdependent range of global migrations being made in professional football's increasingly complex global configuration of teams, leagues and associations is reflective of a range of processes. This chapter has drawn attention, albeit briefly, to some of these processes to show that migration is rarely, if ever, a straightforward transaction conducted between one team and another. It has shown that migration decisions are influenced by a mix of push and pull factors; that migration in professional football can be precarious and sometimes fraught with difficulty; and that the intended actions of migrants, and the teams that recruit them, can result in a range of largely unplanned and unintended consequences.

Whilst this chapter has drawn on a number of specific examples from a range of different football contexts, these are obviously not the limit of the processes that are occurring in the game today. Professional football's global league structure is vast, extending across every continent. It is also dynamic and constantly in flux. Whilst the professional game is bound within a complex power geometry that dictates, in part, the flows of labour within it, the distribution of power in the game is never static, total or exclusive. In this respect, labour flows can and will alter over time – their complexity, however, is unlikely to change.

References

Andreff, W. (2009) The Economic Effect of 'Muscle-Drain' in Sport. In G. Walters and G. Rossi (Eds.) *Labour Market Migration in European Football: Issues and Challenges.* London: Birkbeck Sports Business Centre.

Brand, A. and Niemann, A. (2006) The Europeanization of German football. In A. Tomlinson and C. Young (Eds.) *German Football: History, Culture, Society*. London: Routledge (127–42).

Carter, Thomas F. (2011) *In Foreign Fields: The Politics and Experiences of Transnational Sport Migration*. London: Pluto Press.

Cornelissen, S. and Solberg, E. (2007) Sport Mobility and Circuits of Power: The Dynamics of Football Migration in Africa and the 2010 World Cup. *Politikon* 34: 295–314.

Darby, P. (2002) *Africa, Football and FIFA: Politics, Colonialism and Resistance.* London: Frank Cass.

Darby, P. (2007) Out of Africa: The Exodus of African Football Talent to Europe. *WorkingUSA: The Journal of Labour and Society* 10(4): 443–56.

Darby, P. (2011) Out of Africa: The Exodus of Elite African Football Labour to Europe. In J. Maguire and M. Falcous (Eds.) *Sport and Migration: Borders, Boundaries and Crossings.* London: Routledge (245–58).

Darby, P., Akindes, G. and Kirwin, M. (2007) Football Academies and the Migration of African Football Labour to Europe. *Journal of Sport and Social Issues* 31(2): 143–61.

Deloitte (2012). *Annual Review of Football Finance.* Manchester: Deloitte.

Elliott, R. (2009, June) A Game of Two Halves? Foreign Players in the English Premier League. Paper presented at the Central Council for Physical Recreation European Summit, London.

Elliott, R. (2013a) New Europe, New Chances? The Migration of Professional Footballers to Poland's Ekstraklasa. *International Review for the Sociology of Sport* 48(6): 736–50.

Elliott, R. (2013b) Reinventing the Past: Youth and National Team Development in England and Germany. In A. Waine and K. Naglo (Eds.) *On and Off the Field: Football Culture in England and Germany.* Berlin: Springer (157–64).

Elliott, R. (2014a) Brits Abroad: A Case Study Analysis of Three British Footballers Migrating to the Hungarian Soproni Liga. *Soccer and Society* 15(4): 517–34.

Elliott, R. (2014b) Football's Irish Exodus: Examining the Factors Influencing Irish Player Migration to English Professional Leagues. *International Review for the Sociology of Sport.* Published online 11 February 2014: DOI 10.1177/1012690213519786.

Elliott, R. and Harris, J. (2011) Crossing the Atlantic from Football to Soccer: Preliminary Observations on the Migrations of English Players and the Internationalization of Major League Soccer. *WorkingUSA: The Journal of Labour and Society* 14(4): 555–68.

Elliott, R. and Weedon, G. (2010) Foreign Players in the Premier Academy League: 'Feet-Drain' or 'Feet-Exchange'? *International Review for the Sociology of Sport* 46(1): 61–75.

Fischer, P.A., Reiner, M. and Straubhaar, T. (1997) Interdependencies between Development and Migration. In T. Hammar, G. Brochmann, K. Tamas and T. Faist (Eds.) *International Migration, Immobility and Development: Multidisciplinary Perspectives.* Oxford: Berg (91–132).

Magee, J. and Sugden, J. (2002) 'The World at Their Feet': Professional Football and International Labour Migration. *Journal of Sport and Social Issues* 26(4): 421–37.

Maguire, J., Jarvie, G., Mansfield, L. and Bradley, J. (2002) *Sport Worlds: A Sociological Perspective.* Champaign, IL: Human Kinetics.

Maguire, J. and Pearton, R. (2000) The Impact of Elite Labour Migration on the Identification, Selection and Development of European Soccer Players. *Journal of Sports Sciences* 18: 759–69.

Maguire, J. and Stead, D. (1998) Border Crossings: Soccer Labour Migration and the European Union. *International Review for the Sociology of Sport* 33(1): 59–73.

Merkel, U. (2007) Milestones in the Development of Football Fandom in Germany: Global Impacts on Local Contests. *Soccer and Society* 8(2/3): 221–39.

Mikos, L. (2006) German Football – a Media-Economic Survey: The Impact of the KirchMedia Company on Football and Television in Germany. In A. Tomlinson and C. Young (Eds.) *German Football: History, Culture, Society.* London: Routledge (143–54).

Molnar, G. and Maguire, J. (2008) Hungarian Footballers on the Move: Issues and Observations on the First Migratory Phase. *Sport in Society* 11(1): 74–89.

Poli, R. (2006) Migrations and Trade of African Football Players: Historic, Geographical and Cultural Aspects. *Africa Spectrum* 41: 393–414.

Poli, R., Ravenel, L. and Besson, R. (2013) *Annual Review of the European Football Players' Labour Market*. Neuchâtel: CIES Football Observatory.

Rial, C. (2008) Rodar: a circulação dos jogadores de futebol brasileiros no exterior. *Horizontes antropológicos* 14(30): 21–65.

Roderick, M. (2006) *The Work of Professional Football: A Labour of Love?* London: Routledge.

Roderick, M. (2012) An Unpaid Labor of Love: Professional Footballers, Family Life and the Problem of Job Relocation. *Journal of Sport and Social Issues* 36(3): 317–38.

Stead, D. and Maguire, J. (2000) 'Rite de Passage or Passage to Riches?' The Motivation and Objectives of Nordic/Scandinavian Players in English League Soccer. *Journal of Sport and Social Issues* 24(1): 36–60.

Taylor, M. (2006) Global Players? Football, Migration and Globalisation: 1930–2000. *Historical Social Research* 31(1): 7–30.

Weedon, G. (2011) 'Glocal Boys': Exploring Experiences of Acculturation amongst Migrant Youth Footballers in Premier League Academies. *International Review for the Sociology of Sport* 47(2): 200–16.

3 Football and migration

A contemporary geographical analysis

Raffaele Poli and Roger Besson

As outlined in numerous places within this collection, international migration is a key feature of professional football across the world. While it has historically mainly concerned coaches and players, it is now more and more common for sports directors, scouts, fitness specialists and other associated workers to migrate in search of employment in the game. This process operates in parallel with the transformation of professional football into a global industry. It has become an international business that generates greater revenues year by year.

This chapter focuses on the migration of football players during the past five years. Drawing upon the ongoing research undertaken by the CIES Football Observatory research team, it describes the situation in 31 top-level leagues of UEFA member associations (see Appendix 1), as well as the trends observed since 2009. It is structured around three sections dealing in turn with the import of players, their export and migration channels. In the section on player imports, we analyse international migration to those European leagues surveyed. The section on player exports maps the countries from which expatriate footballers originate. Finally, the section on transfer networks proposes a joint analysis of importing and exporting countries to determine if and how migration routes are changing within the framework of globalisation.

Import of players

On 1 October 2013 almost half (49.3%) of all the players in the 31 top-division European championships analysed had already played for a team outside of the national association in which they grew up (see Figure 3.1). This percentage increased by 3.3% compared to 2009.

During the same period, the percentage of expatriate players also increased slightly. An expatriate player is defined as a player who is playing outside the national association in which they started to play football and from where they departed following recruitment by a club overseas. As Figure 3.2 shows, in October 2013 expatriates represented 36.8% of the players under contract with the 472 clubs in the top-level championships of the 31 UEFA member associations surveyed. The figure is lower than that of players with football-related migratory experience because some of the latter experienced return migration to their home country.

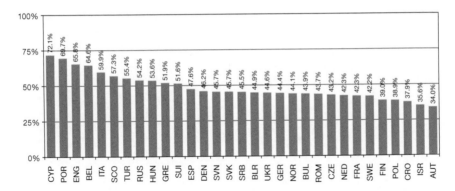

Figure 3.1 Percentage of players with a football-related migratory experience in 31 top division European leagues (2013).

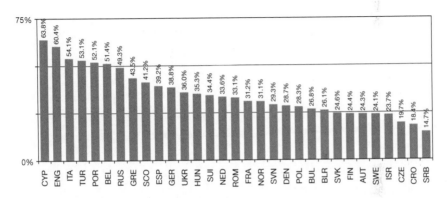

Figure 3.2 Percentage of expatriate players in 31 top division European leagues (2013).

High discrepancies still exist between leagues with regard to the relative presence of expatriate footballers. While more than three players out of five in Cyprus are expatriates, the proportion is lower than one fifth in the Czech Republic, Croatia and Serbia. Generally speaking, as illustrated in Figure 3.3, the greater the sporting level of a league the higher the percentage of expatriate players. The sporting level of a league was calculated on the basis of results achieved in European club competitions by national association representatives during the last five completed seasons.

While expatriates are still over-represented in the best-performing leagues, the highest increase in their relative presence among squad members since 2009 was recorded in the least competitive championships (see Appendix for league categorisation). The data in Figure 3.4 suggest that the ongoing internationalisation trend mainly occurs 'from below', from lower performing leagues that for a long time remained reluctant to recruit players from abroad.

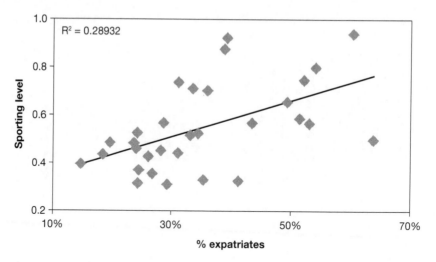

Figure 3.3 Correlation between the percentage of expatriates and the sporting level of leagues (2013).

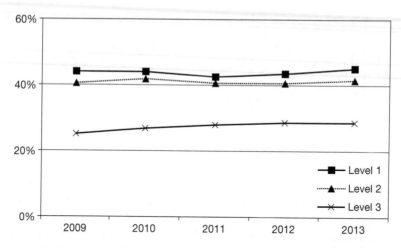

Figure 3.4 Evolution in the proportion of expatriates, according to the sporting level of leagues (2009–13).

Export of players

Within the context of the internationalisation of the labour market for football players, some countries and world areas play a greater role as exporters than others. The map in Figure 3.5 illustrates the high number of intra-European migrations, as well as the key role played by South America and West Africa in the supply of labour to the European market.

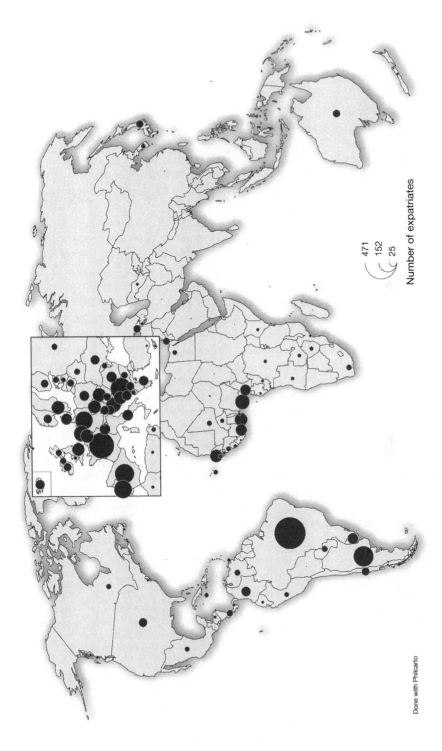

Number of expatriates

471
152
25

Done with Philcarto

Figure 3.5 National association of origin of expatriate players in 31 top division European leagues (2013).

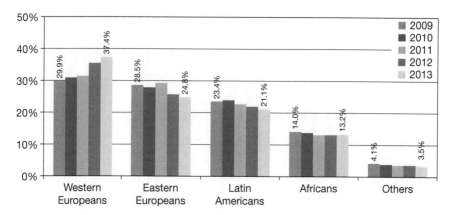

Figure 3.6 Evolution in the distribution of expatriate players according to zone of origin (2009–13).

At national level, Brazil has by far the most representatives in the European leagues surveyed: 471. The number of players from the second most represented donor, France, is also very high: 306. Five other countries have more than 150 representatives abroad in European leagues: Serbia, Argentina, Portugal, Spain and Germany.

On the whole, 117 national associations are represented in the top division European leagues surveyed. However, more than one third of expatriates originate from the five most represented countries. Since 2009 the number of players from Western Europe among expatriates has strongly increased (see Figure 3.6). Henceforth, Western Europeans account for 37.4% of all expatriates (+7.5% compared to 2009).

At national association level, the four biggest increases from 2009 to 2013 were registered for Western European donors: Spain, France, the Netherlands and Germany (see Table 3.1). This reveals the top-level quality of the training programmes developed in these countries.

Table 3.1 Highest increase in the number of expatriate players in 31 top division European leagues, per national associations (2009–2013)

1.	Spain	+121
2.	France	+59
3.	The Netherlands	+47
4.	Germany	+42
5.	Ghana	+37
6.	Portugal	+27
7.	Greece	+18
8.	Colombia	+17
9.	Senegal	+15
10.	Chile	+14

Migration channels

Brazil is the most represented foreign donor in seven leagues out of 31. In Portugal, they account for 47.1% of all expatriates. This example illustrates the importance of historical relationships between territories in the geography of players' migration.

Despite globalisation, proximity also still plays a crucial role in the spatial configuration of flows (see Table 3.2). This can be seen, for example, through the presence of Germans in Austria, French in Belgium and Switzerland, Ukrainians in Belarus, Bosnians in Croatia, Slovakians in the Czech Republic and vice versa, Serbians in Hungary and Montenegrins in Serbia, for example.

In order to test if migration routes are changing within the context of the ongoing internationalisation trend, we analysed the evolution in the distribution of expatriate players according to their zone of origin and the continental area of their employer club (see Table 3.3). Continental areas were defined as follows:

Table 3.2 Most represented origin per country (2013)

Austria	Germany	12
Belarus	Ukraine	23
Belgium	France	52
Bulgaria	Brazil	21
Croatia	Bosnia	17
Cyprus	Portugal	37
Czech Republic	Slovakia	30
Denmark	Nigeria	10
England	France	49
Finland	Nigeria	7
France	Brazil	21
Germany	Brazil	16
Greece	Spain	31
Hungary	Serbia	33
Israel	Serbia	12
Italy	Argentina	48
Netherlands	Belgium	19
Norway	Sweden	19
Poland	Slovakia	15
Portugal	Brazil	98
Romania	Brazil	25
Russia	Brazil	24
Scotland	England	41
Serbia	Montenegro	16
Slovakia	Czech Republic	23
Slovenia	Croatia	23
Spain	France	28
Sweden	Ghana	13
Switzerland	France	10
Turkey	Germany	64
Ukraine	Brazil	39
Total	Brazil	471

Table 3.3 Zone of origin of expatriates, by continental area (2013)

	Western Europeans	Eastern Europeans	Latin Americans	Africans	Total
South	521	224	498	160	1403
West	615	181	162	166	1124
East	172	276	148	68	664
Central	135	348	59	79	621
North	159	35	36	92	322
Total	1602	1064	903	565	4134

Rem: chi^2: 838.3, ddl: 12, p = 0.000, **; phi^2 = 0.46

Western Europe (France, Switzerland, Belgium, Netherlands, Germany, England and Scotland), Eastern Europe (Bulgaria, Romania, Ukraine and Russia), Central Europe (Austria, Czech Republic, Poland, Slovakia, Hungary, Slovenia, Croatia and Serbia), Northern Europe (Denmark, Norway, Sweden and Finland) and Southern Europe (Portugal, Spain, Italy, Greece, Turkey, Cyprus and Israel).

Table 3.3 confirms that some donors are still clearly over-represented in specific continental areas. The probability that the distribution of players per continental area according to their zone of origin is due to chance is close to zero. However, as shown in Figure 3.7, the value of the chi^2 is on the decrease. The chi^2 is a statistical parameter ranging from 0 (lowest concentration) to 1 (highest concentration). This finding reveals that the impact of players' origin in their distribution between different continental areas in Europe diminished between 2009 and 2013.

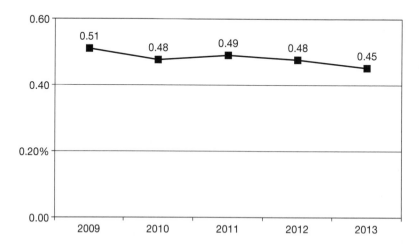

Figure 3.7 Evolution in the chi^2 (2009–13)

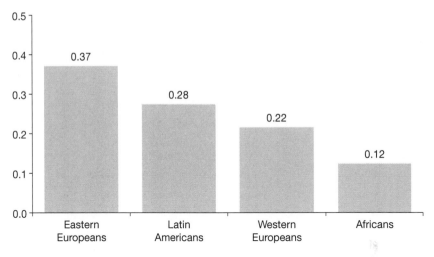

Figure 3.8 Dissimilarity index per origin (2013).

Figure 3.8 presents the results of the dissimilarity test undertaken. We used the segregation index developed by Duncan and Duncan (1955) to analyse the percentage of the expatriate population that should play for clubs located in another continental area than that where they actually play to have a perfect distribution. The lower the index, the better the distribution between continental areas. From this perspective, Africans are the most evenly distributed throughout Europe. At the opposite end of the table are Eastern European expatriates.

Conclusion

Our analysis shows that the transfer and labour market for football players is still evolving towards internationalisation. While some origins are still clearly over-represented in specific areas, a diversification process was observed since 2009. It will be interesting to monitor if this trend continues in the next few years.

Contrary to trends observed in the decade following the Bosman ruling, since 2005 the relative presence of non-European players among expatriates stopped increasing. Instead, in the five-year period analysed in this chapter, the four biggest increases in foreign leagues were registered for representatives of Western European countries: Spain, France, the Netherlands and Germany. This finding challenges the idea that European countries have a competitive disadvantage in training top-level footballers. It also suggests that the top-level quality of training programmes can make a difference beyond the intrinsic talent of local footballers. From this perspective, it will also be interesting to analyse the vast Aspire Academy project developed by Qatar to train Qatari talents in order to produce a competitive team for the 2022 FIFA World Cup.

Appendix

Table 3.4 League surveyed and level category

Name	Clubs	Players	Level
England	20	535	1
Spain	20	498	1
Germany	18	459	1
Italy	20	536	1
France	20	504	1
Portugal	16	399	2
The Netherlands	18	423	2
Ukraine	16	397	2
Russia	16	424	2
Belgium	16	387	2
Greece	18	451	2
Denmark	12	279	2
Turkey	18	473	2
Austria	10	235	2
Switzerland	10	244	2
Romania	18	474	2
Cyprus	14	326	3
Czech Republic	16	366	3
Israel	14	329	3
Sweden	16	370	3
Poland	16	396	3
Norway	16	363	3
Croatia	10	256	3
Belarus	12	283	3
Serbia	16	380	3
Slovakia	12	289	3
Bulgaria	14	351	3
Hungary	16	416	3
Scotland	12	267	3
Finland	12	287	3
Slovenia	10	256	3

References

Duncan, O. and Duncan, B. (1955) A Methodological Analysis of Segregation Indexes. *American Sociological Review* 20: 210–17.

Places

4 Migration and soccer in a football world

The United States of America and the global game

John Harris

This chapter provides an overview of some of the issues relating to soccer and migration in the United States of America (USA). That I refer to the sport as soccer highlights its somewhat marginal status in a football world (see Markovits & Hellerman, 2001; Wangerin, 2008). In looking at where the USA 'fits' in the broader landscape of international football and labour migration, the chapter focuses on the positioning of Major League Soccer (MLS), the case of David Beckham, and the role of the women's game within the USA, as points of departure for discussing soccer and migration in a global perspective.

As outlined in numerous places within this collection, research into the migration of football players has developed markedly over the past two decades. Much of the work on the game, generally regarded as the global sport *par excellence* (see especially Maguire & Stead, 1998; Giulianotti, 1999; Maguire & Pearton, 2000; Lanfranchi & Taylor, 2001; McGovern, 2002; Magee & Sugden, 2002; Darby, 2007; Giulianotti & Robertson, 2009; Elliott & Weedon, 2010), has shown how players move towards the core football economies. As Lanfranchi and Taylor (2001, p.141) note in their history of migration in the sport, "North America has always stood at the periphery of the football world".

There has been significant change in football across the world through the increased intensification of global flows (Giulianotti, 1999; Lanfranchi & Taylor, 2001; Giulianotti & Robertson, 2009). As outlined in Elliott's chapter, the massive developments in the English Premier League from its inaugural season in 1992–3 to the present day capably highlight the magnitude of this change in relation to the number of different nationalities now represented within a particular locale. Such a case evidences the ever-increasing prominence of migration in football during what has been referred to more broadly as the age of migration (Castles & Miller, 1993). Sports scholars, and most notably those interested in football, have written extensively on globalisation as a means of exploring the increased commercialisation and commodification of elite sport. Globalisation is, of course, a contested concept and leading researchers in the sociology of sport have outlined the many layers of this within the sports world (Maguire, 1999; Bairner, 2001). As Giulianotti (2005) posits, we can be neither 'for' nor 'against' globalisation. Instead we should recognise that globalisation has become "an ontological dimension of social life, a kind of multi-faceted social fact"

LIVERPOOL JOHN MOORES UNIVERSITY
LEARNING SERVICES

(Giulianotti, 2005, p.190). Taylor (2007) suggests that much of the writing on football migration has tended to employ the term globalisation uncritically and treats it as an established fact.

In most discussions of globalisation, the USA sits at the centre and assumes a hegemonic status. As Markovits and Hellerman (2001, p.5) note in their discussion of the "American century":

> Whereas it would be quite impossible to write a history of the twentieth century in virtually any field without having the United States present in some prominent (if not necessarily predominant) manner, this is simply not the case in the world of soccer. Crudely put, America did not matter.

There can still be some confusion as to exactly what is meant by globalisation, with some dominant discourse still largely framing it within a language that is presenting a thesis of Americanisation. Whilst there is no denying that the USA has a hegemonic status in many spheres of globalisation, this is not always the case in sport per se and certainly not in football. Writing more broadly about the so-called Americanisation of sport, Bairner (2001) suggests it is doubtful that much of this reflects Americanisation as opposed to "the evolution of capitalism" (p.15). Veseth's (2005) wider analysis of globalisation draws out some of the central issues in highlighting the limitations of the Americanisation thesis and emphasises that much of what is put forward as globalisation and/or Americanisation is actually little more than 'globaloney' – about interests and the arguments that best advance them. In international football the USA has long occupied a peripheral role (Lanfranchi & Taylor, 2001), although this is not to ignore the more central position the country has begun to play, and will likely continue to play, in the contemporary international football business (Giulianotti & Robertson, 2009).

There has been relatively little work undertaken which has examined labour migration into US sport. This is due, in part, to the somewhat insular nature of sport in the USA and the popularity of (American) football, which is played (largely) within national borders. At both the collegiate and the professional level this particular code of football assumes a hegemonic place in the landscape and casts a significant shadow over all other sports (Markovits & Rensmann, 2010). The global sport of association football becomes the 'other' within this particular cultural context and has to compete with many activities in a very crowded sporting space. As noted above, this 'othering' extends to referring to the sport by a different name and also sees the game marginalised and placed in a peripheral position. This discourse often frames soccer in relation to what football is not (Sugden, 1994; Wangerin, 2008). As work on social identities in sport has clearly outlined, these collective identities are focused on notions of difference where boundaries are negotiated and contested (Harris & Parker, 2009).

The US version of football assumes a central and important role in the promotion and representation of dominant ideologies surrounding masculinity and muscularity (Sabo & Panepinto, 1990). This in part helps explain the popularity and success of women's soccer in the USA, where girls and women do not face the barriers to participation evident in many other parts of the world where association football is the national sport and a key marker of masculine identity (e.g. Harris, 2005). Here then we encounter a very different scenario, and in a sport where the country has long sat at the periphery of the men's game the very same nation sits at the core of the women's game, and this is a subject I will return to later in the chapter.

As the various contributors to this collection capably highlight, the migration patterns of football players traverse geographical, political, cultural, ethnic and economic boundaries. These flows have developed steadily with the increasing globalisation of the game, which has witnessed exponential growth in recent years (Giulianotti & Robertson, 2009). Many studies examining migration in football have sought to make sense of the movement of workers by examining the factors influencing players to move (e.g. Maguire & Stead, 1998; Magee & Sugden, 2002; Molnar, 2006; Darby, 2007; Elliott, 2013). Whilst some athletes are obviously significantly influenced by financial gain, as is the case with many other skilled migrant workers, the process of "following the money" (Maguire & Pearton, 2000, p.761) is interconnected with a broader series of processes, which reflect political, historical, cultural and geographical patterns (see Lanfranchi & Taylor, 2001; Taylor, 2007). It is also important to note that the movement of athletic migrants is not always towards the 'core sport economies' but occurs on a number of levels, and for a range of reasons.

Men's professional soccer in the USA: from ASL to NASL to MLS

Allison (2005) noted the USA's curious role in world sport, where domestic competitions achieve a certain primacy and international competition is not considered as important in the most popular sports. Markovits and Hellerman's (2001) work on soccer and American exceptionalism, where the notion of American exceptionalism in the global order is also reflected in the sports space of the nation, offers a cogent account of this positioning. The establishment of this sports space in the late 1800s and early part of the twentieth century was influenced by a desire to 'Americanise' sports introduced from Britain and mark the country as being distinct and different from the old world (Markovits & Hellerman, 2001). One of their key points is that soccer, whilst being an immensely popular activity (what people do), has failed to move into culture (what people talk about). In an overview of the sport in the nation, Collins (2006) noted that in contemporary times there has been a marked growth in the numbers playing the game, although it is also important to recognise that much of this growth is among female players. In this sense, as Markovits and Hellerman (2003) have suggested, the success of women's soccer in the USA may be perceived as yet another form of American exceptionalism.

Limitations of space do not permit a detailed discussion of the history of migration and US soccer here, but, as with many of the other cases discussed in this collection, the migration of players to and from various nations has occurred for a number of years and is not just a recent development. Commenting more broadly on the subject of migration, Lanfranchi and Taylor (2001) note that what has marked out the United States (and Canada) from other countries of immigration is not so much the scale of immigration as its diversity. English players were part of the first professional football league in the USA in the 1890s (Waldstein & Wagg, 1995; Lanfranchi & Taylor, 2001) but many of these men were from established immigrant communities in the nation. The creation of the American Soccer League (ASL) in 1921 was an important moment in the history of the game in the USA and also included a number of players who had moved to the country for work outside of football. Many wealthy companies soon began to target professional players in the United Kingdom though, and numerous Scottish footballers were recruited on salaries far better than those they were receiving from their Scottish clubs (Lanfranchi & Taylor, 2001; Wangerin, 2008). The ASL collapsed in 1931, and the next significant attempt at developing a professional league in the region occurred with the formation of the North American Soccer League (NASL) in 1968.

Part of NASL's strategy to develop the sport involved the signing of some of the best-known players in the world. At the height of NASL's popularity, Franz Beckenbauer (West Germany) George Best (Northern Ireland), Bobby Moore (England) and Pele (Brazil) all played in the league. Yet these players were at the end of their athletic careers, and NASL gained a reputation as a kind of 'football graveyard' for ageing mercenaries from across the world. Pele stated on his arrival that he hoped to make soccer as big as baseball and (American) football (Satterlee, 2001). This was too big a task even for the man widely regarded as the greatest player of all time. On one level it is felt that Pele failed, as NASL folded in 1984 and of course soccer never ascended to the status of the major sports in the USA. Yet, looking at the number of players now registered in youth leagues and the many other developments in the game, it could be argued that this was Pele's real legacy and that he played a significant role in increasing the popularity and profile of the sport (Satterlee, 2001).

In addition to the financial incentives that tempted a number of the well-known players referred to above to move to the USA, the motivation to move can also be linked to a lack of opportunities for career development. The lack of professional opportunities can push an athlete from their home nation, whilst the lure of a specific location may pull them in a particular direction whether on cultural or economic grounds. For some American (male) soccer players during the 1980s and 1990s this was certainly the case, as few opportunities existed to develop a professional career given that no professional league existed in the United States between 1984 and 1996. Players such as Brad Friedel, a goalkeeper for the US national team and someone who has enjoyed a long and successful career in the English Premier League, followed the path of winning a soccer scholarship and gaining a university degree before embarking upon a career in the professional game. The creation of Major League Soccer (MLS) in 1996 offered a new generation of American players the chance to develop a professional career in the game within their home nation.

MLS is quite different from the sports leagues that dominate the American sporting space, as the National Basketball Association (NBA), National Football League (NFL), National Hockey League (NHL) and Major League Baseball (MLB) define themselves as the best leagues in the world in their respective sports. Here the increased inward migration of non-American athletes over recent years has been viewed as having a negative impact upon the popularity of activities such as basketball and baseball to domestic sports fans (Brown, 2005). These leagues though, just like many other sporting competitions all over the world, needed to promote their products and develop their brands in new markets and so embarked upon targeted internationalisation strategies. Such change is not always welcomed. The decision to award the 1994 FIFA World Cup Finals to the USA was a contentious one, and the Fédération Internationale de Football Association (FIFA) insisted that a professional league would have to be developed in the country as part of this agreement. MLS was created as a single-entity structure, meaning that the league is owned and controlled by investors. Part of the rationale for adopting this approach was to control the expenses associated with operating such a league and was a conscious attempt to avoid some of the worst excesses of NASL.

From the beginning MLS promised to learn from the lessons of NASL and implemented a strategy focused on slow consolidated growth and the development of domestic players. From the start of the operation there was a restriction placed on the number of foreign players allowed in the league. Yet as Armstrong and Rosbrook-Thompson (2010) note, the ageing foreign players and marginal foreign-born players who played in MLS were often the 'standout' players in the league. Freddy Adu, a 14-year-old boy born in Ghana who moved to the USA at the age of eight, signed a professional contract one year after gaining US citizenship and was quickly positioned as the next Pele and the future star of MLS. He represented the USA in a number of youth tournaments and made his debut for the senior national team at the age of sixteen, thereby becoming the youngest player to win a full international cap for the country. Adu has failed to match the unrealistic expectations placed upon him and is not the international football star that many hoped he would be. DeSchriver's (2007) study of Adu showed that a so-called 'marquee player' can have a significant impact upon spectator attendance figures in MLS. There have been a number of attempts at bringing in players from outside of the USA to increase attendance figures and boost the popularity of the league.

The signings of high-profile players such as Lothar Matthäus (Germany) and Luis Hernandez (Mexico) drew criticism and prompted Markovits and Hellerman (2001) to suggest that "the league is dangerously approaching the strategy pursued by NASL with such adverse consequences for the game's development at the top level in the United States" (p.188). If these types of signings were reminiscent of the worst excesses of NASL, then the signing of arguably the most famous player in the modern game in 2007 brought with it numerous comparisons with the signing of Pele some three decades before, and I will return to focus on the case of David Beckham later in the chapter. Even since the development of MLS, many members of the USA national team have moved abroad to further their careers and compete at a higher level. The 2006 USA squad that competed in the World Cup finals in Germany included players who were at the time employed by clubs in Belgium, England, Germany and Holland. Players such as Brian McBride, Brad Friedel, Clint Dempsey and Kasey Keller enjoyed long and successful careers in some of the top leagues in Europe. The USA roster for the 2010 World Cup finals in South Africa included only four players registered with MLS franchises. This shows that a number of American players continued to move in search of professional opportunities.

For quite some time a common theme in promoting American identity and difference has been to attack the sport of soccer (Sugden, 1994; Waldstein & Wagg 1995; Delgado, 1997; Wangerin 2008). The popularity of the sport amongst different immigrant groups has also been used by those opposed to the game as a means of highlighting that it is not something that Americans should support and represents a challenge to 'traditional' American values. This of course overlooks and oversimplifies the multiple layers of identities at play in a society built on immigration. In contemporary times, the Latino community in the USA is the largest and fastest-growing minority ethnic population in the country. Delgado (1997) observed that from the very start MLS has targeted younger and lesser-known players, often from Latin America, and, as Armstrong and Rosbrook-Thompson (2010) noted more than a decade later, all MLS teams have Latinos on their roster. Then MLS commissioner Doug Logan noted the xenophobic reaction to the league and the feeling that it was not American (Delgado, 1997). The granting of an MLS franchise to the owner of Mexican club Deportivo Guadalajara (known as Chivas) in 2004 was another concerted attempt to reach the Mexican-American fan base (Wangerin, 2008). Chivas USA shared a stadium with Los Angeles Galaxy, who themselves were soon to make an ambitious attempt to internationalise their brand and the profile of soccer in the USA.

Soccer exists as a somewhat marginal activity at the professional level, despite the fact that it is an incredibly popular recreational pursuit (Collins, 2006). So whilst the sport of (association) football serves as an important part of masculine identity and working-class culture across the globe (Giulianotti, 1999; Giulianotti & Robertson, 2009), in the US it is more of a women's game and also viewed as a suburban activity of the middle classes (Andrews, 1999; Markovits & Hellerman, 2003). Before returning to look at the case of David Beckham, arguably the most famous person to compete in a soccer league, the next section briefly discusses the position of women's soccer in the USA.

US soccer at the centre of the football world

As outlined earlier in this chapter, the position and prominence of a hegemonic code of football have a marked effect on the place of any other football code within a particular locale, and this in turn also affects the opportunities afforded to women in the different codes. Football, in its various forms, is often identified as a marker in the promotion and maintenance of hegemonic masculinity and a site for the reproduction of dominant gender ideologies (e.g. Sabo & Panepinto, 1990;

Clayton & Humberstone, 2006). Given the dominant position of American football in the USA then, women have perhaps faced less resistance to and greater support for taking part in soccer than has been the case elsewhere. As a result of this, the USA was for many years the leading nation in the world in international women's football.

The 1996 Olympic Games in Atlanta provided an important stage for women's soccer in the USA. The USA won the tournament and increased attention was focused on the women who played the sport, although this was nothing compared to the interest that another success on home soil would bring three years later. Major international events often serve as key moments and/or focusing events for different nations in the development of a particular sport, and the 1999 Women's World Cup Finals staged in the USA promised to be a very important event. The 1999 finals marked a significant moment in the history of women's soccer and perhaps even women's sport as a whole (Longman, 2000; Christopherson *et al.*, 2002; Markovits & Hellerman, 2001, 2003). It was declared the largest women's sporting event in history before a ball had been kicked and as the tournament unfolded, with the host nation going on to win the title, the game received widespread media attention and public recognition of a type never seen before (Longman, 2000; Christopherson *et al.*, 2002).

Within (post)modern sport few other issues have been as visible or contested as those surrounding gender. Title IX in the USA was passed in 1972 and states that federal funds can be withdrawn from a school engaging in intentional gender discrimination. This of course had a massive impact upon sport, which had until then largely been considered a male activity in schools and colleges. As a result of Title IX in the USA, the advances of feminism, and the global women's rights movement, opportunities for girls and women in sport have developed markedly in the last 40 years. The team that won the 1999 World Cup are often portrayed as the "poster girls" or "children of/for Title IX" (Longman, 2000). The significant media attention afforded to the team, and the celebration of the successes of 1996 and 1999 meant that there had seemingly never been a better time to develop a professional soccer league in the country.

The Women's United Soccer Association (WUSA) was founded in 2001 and, alongside the launch of MLS five years before, was hailed as proof that soccer had finally arrived as a professional sport in the USA. Unlike MLS though, WUSA was the premier league in the world and was launched with an ambitious five-year business plan to develop the product as a viable television commodity (Southall & Nagel, 2007). Giardina and Metz (2005) note how WUSA marketed itself on the promotion of traditional family values and popular conservatism. Southall *et al.* (2005) suggest that the organisation attempted to use three marketing theories interchangeably and seemed confused as to what it was trying to sell. Southall and Nagel (2007) further contend that the league failed to recognise its perceived value amongst sports fans and prospective business partners. The league did not make the leap from "a novelty item that spectators went to see once a year to a sport that had enough true fans to support it" (Southall & Nagel, 2007, p.382). The failure of WUSA, in the country where a professional women's league had arguably the best chance of succeeding, was a significant blow for the game in an international context. Many of the best female players in the world had been recruited to WUSA, and for a number of them the league represented their only chance of a professional career in the game. Southall and Nagel (2007) speculated that WUSA would be seen as the women's equivalent of NASL – a league ultimately doomed to fail but one that would lay the groundwork for future success.

Some years later another attempt at developing a professional women's league was made with the creation of Women's Professional Soccer (WPS). Like MLS, WPS was focused on a more consolidated growth than its predecessor and a more realistic financial plan. Yet, despite this, WPS would only last for three seasons and various internal organisational struggles led to the suspension of the 2012 season. At the time of writing yet another league has been in operation for one season, but it is even more modest than WPS. The National Women's Soccer League (NWSL) started in 2013 and is subsidised by the soccer federations of Canada, Mexico and the USA, which pay the salaries of a number of national team players, and this then frees up space under a very modest salary cap to recruit international players from other nations.

Given the position of soccer in the USA, the first two attempts at a professional league offered an attractive proposition for the best foreign players in the game. Many of the leading players in the world, including Marta (Brazil), the five-time FIFA World Player of the Year, were tempted to the USA. Because there have been so few opportunities for female football players to develop a professional (or, more realistically, semi-professional) career in the sport, globally the USA has often been seen as the most desirable destination in the game. Some of the top international players, such as England's Kelly Smith (Seton Hall University), first came to the USA on a soccer scholarship.

The excitement of the promise of a professional league was a central narrative in the film *Bend It like Beckham*, in which two young women from England dreamt about the chance of a soccer scholarship at a US university and then being paid to play the game, something they could not possibly envisage in their home nation. Beckham did not appear in the film but was to make the move to the USA himself in the most ambitious attempt to develop the game there since the signing of Pele. The signing of David Beckham brought international media attention to soccer in the USA, and for a brief period the sport became an important news story within the country. His case (although somewhat 'exceptional') represents an interesting point of departure to consider the migration of football players into this particular sporting space in contemporary times and reflect some more on the current positioning of men's soccer in the USA and its relationship to the wider football landscape.

Celebrity football players, students, journeymen professionals and migration: Beckham and friends

In signing a big money contract with the Los Angeles Galaxy, with the stated aim of taking the sport of soccer to 'another level', Beckham was (re)presented as both a football mercenary and a soccer missionary. The news of Beckham's signing attracted massive media attention on both sides of the Atlantic, prompting headlines such as "US Soccer Bends over Backwards" (*Washington Post*, 12 January 2007) and "Posh and Bucks" (*The Sun*, 12 January 2007). In an international football context, Beckham's transfer was promoted as a sign that the league would now compete with other top leagues throughout the world (or perhaps more specifically in Western Europe, where football's core economies are located). Yet this ignored the unique positioning of 'Brand Beckham' and his capacity to transcend boundaries in a way that no other football player could (Vincent *et al.*, 2009; Wahl, 2009). When Beckham arrived in the USA, no other players on MLS team rosters had anything resembling his achievements in terms of domestic league titles in England and Spain, a European Champions League medal, and second place in the World Player of the Year polls.

Research focusing on the economics of professional football has included work on MLS (e.g. Haas, 2003; Kuethe & Motamed, 2010; Lee & Harris, 2010, 2012). These studies identified major performance-related determinants of player salaries. MLS differs from the majority of elite professional leagues throughout the world, as there is no promotion or relegation (commonplace in Europe and other major football regions), the league operates as a single-entity structure, and there is also a salary cap imposed upon teams. This restriction was lifted and the designated player rule, also widely referred to as 'the Beckham rule', was introduced in 2007, allowing some franchises to target high-profile players and pay this individual a figure above the league's designated salary budget. This has since been extended and teams can now have three players outside of the salary cap.

Some commentators excitedly suggested that Beckham's signing would pave the way for other high-profile soccer players to move to the USA, although this ignored the unique contract Beckham had signed and the wider commercial factors shaping the Beckham brand (see Vincent *et al.*, 2009; Wahl, 2009). Other famous names are now part of the league, highlighting that there may be evidence of a shift towards increasing the quality of international imports. The former French international Thierry Henry joined New York Red Bulls from Barcelona in Spain. Henry had himself experienced considerable success with Arsenal in England and, in terms of trophies won, was a more successful athlete than Beckham, having been part of World Cup and European Championship winning teams with France. Here someone also described as a global star alongside Beckham (Simmons, 2007) was identified as an important figure in the next stage of development.

Yet below the handful of marquee signings used to boost the popularity of the league a very different picture emerges when we begin to look more closely at the migrant athletes on MLS rosters. Amongst a number of other English players appearing in MLS in the 2007 season, Beckham's first in the league, were his former youth team colleague at Manchester United Terry Cooke. Other English-born players to have appeared in MLS include John Cunliffe, who moved to the USA to study (and play soccer) at Fort Lewis College (CO), Jason Griffiths (University of Kentucky to New England Revolution) and Andy Dorman. Dorman was drafted by the New England Revolution from Boston University but moved to

Scotland at the end of 2007 and subsequently gained a Welsh cap, thus further highlighting the many layers underpinning athlete migration and identification.

Bale's (1991) work on the migration of student-athletes to the USA highlighted that collegiate soccer had a significant foreign presence and noted that "there has been something of a tradition of importing foreign recruits for the round-ball game" (Bale, 1991, p.55). Whereas American football uses the collegiate game as a kind of 'minor league' system and recruits its athletes through these institutions, soccer is quite different. Male players from the core football economies would (usually) only sign up to a college scholarship in the USA if they were not good enough to develop a professional career in their home nation. Bale (1991, p.56) noted that "it is rare for top foreign professionals to have been nurtured on, or even to have experienced, US college soccer", and the same is still true today.

A number of the players who appear in MLS are individuals who have been released by clubs in their home countries, and so for them the league may be one of their few options to continue playing professionally. In this sense some of the migration patterns to be found in MLS are similar to those found in the North American sports played in the British Isles (e.g. basketball and ice hockey), where players move overseas because they have failed to establish themselves in their home country's sporting environment or wish to prolong a professional engagement with their sport towards the end of their career (Elliott & Maguire, 2008).

As noted earlier, NASL was seen as something of a 'football graveyard' for ageing professionals who wanted one last big payday before they retired from the game. Whilst it is doubtful that in contemporary times players of the calibre of Beckham, Thierry Henry, Robbie Keane and Freddie Ljungberg make a move from Europe to the USA solely for financial reasons, such movement represents an interesting subject and is certainly an area that needs to be looked at further, for we know little about the experiences of wealthy athletic migrants nearing the end of their sporting careers.

Elliott and Harris (2011) suggested that three main groupings can be identified to explain the movement of English players into MLS. The first group comprises those who moved to the USA to attend college and subsequently stayed to play professional soccer. The second consists of players not deemed good enough by teams in their home country. The third group comprises ageing players looking to prolong the engagement with their sport at the end of their careers. Elliott and Harris (2011) also recognise that typologies represent somewhat ideal type categories and that for each individual there is usually a combination of factors that influence their movement to work in a different nation. In this sense then there are probably numerous similarities between many of the migrant players who moved to MLS and their predecessors who made the journey to the NASL many years before.

Concluding remarks

This chapter has attempted to better locate the position of soccer within the wider football world. In focusing on men's and women's soccer, it has shown some of the challenges and possibilities for migrant athletes moving to and from the USA. The signing of David Beckham represented a bold move by MLS to develop the product and reflects the increasing internationalisation of elite sport which is now a central marketing strategy for the recruitment of athletes across the world. The buzzword in much of international sport is legacy, and it is still too early to really tell just what Beckham's legacy will be. Beckham was paid more than 400 times the salary of some of his team-mates in his first season, for a return of five games and two goals (Lee & Harris, 2010).

During his second season in MLS he continued to be selected for the England national squad despite the fact that many saw his moving to the USA as definitively signalling the end of his international career. This presented those involved with the governance of MLS with a new, and unanticipated, problem, as international call-ups often meant that Beckham was unavailable for matches in the domestic competition. As the MLS season runs at a different time from many other leagues across the world, this could present a major problem if the aim is to attract current international players from Europe and other core football nations who continue to remain active as international footballers.

In the early part of 2009 Beckham agreed a loan deal with AC Milan in Italy, as he wanted to stay 'match fit' and try to hold on to his place in the England squad (as MLS did not resume its season until March). The opportunity to play once again in one of the top leagues in the world was something Beckham desperately wanted (Wahl, 2009), and there was some discussion suggesting that MLS was not of a level commensurate with that of an international football player. For those looking from outside then, this suggested that MLS was not really a part of the football world and remained a soccer league far removed.

As with many other parts of his career and wider celebrity profiling, Beckham's positioning is unique and his is a markedly different case from that of other international players who have moved to MLS. Although Beckham could command a salary 35 times that of the average annual salary for an MLS midfield player (Lee & Harris, 2010, 2012), it is also important to note that the average annual salary for an MLS player would equate to less than one week's wages for a top player in the European leagues. Some of the overseas players who are currently registered with MLS clubs first came to the USA on soccer scholarships and so there are similarities here between male and female players from different nations who continue to try to carve out a professional career in US soccer.

As evidenced at different places in this collection, the alleged effect of inward migration on the performances of national football teams has been a point of some contention. In England, for example, the increasingly high number of foreign-born players in the top league has been viewed as a key factor in the perceived sub-standard performances of the men's national team in major tournaments (see Elliott's chapter in this collection), but few would guess that there have been more nationalities represented in MLS than in the EPL despite the fact that the former is also a newer league. There is also much more to learn about the experiences of female soccer players who move to the USA to pursue a professional career in the game. After two false dawns in a little over a decade, even in the country where everything is seemingly in place to see women's professional soccer succeed, there is still no clear sign that it has a viable and sustainable future. Research may also explore the migration of football coaches and managers, as this is an area that has received scant attention in the migration research to date.

Whilst men's professional soccer in the USA has developed markedly over the last few years, it remains to be seen whether MLS can become an important league in an international context. It is important to note that in terms of its longevity MLS is already the most successful attempt at professional soccer in the USA and is generally viewed far more positively in an international context than has often been the case in the past. One key individual in the next stage of development could be the ubiquitous David Beckham, who has been positioned as many things from an ageing mercenary to the saviour of US soccer. The popularity of the sport amongst females, and for both sexes at the recreational level, has clearly shown the game has never been in need of 'saving'. Kuper and Szymanski (2009, p.164) note that MLS is not American soccer but "just a tiny piece of the mosaic". Beckham's contract when signing for LA Galaxy in 2007 included a clause that would allow him the opportunity to own an MLS franchise, and after being touted as "the saviour of United States soccer, he may well become one of its custodians" (Armstrong & Rosbrook-Thompson, 2010, pp.366–7). In February 2014 it was announced that Beckham would launch a new MLS franchise in Miami. Wangerin (2008, p.338) suggested that "there has never been a better time for soccer in a football world", and it will be interesting to see just what the next few years will bring for the global game in the USA.

References

Allison, L. (2005) The Curious Role of the USA in World Sport. In L. Allison (Ed.) *The Global Politics of Sport*. London: Routledge (101–17).

Andrews, D. (1999) Contextualising Suburban Soccer: Consumer Culture, Lifestyle Differentiation and Suburban America. *Culture, Sport, Society* 2: 31–53.

Armstrong, G. and Rosbrook-Thompson, J. (2010) Coming to America: Historical Ontologies and United States Soccer. *Identities* 17(4): 348–71.

Bairner, A. (2001) *Sport, Nationalism and Globalisation*. Stonybrook, NY: State University of New York Press.

Bale, J. (1991) *The Brawn Drain: Foreign Student-Athletes in American Universities*. Urbana: University of Illinois Press.

Brown, S. (2005) Exceptionalist America: American Sports Fans' Reaction to Internationalization. *International Journal of the History of Sport* 22: 1106–35.

Castles, S. and Miller, M. (1993) *The Age of Migration*. London: Macmillan.

Christopherson, N., Janning, M. and McConnel, E. (2002) Two Kicks Forward, One Kick Back: A Content Analysis of Media Discourse on the 1999 Women's World Cup Soccer Championship. *Sociology of Sport Journal* 19: 170–88.

Clayton, B. and Humberstone, B. (2006) Men's Talk: A (Pro)feminist Analysis of Male University Football Players' Discourse. *International Review for the Sociology of Sport* 41(3–4): 295–316.

Collins, S. (2006) National Sports and Other Myths: The Failure of US Soccer. *Soccer & Society* 7(2–3): 353–63.

Darby, P. (2007) Out of Africa: The Exodus of African Football Talent to Europe. *WorkingUSA: The Journal of Labor and Society* 10(4): 443–56.

Delgado, F. (1997) Major League Soccer: The Return of the Foreign Sport. *Journal of Sport and Social Issues* 21: 285–97.

DeSchriver, T. (2007) Much Adieu about Freddy: Freddy Adu and Attendance in Major League Soccer. *Journal of Sport Management* 21(3): 438–51.

Elliott, R. (2013) New Europe, New Chances? The Migration of Professional Footballers to Poland's Ekstraklasa. *International Review for the Sociology of Sport* 48(6): 736–50.

Elliott, R. and Harris, J. (2011) Crossing the Atlantic from Football to Soccer: Preliminary Observations on the Migration of English Players and the Internationalization of Major League Soccer. *WorkingUSA: The Journal of Labor and Society* 14(4): 557–70.

Elliott, R. and Maguire, J. (2008) 'Getting Caught in the Net': Examining the Recruitment of Canadian Players in British Professional Ice Hockey. *Journal of Sport and Social Issues* 32(2): 158–76.

Elliott, R. and Weedon, G. (2010) Foreign Players in the Premier Academy League: 'Feet-Drain' or 'Feet-Exchange'? *International Review for the Sociology of Sport* 46(1): 61–75.

Giardina, M. and Metz, J. (2005) All American Girls? Corporatizing National Identity and Cultural Citizenship with/in the WUSA. In M. Silk, D. Andrews and C. Cole (Eds.) *Sport and Corporate Nationalisms.* Oxford: Berg (109–26).

Giulianotti, R. (1999) *Football: A Sociology of the Global Game.* Cambridge: Polity.

Giulianotti, R. (2005) *Sport: A Critical Sociology.* Cambridge: Polity.

Giulianotti, R. and Robertson, R. (2009) *Globalization and Football.* London: Sage.

Haas, D. (2003) Technical Efficiency in the Major League Soccer. *Journal of Sports Economics* 4(3): 203–15.

Harris, J. (2005) The Image Problem in Women's Football. *Journal of Sport and Social Issues* 29(2): 184–97.

Harris, J. and Parker, A. (2009) (Eds.) *Sport and Social Identities.* Basingstoke: Palgrave Macmillan.

Kuethe, T. and Motamed, M. (2010) Returns to Stardom: Evidence from U.S. Major League Soccer. *Journal of Sports Economics* 11(5): 567–79.

Kuper, S. and Szymanski, S. (2009) *Soccernomics.* Philadelphia, PA: Nation Books.

Lanfranchi, P. and Taylor, M. (2001) *Moving with the Ball: The Migration of Professional Footballers.* Oxford: Berg.

Lee, S. and Harris, J. (2010) An Analysis of the Relationship between Player Performance and Salary in Major League Soccer. *International Journal of Sport Management* 11(3): 360–72.

Lee, S. and Harris, J. (2012) Managing Excellence in USA Major League Soccer: An Analysis of the Relationship between Player Performance and Salary. *Managing Leisure* 17(2–3): 106–23.

Longman, J. (2000) *The Girls of Summer: The U.S. Women's Soccer Team and How It Changed the World.* New York: Harper Collins.

McGovern, P. (2002) Globalization or Internationalization? Foreign Footballers in the English League, 1946–95. *Sociology* 36(1): 23–42.

Magee, J. and Sugden, J. (2002) 'The World at Their Feet': Professional Football and International Labour Migration. *Journal of Sport and Social Issues* 26(4): 421–37.

Maguire, J. (1999) *Global Sport: Identities, Societies, Civilizations.* Cambridge: Polity Press.

Maguire, J. and Pearton, R. (2000) The Impact of Elite Labour Migration on the Identification, Selection and Development of European Soccer Players. *Journal of Sports Sciences* 18: 759–69.

Maguire, J. and Stead, D. (1998) Border Crossings: Soccer Labour Migration and the European Union. *International Review for the Sociology of Sport* 33(1): 59–73.

Markovits, A. and Hellerman, S. (2001) *Offside: Soccer and American Exceptionalism.* Princeton, NJ: Princeton University Press.

Markovits, A. and Hellerman, S. (2003) Women's Soccer in the United States: Yet Another American Exceptionalism. *Soccer & Society* 4: 14–29.

Markovits, A. and Rensmann, L. (2010) *Gaming the World.* Princeton, NJ: Princeton University Press.

Molnar, G. (2006) Mapping Migrations: Hungary Related Migrations of Professional Footballers after the Collapse of Communism. *Soccer & Society* 7(4): 463–85.

Sabo, D. and Panepinto, J. (1990) Football Ritual and the Social Reproduction of Masculinity. In M. Messner and D. Sabo (Eds.) *Sport, Men and the Gender Order.* Champaign, IL: Human Kinetics (115–26).

Satterlee, T. (2001) Making Soccer a Kick in the Grass: The Media's Role in Promoting a Marginal Sport, 1975–1977. *International Review for the Sociology of Sport* 36: 305–17.

Simmons, R. (2007) Overpaid Athletes? Comparing American and European Football. *WorkingUSA: The Journal of Labor and Society* 10: 457–71.

Southall, R. and Nagel, M. (2007) Marketing Professional Soccer in the United States: The Successes and Failures of MLS and the WUSA. In M. Desbordes (Ed.) *Marketing and Football: An International Perspective.* Oxford: Butterworth Heinemann (366–94).

Southall, R., Nagel, M. and LeGrande, D. (2005) Build It and They Will Come? The Women's United Soccer Association: A Collision of Exchange Theory and Strategic Philanthropy. *Sport Marketing Quarterly* 14(2): 158–67.

Sugden, J. (1994) USA and the World Cup: American Nativism and the Rejection of the People's Game. In J. Sugden and A. Tomlinson (Eds.) *Hosts and Champions: Soccer Cultures, National Identities and the USA World Cup.* Aldershot: Arena (219–52).

Taylor, M. (2007) Football, Migration and Globalization: The Perspective of History. Retrieved 7 November 2013 from: http://www.idrottsforum.org/articles/taylor/taylor070314.html.

Veseth, M. (2005) *Globaloney: Unravelling the Myths of Globalization.* New York: Rowman and Littlefield.

Vincent, J., Hill, J. and Lee, J. (2009) The Multiple Brand Personalities of David Beckham: A Case Study of the Beckham Brand. *Sport Marketing Quarterly* 18: 173–80.

Wahl, G. (2009) *The Beckham Experiment.* New York: Three Rivers Press.

Waldstein, D. and Wagg, S. (1995) UnAmerican Activity? Football in US and Canadian Society. In S. Wagg (Ed.) *Giving the Game Away: Football, Politics and Culture on Five Continents.* London: Leicester University Press (73–87).

Wangerin, D. (2008) *Soccer in a Football World.* Temple, PA: Temple University Press.

5 Circulation, bubbles, returns

The mobility of Brazilians in the football system

Carmen Rial

This chapter deals with the transnational circulation of Brazilian football players, many of whom are celebrities, and their lifestyle abroad, which is characterised by the experience of life in an institutional bubble which serves to keep them away from local cultural contexts. The ethnographic study was conducted in more than 15 countries. It concludes that the permeability of the bubble varies according to an athlete's age, original social class, the ranking of his or her club in the football system, and the duration of their stay abroad. As studies of other transmigrants have found, the experience abroad led many of the footballers to have a sharper political awareness.

Football today "is an economically significant, highly popular, globally networked cultural form" (Smart, 2007, p.114); it is an integral part of consumer culture and is focused on celebrities. The global expansion of football is linked to growing interest by the media in the sport and to the development of media technologies, such as satellite TV and the internet. Football games are the world's most widely watched events. This mediascape hegemony (Appadurai, 1990) fosters a global circulation of people and money, in which Brazil is one of the top protagonists, given its football dominance in recent decades. Brazil is the only country with five football World Cup titles, the only one that took part in every World Cup, the country that has led the FIFA ranking for the longest time in recent decades, and whose athletes have received the most FIFA best-player awards (men and women). Brazil is not the only large exporter of football players. In Latin America, Argentina and Uruguay export more footballers per capita, but Brazil leads in absolute numbers.

Sports stars are elevated to an iconic global celebrity status yet still represent local and/or national communities. "The celebrities serve as role models, as objects of adulation and identification, but also increasingly as exemplars of consumer life-styles to which spectators and television viewers alike are enticed to aspire" (Smart, 2007, p.22).

Drawing on Bourdieu's (1987) notion of *field*, I use the term *football system* to refer to the assemblage of various fields related to the practice of football, whose origins date back to the nineteenth century (Guttmann, 1978; Elias & Dunning, 1986; Bottenburg, 2001). The football system includes the football field, which ranges from amateur football in schools for children and makeshift facilities, to the spectacle of professional football. As a transnational institution, FIFA plays a central role in the system by acting through regional federations and national confederations to organise, oversee and regulate its practice. But the football system is not limited to the football field; it includes others such as the journalistic field and the economic field. Drawing on Bourdieu's concepts of cultural, social and symbolic capital (Bourdieu, 1987), we can consider football capital the sum total of knowledge particular to the football field, be it corporal (to know how to deploy one's body during football performances), social (to know important people who will help a player to ascend in the field) or economic knowledge (to know how to manage contracts and capital expenditure).

Since 2003 I have been studying the transnational circulation of Brazilian football players, many of whom are celebrities. My research has led me to conclude that a product valued in the football field does not necessarily have the same value in the football system, as in the latter the journalistic field plays a major role. For instance, few fans in the world are able to recall the names of the Greek players who won the 2004 European Championships, but many know Real Madrid's 2004/2005 starting line-up, even though they didn't win any major title that year. The value of the Greek footballers who became European champions in Portugal is a far cry from that of Real Madrid's 'galactic' stars. In the 'star system' (Morin, 2007) that characterises the current football system, victory in a major competition does not necessarily mean placement at the apex of the football systems hierarchy.

Of the approximately four million Brazilians living abroad, four thousand[1] are estimated to be football players. This emigration is highly visible in the global media. Ronaldinho, Pelé, Ronaldo and Neymar are certainly among the world's best-known Brazilians.

The global dissemination of Brazilian football players, even if not recent, has heightened in the twenty-first century, representing a large symbolic impact given football's strong presence in the global media and its colonisation of masculine imaginations. In addition to the player-celebrities at global clubs in Europe, there is also a numerically significant flow of non-famous footballers looking for work in countries that are unlikely destinations for other Brazilian emigrants, such as Russia, China, India, Korea, Morocco and Saudi Arabia. There is also a nearly invisible flow of Brazilian women football players who seek out the United States of America (USA) and northern European and even African[2] countries to practise the sport in which they have been historically discriminated against (Rial, 2014). These men and women are unknown in Brazil, and if they had remained in the country would probably have had contracts at the minimum wage[3] and of short duration with local clubs, which would require them to spend part of the year unemployed, given the schedule of the Brazilian Football Confederation (CBF). I found that some of them are (or were) living lives abroad with a certain degree of economic precariousness, but in a better economic situation than they had in Brazil, and the large majority earn far less than the millions of dollars in annual income of the celebrities I initially contacted.

Background to the contemporary emigration of football players

Although portrayed by the media as unprecedented, the emigration of South American football players[4] is not a recent phenomenon. The first wave took place in the 1930s, after the first World Cup, which was held in Uruguay. The main destination for Brazilians was Italy, the homeland of the ancestors of many of the emigrating players, which in a way turned this displacement into a homecoming return.

Although it has occurred since the early decades of the twentieth century, this emigration has intensified in the last few years, partly as an effect of changes in European legislation because of what is known as the Bosman ruling (which in Brazil took shape as the so-called Pelé Law of 1998).[5]

The new law meant that footballers became workers with control over their own labour, the right to choose where to play, control over transfers from one club to another, and so forth. This control was to be regained at the end of each contract with a club, thus favouring the circulation of players between clubs within the same country or among different countries. It also favours short contracts and therefore the unemployment of footballers at regional clubs. The athletes have more 'freedom', but this means that they no longer continue to receive a salary and medical assistance as they previously did at the end of a contract.

One of the consequences of the Bosman ruling was that, since the barrier of national origin for European players was partially removed, economics became the primary factor in player circulation among countries and favoured importation. Talent became increasingly concentrated in wealthier global clubs[6] in Europe to the point where some teams are now made up almost exclusively of foreign athletes.

In the first period of 2013, Latin American countries shipped off about 5,000 footballers worth over US$1.1 billion. Argentina and Brazil alone exported over 3,000 football players, or over $400 million in talent. Latin America as a whole exported more value in football players in the first half of 2013 than live animals in the entirety of 2011 (Ferdman & Yanofski, 2013).[7] The export of Brazilian players has yielded over one and a half billion dollars since 1993, when Brazil's Central Bank began to account for the transfer of players under the category of 'services'.

The entire value of some of these transactions may not be officially recorded, since funds can be directly channelled to bank accounts in fiscal havens such as Switzerland, but these are likely to be minor deviations. The largest share of foreign remittances to Brazil from emigrants comes from this group of players. Since large amounts of the players' salaries return to the country and since those who emigrate do so for pay higher than they would earn in Brazil, this emigration clearly entails significant financial contributions. This is true even if only a few players earn ten million euros a year, as do some celebrities at the wealthiest clubs, where their salary is complemented by 'image rights' (paid by the club for the right to use the player's image commercially) and by advertising contracts.

While this migratory flux has some impact on the national economy (though much smaller than its symbolic impact), its economic relevance for Latin American clubs is substantial. Player transfers have become a vital source of financial support, without which clubs would not be able to maintain the current high salaries paid to other professionals. This situation has been changing since 2008, in part because Europe and the European clubs were harder hit by the global financial crisis than Brazil, which provoked a wave of returns of Brazilian emigrants to the country, but also because many of the players who had gone to Europe and had successful careers had reached retirement age and returned to play a few more years for clubs in Brazil.

As Poli and Besson have shown in their analysis in Chapter 3, Brazilian players are found in most of the 208 countries and territories where football is controlled by FIFA, in social, political and sporting contexts that often do not have the same security offered by clubs in Europe or North America. Even countries that are unlikely destinations for Brazilian workers have received football players, so much so that Brazil's Ministry of Foreign Relations prepared a pamphlet to warn football players[8] about potentially dangerous ties with unscrupulous managers in countries such as Armenia, Singapore, South Korea, China, Greece, India and Thailand. Despite the brochure's good intentions, and the fact that each of these countries has a different social and cultural reality, I have personally been to all the countries mentioned except Armenia, and although some footballers had problems in Saudi Arabia, I did not find anything that could be characterised as human trafficking.[9]

Football players as specialised workers constitute a quantitatively and eco-nomically significant group of emigrants, who do not consider themselves to be emigrants or immigrants and are not considered to be so in their places of origin or in their destination. They emigrate with assurances of institutional support (the clubs take care of their work visas, air fares and hotels and help them to find housing, at times providing a translator and other services).If they are transferred to a club in another country, the clubs take care of the travel and work documents, as occurs with the workers studied by Gustavo Ribeiro (1992), the transnational professionals analysed by Alain Tarrius (1992) and the skilled, student and expert workers focused on by Adrian Favell (2006). Studies on the migration of specialised workers tend to focus on intellectual labour, the so-called brain drain (such as that to the USA's Silicon Valley, where communities of intellectuals of different ethnic origins work in computer and electronics firms). But countries like Brazil, Uruguay and Argentina have provided wealthy (and not so wealthy) specialised labour of a particular kind, such as football players who move abroad in the hope of ascending socially thanks to their talent in the sports field.

Furthermore, football players are special emigrants in the sense that they are both a labour force and commodities (Marx, 1978). As many studies have shown, footballers concentrate in themselves others' labour and circulate as commodities; in doing so, they render profits to third parties. Although the football lexicon echoes that of slavery ('to be sold', 'to belong to a club' are phrases very much present in the field), there is no doubt that the exchange of athletes is fully incorporated into late capitalist models.

Today's global circulation creates some nodes that are more important than others where the main clubs and players are concentrated. To draw an analogy with Sassen's work (Sassen, 1991, 2003), global cities in the contemporary football system are those where global clubs are located: Madrid, London, Milan and Barcelona. On the other hand, cities with little political-economic power, such as Seville, Eindhoven and Munich, have a more significant position in the football system than New York, Paris, Berlin or Los Angeles. As global cities, global football cities are less domestic territorial units than nodes of fluxes that cross national borders. It is to these global football cities, or more precisely to the global clubs they harbour, that the 60-odd Brazilian players I have spoken to aim to migrate. Their professional project is representative of most footballers in the world today.

The constant changes of institution (club) and country, and the large number of footballers who are 'repatriated' (about one third of those who leave Brazil return after one year and very few remain abroad when they retire), characterise this migration movement as circular. Brazilian players speak of their circuitous paths as the 'rodar', while attributing to it the positive value of gathering 'experience' and learning ('football teaches us', as many have told me).

The value of football players

Playing football is not an occupation typical of the extremely poor. Certain resources are needed for a young player to become a professional (football boots, contacts with clubs, bus tickets, days off from work). It is not typical of the upper social classes either, whose projects (Schütz, 1987; Velho, 1981, 1999) for reproducing social capital prescribe that heirs – preferably sons – take up leadership positions in business. Football is thus a possible occupation for a broad stratum of the Brazilian population, the subaltern classes, which range from the poor to the lower middle classes. Indeed, most of my interlocutors came from these layers, and their parents were workers in the greater São Paulo metropolitan region with backgrounds as rural workers, locksmiths, carpenters, plumbers, street vendors, domestic maids, re-sellers of goods, and sailors. The stories I heard have many commonalities. They are life histories of families who, as they themselves acknowledge, did not starve but could barely make ends meet.

Thus, a pattern for the displacement of Brazilian footballers may be sought in terms of their placement in social hierarchies, information elicited by asking about the occupation of their parents and sometimes grandparents. Most of the migrating players come from the subaltern classes (among my interlocutors this was true of 90% of all cases). Some came originally from the lower middle classes (around 9% – the sons of a police detective, a nurse, some teachers), and only one of the footballers I contacted directly in Europe came from the middle class (his father was a doctor). In this respect, they are not very different from other Brazilian emigrants, for generally it is not the poorest who migrate.

Most footballers I interviewed had only attended elementary school; around 10% had been able to finish high school; one had applied for college (and dropped out when he moved abroad), and only one had a higher education. This was also the case for only two of their wives, although there is a general tendency for the wives to have higher schooling than the athletes.

Literature about emigration has demonstrated the inappropriateness of thinking about this population in terms of poor or lower-class individuals who migrate mainly as a strategy for working out economic problems (Kearney, 1995, 1996). These studies have shown that emigration is a collective project of social mobility, mainly by families who choose from among their members those who are regarded as better fit for the adventure of migration.[10]

Professional careers (Hughes, 1993) that involve the international displacement of their practitioners are neither extraordinary nor novel. They have been studied in recent decades by scholars interested in the consequences of cross-border living and a cosmopolitan lifestyle. But such careers have typically involved social actors with high cultural capital (students, professors, scientists, diplomats, executives of multinational corporations, etc.). This is rarely the case for workers from the subaltern classes (for instance, employees in offshore oil-drilling platforms). For this reason, cosmopolitan identities have been extensively related to aesthetic and consumption habits (Hannerz, 1996) which are typical of an elite who move among global cities as if they were in their own home town, visiting museums, art galleries, theatres and restaurants with the familiarity that is proper to those who have spent much of their lives in these environments.[11] This was not true of the players (or their families) I contacted. Rather than consuming luxury or cultural goods related to an individualist attitude (Dumont, 1986), it was more important to them to share their earnings with their family and be close to friends. Family, friends and religion appear as central values in their lives.

All were aware that upward mobility in their lives was only made possible by football. They impart to a divine will the fact that they have ascended, as if they had been chosen. Comments such as 'everything I am, I owe to God', 'that's God's will' and 'thank God' punctuate their speech, in acknowledgement of the fact that the talent for football, even while potentiality found in many, is only developed by a few. God – and not religion, as some have emphasised – is a central value in their lives. Most players are neo-evangelicals, and some are Catholics. The Bible is read and taken along on trips. Some get together to read it at each other's homes along with their families or at the training facility. They take short trips to find neo-evangelical churches. Belief in God has a fundamental role in consolidating a righteous personal ethic ('God helps to sort out evil from good'; 'before, I used to drink and do wrong things'). It establishes and consolidates friendship ties with other Brazilian players and provides them with support in an extremely competitive professional field; 'God is a friend who is always with me', declared Edu (Rial, 2012).

Transmigrants living in a bubble

These footballers and their families seek to maintain as much contact as possible with Brazil. The visits of friends and relatives are frequent; their housekeepers are Brazilians; their friends are Brazilian footballers or other Brazilian (or South American) emigrants; they attend churches of Brazilian evangelical denominations and regularly consume foods similar to those that they had at home, thus reactivating with each meal the link with their place of origin (Rial & Assunção, 2011). The club, in turn, provides them with housing, and if they gain a certain status in the football system,[12] with translators, secretaries, cars, help to open bank accounts and anything that they may need so that they do 'not have adaptation problems'. Their lifestyle focused on their country of origin, and the condition of being overprotected by clubs and managers and subject to rigid hours and discipline, led me to characterise the daily life of these athletes as being contained in a *bubble* within which they are isolated from local social connections – hotels, training centres, physical therapy clinics and residential condominiums. Inside the bubble, contact with common mortals is minimal (Rial, 2012).

'Here it's just like in Sweden', the aunt of one of the football players who lived with him in Holland told me, an affirmation that in some way also appeared in numerous statements made by footballers who had already circulated in different countries. Evidently, this bubble is more or less permeable to the local cultures, depending on factors such as the importance of the club (global clubs create thicker bubbles for their stars), the salary, age, the country of residence, the length of stay abroad, and the social class of origin. I found greater permeability of the bubble among the younger footballers, those who remained longer outside the country, those who had lower salaries, and those who came from the middle classes. Athletes transferred to Europe when they are very young tend to learn the local language and to have girlfriends born abroad, and thus a greater opportunity to leave the bubble.[13] Athletes who have been in Europe for more time, and who send their children to school there, establish important local ties. And in the same sense, the football players with lower salaries, with less chance to bring Brazil to the places where they work, have greater permeability to the local contexts. In all cases, this greater insertion into the local context does not make them lose their strong sense of belonging to their place of origin.

In fact, as a general rule, I found that although they circulate among many countries, these players were far from being cosmopolitan. On the contrary, they reveal an extreme ethnocentrism that at times emphasises the importance of their place of origin (the neighbourhood, the city, the region) more than a sense of nationalism. They tend to experience their stay abroad as a sacrifice to support their families, and the daily reading of the Bible was an important consolation. For this reason, they prefer to spend their holidays in their cities of origin, even when this is a remote place like the tiny village of Humaitá in the Amazon jungle. Because of their efforts to maintain contact with familiar foods and products, it was not rare for me to find curious cases such as the importation by footballers of rice to Korea or of orange juice to Spain.

Although many recognise that they have had an important personal education by living outside Brazil, those I found with cosmopolitan tastes came from the middle classes or were those who went abroad very young or were there for many years. In general, what I found is a strong sense of belonging (to family, place of origin) which is often not understood by journalists or fans, who imagined that the economic ascent is automatically reflected in radically different personal values.[14] The recent return of many stars indicates that they kept to the plan that they presented to me in interviews: to live in Brazil when they retire, if possible working at the original Brazilian clubs where they began their careers, even with salaries lower than they could earn in other parts of the football market, as a type of moral counter-gift (Mauss, 1990) to the institution that helped them at the beginning of their careers.

Strategic nationalisations at the global clubs

Global clubs are strongly internationalised institutions in the football system. They are dominated by international capital and built upon the labour of emigrants (footballers), who have a daily presence in the global media and are the object of feelings of loyalty and belonging for individuals from various nation-states (their fans).

The importance of Brazilian players to the global clubs can be calibrated quantitatively: Brazil was the nation with the highest number of players in Europe's Champions League in 2013/14, as it was in previous years. Brazilian footballers have not only an important numeric presence but also, and more importantly, a qualitatively pivotal presence. They often occupy leading positions in their teams – they are the stars, be it as forwards (the role in which most outstanding Brazilian players have been historically acknowledged) or as defenders (a more recent development, as defenders have rarely figured among a team's most popular stars).[15] At the FIFA 2013 Club World Cup, held in Marrakesh in December 2013, Bayern Munich became champions but only one goal was scored by a German. The tournament had many more goals scored by Brazilians from a variety of clubs: Bayern (2), Guangzhou Evergrande (4) and Atlético Mineiro (4).

The market for foreign players at these global clubs is, however, restricted, as is their time of stay, since players rarely play beyond the age of 30. Moreover, after the Bosman ruling, legal obstacles in most European countries have prohibited the simultaneous use of four foreigners as starters in one team in any given match.[16] 'Nationalisations' are therefore vital for this market to remain open. In this, as in other aspects, the contemporary migratory flows repeat the nationalisations pioneered by Italian-Brazilians during the exodus of players to Italy after the 1930 World Cup. As descendants of Italian emigrants, players obtained Italian passports, which granted them free entry to the country. Today citizenship of a European country is still coveted and remains the prime way to circumvent legislation controlling access to clubs in the countries with the biggest football markets.

Obtaining citizenship in the host country by no means implies gaining nationalist sentiments towards it, or even an identity other than as a Brazilian. 'Brazilianness' remains the sole identity of ethnic belonging of the nationalised athletes. The footballers I contacted, for instance, did not speak of becoming citizens, but of 'being able to get a community passport' – a formula in itself legally impossible, since there is no such thing as a community passport (the passport is granted by each member country of the European Community, now the European Union). But this statement aptly encapsulates the motivation behind nationalisation: the ability to circulate freely among the member countries of the European Union. The main reason for this lies not so much in the security it provides that athletes will be able to stay in the country (they are legal immigrants; the clubs have means to justify their presence), as in making room for another Brazilian to join the club (given the limits imposed by the football system's national legislations) and to be able to circulate freely between clubs.

Obtaining a new national passport does indeed change the legal status of the player, as he now becomes a full citizen of that country. But it is merely a strategic nationalisation. While legally the footballers obtain dual citizenship, they continue to see themselves (and to be seen) as only Brazilian.

Therefore, nationalisation interferes with circulation not only by making it possible for another foreigner to join the club, but also by granting the player some benefits and imposing some constraints. Among the latter, the most significant is probably that the player is required to pay income tax in the host country (in Spain this could mean a tax as high as 43% of earnings). This can be a strong stimulus to move, preferably to another global club in a country with lower taxes. Thus, paradoxically, nationalisation into a European country could favour the movement rather than the permanence of football players in these countries, which is in sharp contrast to other modalities of international emigration. It favours the increased circulation of footballers, since those who are 'nationalised' move from the restrictive category of foreign commodity (subject to limits imposed by trade barriers against imported commodities) to the category of a European Union commodity (and therefore, in principle, able to circulate freely in the European Union market).

Nationalisation is not regarded by players as increasing their distance from Brazil. The same holds true for the increasing participation of Brazilian players in foreign national teams.[17] The athletes constantly reaffirm their closeness to their native country and, as I have been able to verify, particularly through daily consumption practices that compound their lifestyle.

For these reasons, even footballers who become citizens of other countries can be characterised as transmigrants, that is, "immigrants who develop and sustain multiple relations – family, economic, social, organizational, religious and political – that traverse borders" (Basch *et al.*, 1994, p.7).

Local matters: the US exception

There is a great similarity in how players in Europe, other parts of the world and those in the USA maintain their ties with Brazil, but I noticed some marked differences in tastes and lifestyles, which in this case appear to relate more to the player's original social layer than to the country where he is found.

In the USA, I expected to find Brazilian players living in a bubble, as those in Europe do. I expected that they would have strong religious values and that the presence of neo-Pentecostalism would be hegemonic. Finally, I expected to find athletes from the humble social origins that are common to the large majority of football players with whom I had had previous contact, even those who had become celebrities. To my surprise, I found a considerable number of players from middle class families, which I did not find in any of the 14 other countries where I conducted research. And among many Brazilian athletes in the USA I also found a pronounced local insertion. These are distinctions in terms of the global circulation of players.

For example, along with expressions of nationalism and patriotism towards Brazil, I also found expressions of a cosmopolitan taste – the use of other languages, references to US music, Mexican food and American brands, attendance at basketball games and going bowling. These tastes are not common among the athletes I had been in contact with in Europe, Asia and Africa, and were more likely to be found among middle class students in Brazil.

Why are young middle class Brazilians practising a profession in the USA that in Brazil and the rest of the world is occupied by youth from the lower classes? Part of the answer is to be found in the way that they were recruited in Brazil. Contrary to the common use of scouts to find players, some of these athletes had registered in 'exchange' programmes that sought to place students in schools where they could practise the sport and receive a grant to do so.

This method of recruiting young Brazilian players, because of its form and costs, attracts the middle classes. It is common for middle class Brazilians to dream of sending their children to the USA, and for most the only way to get a visa is through a study programme. But studies in the USA are expensive and usually undertaken only by young people from Brazil's economic elite and rarely by those from the middle classes. When they do, it is through exchange programmes.

One of the programmes that organises trips to the USA is 2SV, an 'exchange' agency that arranges for young Brazilians to attend US schools. Here I found various Brazilian football players playing as 'amateurs'.[18] 2SV recruits players through an internet questionnaire, and football (soccer) is one of various sports it offers. After undergoing tests of their athletic abilities (try-outs), the players who pass are sent to the USA and registered in high schools, colleges or universities, where they hope to win a place on a school team. In the selection for 2012, more than 100 student-athletes were chosen.

The existence of training centres for players in the Global South dedicated to preparing them to be athletes in the North is nothing new. This is one of the forms of recruitment of new footballers in the second globalisation phase (Giulianotti and Robertson, 2007). Many of the large European clubs have *soi-disant* philanthropic centres in their former colonies (especially in Africa but also in Indonesia). As Cornelissen and Solberg (2007, p.295) have shown,

> Africa is a primary source for football flows to Western Europe, an aspect that is mostly viewed as exploitative and an extension of neo-imperialist relations between the continent and its former colonial powers. Over the past decade, however, South Africa has emerged as an important alternative destination for many of Africa's departing footballers.

Because its laws are less restrictive than those in the North concerning required schooling, these centres are able to more quickly develop athletic bodies and a player *habitus* (Mauss, 1968) among poor young people. With more 'free' time out of school, they can spend many more hours training.

The novelty of the US context is the existence of centres aimed at the middle classes, and the fact that this recruiting occurs among middle class Brazilian youth. They are recruited in the southern portion of Brazil, where incomes are higher, through companies such as 2SV that operate over the Internet, a tool that still excludes large contingents of the Brazilian population, although its use is growing rapidly in Brazil. A large majority of these student athletes return to Brazil once they graduate, but some are able to find a place on professional teams in Major League Soccer (MLS),[19] and others return to Brazil to play football at good clubs.[20]

Russian sailors? Final considerations

Brazilian players in Europe come from the subaltern classes, but those located above the poverty line. They seek, through transnational circulation, a salary to guarantee a better life for their extended families, and they maintain close emotional and material ties with Brazil, remaining in permanent contact through Brazilian TV channels and social media on the Internet. Brazil, or more precisely their city of origin, is where they spend their holidays, invest money and, if they can, recover from serious injuries. Their attendance at Brazilian neo-Pentecostal churches located where they live, and the consumption of Brazilian products, are central to the constitution of a translocal daily life. I prefer this term to transnational, because the relations are established with the location of origin, even if they are small towns in the interior.

We can imagine that, living in a bubble, Brazilian footballers come and go unscathed, maintaining their ideas and cultural values intact, as the ethnocentrism of their statements indicates. Nevertheless, this is not always the case. Migration studies show that transmigrants can develop political organisations abroad with a strong impact on their countries of origin, as was the case for Filipinos living in the USA who were central protagonists of the democratisation of the Philippines. In the case of Brazilian footballers, the experience in other countries and clubs transforms these athletes, despite the fact that they live in a bubble and prefer to speak only Portuguese and consume Brazilian products, that is, maintain a lifestyle similar to the one they had before they left. They do not study abroad, but their cultural capital grows with what 'football teaches', as many of them told me. They learn other languages; they are exposed to different disciplinary rules by the clubs; they meet footballers from other countries; they observe the trajectory of their children – who are more integrated into local cultural contexts – and change.

Proof of this came in 2013 with the organisation of a national movement in Brazil, the Good Sense FC, led by footballers who had lived abroad for many years, especially in Europe and the USA (Paulo André, Alex, Edu, Juninho

Paulista, Dida and others). The movement demanded that the Brazilian Football Confederation make changes, including the political participation of athletes in decision-making. Their manifesto was signed by more than 300 footballers from large Brazilian clubs and sought changes in the Brazilian football calendar, holidays, a pre-season, financial fair play (loss of points for clubs who failed to pay salaries) and participation for players on the technical councils of the entities that control football in Brazil.

The Good Sense FC was a surprise because, with rare exceptions, Brazilian players have always been estranged from politics in the country or in the sport, or have adhered to conservative positions, even during the military dictatorship (1964–89).[21] Like the farmworkers who had to become sailors in order to return to their country to lead a revolution in Russia, the footballers who circulated abroad and particularly to the global clubs as transmigrants are today the main force seeking changes in the institutional framework of Brazilian football.

Notes

1 One of the Brazilian Football Confederation's directors of records, Luiz Gustavo, estimated that there are four thousand Brazilian footballers playing abroad (Souza, 2007: 45). But it is hard to know for sure, as the Brazilian Football Confederation (CBF) has only published data from 2005 on.

2 As Martha Saavedra called to my attention, Equatorial Guinea's national team, which won the eighth African Women's Championship in 2012 (making them the only African country apart from Nigeria to win this competition), had 11 Brazilians who had been naturalised among its 21 registered players. Guinea's national teams have had more than 30 Brazilian athletes, men and women, in recent years.

3 The minimum wage in 2014 is 226 euros per month.

4 'Football player' or footballer is used here to denote a professional player in the football field. Amateur and futsal players have also emigrated.

5 The Bosman ruling, enacted by the European Court of Justice on 15 December 1995, abolished quotas for European football players in clubs from the European Union's 27 nations or from the European economic area (which also includes Norway, Iceland and Luxembourg). Moreover, after the Bosman ruling, agreements were signed with the Russian Federation, and African and Caribbean countries, clearing the free movement of players in these (and especially from these) countries.

6 Global clubs are strongly internationalised institutions in the football system. They are dominated by international capital, centred around the labour of emigrants (players), daily present in the global media, and are the object of feelings of loyalty and belonging among individuals from various nation-states (their rooting fans).

7 According to Euroamericas Sport Marketing, International Trade Centre. I thank Jeffrey Hoff for calling my attention to this article.

8 The pamphlet is also aimed at models, capoeiristas and Brazilian barbecue cooks, which are professions thus curiously seen as posing threats to Brazilian emigrants. I thank Maya Spandell for calling my attention to this brochure.

9 I have found media reports about football players in Arab countries, especially Saudi Arabia, who declared they had their passports withheld, their residential water and electricity cut off, and so forth.

10 I say 'adventure' (Sarró, 2009; Simmel, 1936) because the journey of a common emigrant is often an illegal and risky activity – as is the case with Brazilians who have headed to the US since the 1970s (Assis, 1995; Margolis, 1994; Reis and Sales, 1999).

This is not true of football players. Their displacements are registered by FIFA and supported by the clubs.

11 Hannerz (1996, p.168) came up with a more sophisticated definition: "A more genuine cosmopolitanism is, above all, an orientation, a willingness to commit with the Other. It upholds an intellectual and aesthetic attitude which is open to divergent cultural experiences, a search for contrasts rather than uniformity. To become familiar with more cultures is to become an enthusiast; it is to see these cultures as if they were works of art."

12 Even players at smaller clubs, like those I found in Marrakesh or Hong Kong, received institutional protection from the clubs in the form of housing, healthcare and at times private attendants to do their clothes shopping and make dental appointments, as I found on more than one occasion. In one extreme case, which probably points to what will be the future for many, Ari in Alkmaar had a secretary hired by the owners of his rights who, in addition to being a translator and driver, each day sent a report to his manager about all of Ari's movements; this supervision extended to the private domain, as he lived with the athlete.

13 This tendency for footballers to leave at younger and younger ages emerged strongly after the change of rules at UEFA which pushed clubs to develop athletes within their own youth systems.

14 The striker Adriano, a former member of the Brazilian national squad, was rumoured to have been kidnapped for three days in the favela where he grew up, and where he went to see childhood friends and family, some of whom were known drug dealers. The media could not accept that a millionaire would spend three days in a favela, and so rumours spread that he had been kidnapped.

15 Such is the case of Lúcio and Dante, who played in Germany, and also of Gomes and Alex in the Netherlands, Luisão in Portugal, Pepe in Spain, Thiago Silva in France, David Luiz in England,.

16 Among the exceptions is England, where Chelsea, owned by the Russian billionaire Roman Abramovich, has played matches with as many as 11 foreign starters.

17 The dispute between Brazil and Spain over Diego Costa in 2013 was a good example. He chose to play for the Spanish national team, but when asked where he would like to live after retirement, he did not hesitate to indicate his home town in Brazil.

18 The agency said it had the support of Disney and ESPN.

19 Ricardo, from Real Salt Lake, was one of those recruited by 2SV.

20 As did Caio – who was unknown in Brazil because he had lived in and become a player in the United States – who returned to Brazil and was able to play for first division teams like Botafogo and Figueirense.

21 The case of Didi Pedalada is famous. Upon retiring from football, he became a torturer and participated actively in Operation Condor, a clandestine consortium of South American dictatorships that sought to exchange information, techniques of torture and political prisoners. There were exceptions such as Sócrates or Afonsinho, who were against the military regime and rebelled against disciplinary rules such as *concentração* before games (a period of time on the eve of games when athletes are restricted to their hotel or accommodation and banned from having contact with friends and family) or the prohibition against the growing of beards.

References

Appadurai, A. (1990) Disjuncture and Difference in the Global Cultural Economy. In M. Featherstone (Ed.) *Global Culture*. London: Sage (295–310).

Assis, G. (1995) Estar aqui, estar lá . . . uma cartografia da vida entre dois lugares. Unpublished MA thesis, Social Anthropology, Federal University of Santa Catarina, Florianópolis, Brazil.

Basch, L., Glick-Schiller, N. and Szanton-Blanc, C. (1994) *Nations Unbound: Transnational Projects, Postcolonial Predicaments and Deterritorialised Nation-States*. Langhorne, PA: Gordon & Breach.

Billig, M. (1995) *Banal Nationalism*. London: Sage.

Bottenburg, M. (2001) *Global Games*. Urbana: University of Illinois Press.

Bourdieu, P. (1979) *La distinction: critique sociale du jugement*. Paris: Minuit.

Bourdieu, P. (1980) Comment peut-onêtre sportif. In P. Bourdieu (Ed.) *Questions de sociologie*. Paris: Minuit (173–95).

Bourdieu, P. (1987) *Choses dites*. Paris: Minuit.

Cornelissen, S. and Solberg, E. (2007) Sport Mobility and Circuits of Power: The Dynamics of Football Migration in Africa and the 2010 World Cup. *Politikon: South African Journal of Political Studies* 34(3): 295–314.

Dumont, L. (1986) *Essays on Individualism: Modern Ideology in Anthropological Perspective*. Chicago, IL: University of Chicago Press.

Elias, N. and Dunning, E. (1986) *Quest for Excitement: Sport and Leisure in the Civilizing Process*. Oxford: Blackwell.

Favell, A. (2006) *The Human Face of Global Mobility*. London: Transaction.

Ferdman, R.A. and Yanofski, D. (2013) Latin America Earns More from Exporting Soccer Players Than Live Animals. Retrieved 7 January 2013 from: http://qz.com/109317/latin-americas-soccer-player-exports-are-worth-more-than-its-animal-exports/.

Giullianotti, R. and Robertson, R. (2007) *Globalization and Sport.* Oxford: Blackwell.

Guttmann, A. (1978) *From Ritual to Record: The Nature of Modern Sports*. New York: Columbia University Press.

Hannerz, U. (1996) Cosmopolitas y locales en la cultura mundial. In U. Hannerz (Ed.) *Conexiones transnacionales: cultura, gente, lugares*. Madrid: Ediciones Cátedra (165–80).

Hughes, E.C. (1993) *The Sociological Eye: Selected Papers*. New Brunswick, NJ: Transaction.

Kearney, M. (1995) The Local and the Global: The Anthropology of Globalization and Transnationalism. *Annual Review of Anthropology* 24: 547–65.

Kearney, M. (1996) *Reconceptualizing the Peasantry: Anthropology in Global Perspective*. Boulder, CO: Westview Press.

Majer, L. (2008) Ir, ficar ou voltar: objetivos, anseios e dificuldades de brasileiros que emigraram a Israel. Unpublished honours thesis, Social Sciences, Federal University of Santa Catarina, Florianópolis, Brazil.

Margolis, M. (1994) *Little Brazil: An Ethnography of Brazilian Immigrants*. Princeton, NJ: Princeton University Press.

Marx, K. (1978) *Capital: A Critique of Political Economy, vol. 1*. Moscow: Progress Publishers.

Mauss, M. (1968) Les techniques du corps. In *Sociologie et anthropologie*. Paris: PUF.

Mauss, M. (1990) *The Gift: Forms and Functions of Exchange in Archaic Societies*. London: Routledge.

Morin, E. (2007) *Les stars*. Paris: Seuil.

Reis, R. and Sales, T. (1999) (Eds.) *Cenas do Brasil migrante*. São Paulo: Boitempo.

Rial, C. (2006) Os jogadores brasileiros na Espanha: emigrantes porém. *Revista de Dialectología y Tradiciones Populares* 61(2): 163–90.

Rial, C. (2012) Banal Religiosity: Brazilian Athletes as New Missionaries of the Neo-Pentecostal Diaspora. *Vibrant* 9(2): 128–58.

Rial, C. (2014) New Frontiers: The Transnational Circulation of Brazil's Women Soccer Players. In S. Agergaard and N. Tiesler (Eds.) *Kicking the Globe: Women, Soccer and Transnational Migration.* London: Routledge (86–101).

Rial, C. and Assunção, V.K. (2011) As viagens da comida: notas a partir de etnografias de brasileiros emigrantes na região de Boston e com futebolistas que circulam pelo mundo. In S. Arend and J. Pedro (Eds.) *Diásporas, Mobilidades e Migrações.* Florianópolis: Editora Mulheres (191–220).

Ribeiro, G.L. (1992) Bichos-de-Obra: fragmentação e reconstrução de identidades. *Revista Brasileira de Ciências Sociais* 18: 30–40.

Sarró, R. (2009) La aventura como categoría cultural: apuntes simmelianos sobre la emigración subsahariana. *Revista de Ciências Sociais* 43(2): 501–21.

Sassen, S. (1991) *The Global City: New York, London, Tokyo.* Princeton, NJ: Princeton University Press.

Sassen, S. (2003) *Contrageografías de la globalización: género y ciudadanía en los circuitos transfronterizos.* Madrid: Traficantes de Sueños.

Sassen, S. (2008) Strategic Gendering in the Global Economy. In *La Igualdad no es una utopía.* Nuevas Fronteras: Avances y Desafíos. Conferencias plenarias. Madrid: Thomson-Aranzadi.

Schütz, A. (1987) *Le chercheur et le quotidien phénoménlogie des sciences sociales.* Paris: Meridien Klincksieck.

Simmel, G. (1936) *Cultura femenina y otros ensayos.* Madrid: Revista de Occidente.

Smart, B. (2007) Not Playing Around: Global Capitalism, Modern Sport and Consumer Culture. In R. Giulianotti and R. Robertson (Eds.) *Globalization and Sport.* Oxford: Blackwell Publishing (113–34).

Souza, M.M. de (2007) Bola dividida. *Zero Hora*, Porto Alegre, 18 June.

Tarrius, A. (1992) *Les fourmis d'Europe.* Paris: L'Harmattan.

Velho, G. (1981) *Individualismo e cultura: notas para uma antropologia da sociedade contemporânea.* Rio de Janeiro: Zahar.

Velho, G. (1999) *Projeto e metamorfose: antropologia das sociedades complexas.* Rio de Janeiro: Zahar.

6 The migration of Irish professional footballers

The good, the bad and the ugly

Seamus Kelly

Since the 1960s the modest ordinary professional hero has been transformed, aided by media discourse, into a contemporary sporting hero who, as a performer and celebrity, can acquire immense wealth and lead an exuberant celebrity lifestyle (Taylor, 2001; Whannel, 2002). The English Premier League, with its increased glamorisation, global profile and media obsession (Buckley, 2004), has witnessed a new generation of celebrity players who are viewed as cultural icons and contemporary heroes (Williams, 2006). The widely held assumption by football fans is that these idols travel an inevitable path to fame and glory. However, behind the scenes a different picture emerges and the path to becoming a professional football player is rarely so uncomplicated.

Ethnographic research dispels many of the myths portrayed by the media concerning contemporary players' glamorous and affluent lifestyles; in fact, chronic insecurity, loneliness and rejection are prominent characteristics (Parker, 1996; Roderick, 2006, 2013). Moreover, significant aspects of professional football culture incorporate anti-intellectualism, ruthlessness and laddish banter (Parker, 1996, 2006; Gearing, 1999) and hyper-masculine workplaces epitomised by authoritarian styles of management and coaching (Kelly & Waddington, 2006; Roderick, 2006; Potrac & Jones, 2009). Building on previous research that examined young Irish migrant professional players' experiences in the UK (McGovern, 2000; Bourke, 2002, 2003), this chapter examines young Irish migrant players' socialisation into professional football culture and the difficulties they encounter in attempting to realise their dream.

Athletes' socialisation into sport subcultures involves both the creation and confirmation of role identities (Donnelly & Young, 1988; Stevenson, 1990). While Roderick (2006, 2013) has examined many aspects of this process in professional football, Parker (1996, 2001, 2006) provides a revealing insight into the daily routines of young apprentices and identifies official and unofficial institutionalised norms, values and behaviours which serve to shape masculine identities through the players' experiences concerning heterosexual relations, wealth and consumption. This chapter examines a crucial and often neglected aspect of identity construction and confirmation in professional football, the micro-cultural features of professional football dressing rooms. Arguably, socialisation into professional football in general and dressing room culture in particular extends to all young migrant players. Particular attention will focus on how young migrant players cope with chronic insecurity and deal with the deconstruction of their identity following rejection from professional football. This is achieved by drawing on the author's experience as a former professional footballer and coach in the UK and Ireland. Before examining these issues, the following section briefly contextualises the outward migration of players from Ireland.

Irish player migration

Professional club academies or youth trainee schemes are one of the most realistic opportunities for young migrant players to realise the dream of playing professional football (Relvas *et al.*, 2010). English clubs have a long history of recruiting young Irish players, which constitutes a form of 'demonstration effect' in which the success (or failure) of previous Irish migrant players influences future recruitment decisions (Maguire & Stead, 1998: Maguire & Pearton, 2000; Elliott, 2014). In this regard, there is a widely held perception that young Irish players possess both natural and contextual talent, the latter concerning how a player "fits in with the team ethos and style of play" in the UK (Brady *et al.*, 2008, p.63).

Of the total number of Irish players (241) currently registered with professional clubs in the UK, 48 are with English Premier League clubs. Historically, Irish players were recruited from places like Belfast and Dublin. In particular, the Dublin District Schoolboy League (DDSL) attracts considerable attention from English clubs, due in part to its high concentration of young players. With over 200 clubs and 16,000 players, the DDSL is arguably one of the largest schoolboy leagues in Europe (Bourke, 2007; Curran, 2014). Local and international youth competitions in Dublin (the Kennedy Cup) and Northern Ireland (the Milk Cup and the Foyle Cup) are viewed as a 'showcase' of the best young talented players on offer (Curran, 2014). In addition to concerns over the motivations of some youth clubs and their coaches towards player development, the practice of tapping up and poaching young adolescent players is widespread.

Most young Irish players are produced for the export market to the UK due to the many formal links that English clubs have with Irish clubs, which act as feeder clubs or nurseries that supply them with young talent (Curran, 2014). While estimates of the number of Irish players who are signed via this route are difficult to obtain, thousands of players, despite an age restriction of 16, are invited to train with English clubs from as young as 14. However, most young players attempting to realise their footballing dreams have limited knowledge of this cut-throat and ruthless industry. In reality, players are viewed as marketable assets and commodities that are bought, sold and discarded by clubs once their playing value dissipates (Darby *et al.*, 2007; Potrac & Jones, 2009). The opportunity to sign with an English Premier League club is an option few young players are willing to forgo. The difficulties of convincing them, and their parents in particular, to stay in Ireland may be due, in part, to the considerable monies on offer and their lack of interest in domestic football or formal education.

In short, many young players view staying in Ireland 'as a missed opportunity', should the option to realise their dream present itself. Because most young players fail to make the grade and then return to Ireland, it has been suggested that these players would be better served continuing their academic and football education in Ireland (Curran, 2014). I will return to this point later. While most UK clubs remain focused on youth development, some clubs have placed a greater emphasis on the recruitment of cheaper, more experienced high-profile players from abroad (Walters & Rossi, 2009). Given the insecure nature of the football manager's position and the pressure for immediate results, relying on long-term youth development strategies for playing talent is a luxury few managers can afford (Gilmore & Gilson, 2007). Moreover, the considerable influx of foreign players in general and to the English Premier League in particular has an obvious impact on young players' potential to progress (see also the chapters by Elliott and by Weedon in this collection).

Following their arrival in the UK, many young migrant players experience difficulties in settling down and adjusting to the host national culture, which is viewed as a form of cultural dislocation or culture shock (Stead & Maguire, 2000; Magee & Sugden, 2002; Bourke, 2003; Weedon, 2012). Acculturation "is a continuous process" in which "an individual may adopt different strategies at different times" as they encounter and interact with new cultural forms (Sam and Berry, 2006, p.19). The process of acculturation might apply to senior migrant players in general and to youth migrant players in particular, who, as migrants and elite athletes, have to undergo social, cultural and physiological phases of development in a highly competitive and unfamiliar setting (Weedon, 2012). Young migrant players may also have to deal with the potential for "glocal" resistance from the host national culture (Weedon, 2012), where a particular 'nation's' exploitative and/or supportive treatment may also be a significant factor (Maguire & Stead, 1998). Migrant players need to be cognisant of the fact that attitudes towards certain nationalities and national stereotyping exist in professional football (see also Molnar's chapter). In addition to the socio-cultural problems of adjustment and dislocation (Maguire & Pearton, 2000; Roderick, 2006), additional factors, as discussed later, may account for the limited number of players progressing from youth to senior levels in the game.

Socialisation into professional football culture

Socialisation has been identified as a process of identity formation where the individual is seen as an active and self-reflective participant who is concerned with the process of developing appropriate or desired attitudes and behaviours that support certain role identities (McCall & Simmons, 1978; Van Maanen & Schein, 1979; Bauer *et al.*, 1998; Cable & Parsons, 2001). When a young football player signs a contract with a professional club, he is socialised into what are considered to be appropriate values, attitudes and behaviours (Gearing, 1997). Both Gearing (1997) and Parker (1996) provide examples of cultural practices and behaviours that young aspirant professionals are socialised into, such as dressing-room banter, gambling, drinking and male promiscuity. Such practices are still prevalent today, the only difference being the method of consumption. For example, mobile phones have replaced trips to betting shops, drinking sessions are carefully organised in VIP rooms and private members' clubs, while male promiscuity is facilitated by social networking sites. Examples of appropriate values and attitudes include "obedience, collective ability and an ability to conform", the adoption of which demonstrates to club coaches signs of young players progress and personal maturity (Parker, 1996, p.200).

One specific aspect of what is considered an appropriate attitude in professional football concerns the adoption of 'good habits', which pertains to such things as punctuality and mental and physical preparation for training and matches. The importance of developing a good attitude is impressed on young players from the moment they sign with a professional club. These attitudes become ingrained over time and constitute a normative form of control that attempts "to shape work culture and workers' subjectivity in order to ensure compliance" (Ezzy, 2001, p.632). When a young player is "seen to comply with appropriate attitudes and values, this quite often will generate increased favour in terms of managerial preference" (Parker, 1996, p.111). Failure to develop a healthy professional attitude or accept such values may generate unfavourable reactions from coaches and team-mates, which can result in players being stigmatised. This is an important point because many young migrant players are unaware of the culture of professional football in general and football clubs in particular, as both have their own specific cultural environment, subcultures, traditions, values and working practices (Parker, 2000, 2001, 2006; Potrac *et al*., 2002; Brady *et al*., 2008).

Professional football in the UK is characterised by a ruthless, macho culture in which heightened levels of performance expectation exist alongside a reduced tolerance for failure (Reilly *et al*., 2008). Professional football is a 'work role' where participation in training and games is deemed a central value of professional football culture and the context through which the highly masculine identities of players are given meaning (Parker, 1996; Roderick, 2006). Because a footballer's sense of self is invested in their physical body, below-par performances in training or matches, or a bad injury in particular, can be viewed as a disruption of the self and severs the legitimisation of such powerful self-definitions, where players can feel unwanted and isolated from their team-mates, both physically and emotionally (Roderick, 2006). Moreover, insecurities are an integral feature of the lived experiences of professional footballers where ruthless competition for places and the concomitant production of individualistic workplace attitudes exist (Ezzy, 2001; Roderick, 2006). Thus, for young players in particular, the pressures to conform to the norms, the threat of losing recognition amongst their peers and significant others and the potential loss of a prospective professional contract consume their lives (Christensen & Sørensen, 2009). One key aspect of the process of informal socialisation concerns how young players learn to "deal with the fears and uncertainties associated with their work, particularly in terms of presentation of self" (Roderick, 2006, p.260).

Impression management

When faced with chronic uncertainty, players learn to become skilled manipulators of self and workplace reputations in the eyes of their fellow players and coaches, and they distance or hide their feelings about their present situations behind a demeanour of enthusiasm for the job (Goffman, 1959; Roderick, 2006). What this means is that players must convince not only their coaches but also their team-mates that, "at least on the surface, they are committed to workplace interests and goals" (Roderick, 2006, p.255). Thus, players adopt impression management tend as a means of communication via the "front regions", where they appear to accept feelings of rejection, insecurity and fear while avoiding their surrender of self among team-mates and employers (Roderick, 2006, p.260). This ability to manage the impressions portrayed to significant others can be viewed as a process in which players adopt "dramaturgical selves" (Collinson, 1988), which is viewed as a form of survival strategy within an occupation characterised by conspicuous visibility. Developing "dramaturgical selves" is also a means by which players may distance their selves from authoritarian coaches and managers. In the company of their team-mates and coaches in general, and in the dressing room in particular, players never let their true feelings show, never complain and, as we shall see later, employ humour when dealing with potentially difficult situations (Collinson, 1988).

The perception of professional football players as being macho and displaying a hard front when dealing with insecurity and rejection contrasts significantly with their underlying worries and fears concerning their future in the game. In addition, impression management plays a crucial role in helping us to understand how young players deal with other aspects of professional football culture. More specifically, one often neglected aspect of the construction and confirmation of a player's identity concerns the role and significance of dressing-room culture. The following sections examine the informal process of socialisation by focusing on the micro-cultural aspects of football culture which contribute significantly to young players' identity construction and conformation.

The good

Young migrant players' first impressions of their new working environment comprise many highlights: the marbled halls of the stadium, state-of-the-art dressing rooms, impressive stands and the first sight, touch and feel of the immaculately prepared pitch. For young players, the first day at the training ground can involve heightened levels of excitement generated by the high-tech performance analysis suites, chill-out rooms with couches, pool tables and the sight of the senior pros arriving.

One key highlight for all young migrant players concerns the allocation of training kit, which signifies your initial entry into the game. In professional football, considerable significance is placed on club gear as an expression of the hierarchical structure. For example, staff (coaches, managers and physiotherapists etc.) tend to have their initials imprinted on their kit, as do most first-team squad members, while youth players tend to be allocated squad numbers. For youth players, squad numbers can signify the particular moment in time of your entry into the club, the number 88, for example, suggesting your late entry to a particular squad. In terms of the (re)allocation of squad numbers, some managers and coaches like to play mind games with both senior and youth players. For example, being allocated number 29 on your kit after having worn number 9 the previous season has obvious implications in terms of signifying your current standing within the squad. Players can view this as being 'put up to them' in terms of the importance of prospective performances in the forthcoming pre-season training. While most players tend to get on with it, some 'bite' and 'snap', with their initial reaction being the source of considerable banter in the dressing room. As players arrive for their first training session and the dressing room fills up, first impressions of their fellow team-mates begin to form.

Walking the walk, talking the talk, and 'the look'

The contemporary professional football dressing room, at youth level in particular, consists of overt displays of male prowess, conspicuous consumption and masculinity. This is particularly evident in the display of designer clothes, hairstyles, flexed pecs, trimmed bodies, beards and even nails. The first pay cheque, which most players tend to keep, signifies a moment in time that confirms, in part, your identity as a professional footballer. For young players, pay-day is usually followed by a trip to town to purchase any combination of designer clothes, watches and accessories that replicates the senior pros' identity: flip-flops, wash bags, sun glasses, headphones, jewellery and, of course, tattoos. Anything that signifies professional footballing identity is purchased and conspicuously displayed thereafter. Some young players find such conspicuous consumption quite intimidating but, in an attempt to attain peer-group identity and credibility, tend to go with the flow. However, as we shall see later, such displays of conspicuous consumption hide the many daily insecurities professional footballers experience. More importantly though, once players assemble the look, they soon realise what 'the look' really means.

One aspect of professional football culture, understood mainly by those in the game, concerns formal and informal symbols that legitimise their footballing identity. For example, one significant contribution to identity confirmation concerns the attainment of formal awards. Such formal awards recognising a player's performance may come from fans, managers, coaches and fellow players, the latter being viewed as more valuable by players. Moreover, in terms of identity confirmation, responses from coaches and fellow players towards their footballing prowess also serve to reinforce this identity (Stevenson, 1990; Brown & Potrac, 2009). One such award, characteristic of the culture of professional football in general and the dressing room in particular, is referred to as 'the look'. 'The look' is a simple, yet highly valuable and informative, nod of acceptance or appreciation from fellow players. Sometimes this is communicated to players on the pitch, by senior pros, or in the dressing room. It signifies acceptance, a considerable form of non-verbal communication that you have 'made it' or 'you'll do for me'. For professional football players, this is *the* most valuable confirmation of their identity as a footballer; a critical moment of truth that signifies to them when they have 'made it' or are on course to 'making it'.

While success, in terms of progression to the senior ranks or the awarding of a new contract, may not materialise, these are significant moments of truth players 'latch on to' and reflect upon to legitimise their footballing identity. Getting the nod or look is deemed far more meaningful than the overt displays of masculinity and wealth because, in professional football, players talk the talk and walk the walk but can they do it where it counts most, on the pitch? More specifically, within the confines of the dressing room and on the training pitch in particular, there are no hiding places and players get 'found out' very quickly. Quite often, it is the most vociferous or 'cocky' players in the dressing room who fail to perform on the training pitch. Failure to perform in footballing terms is one aspect of professional football that is often the subject of much banter in the dressing room. For example, comments such as 'put your medals on the table' and 'played a few games, have we?' explicitly put players with a misplaced sense of achievement back in their place. In football parlance, 'the young bucks, flash dans or peacocks' tend to be the focus of senior pros who deem their performance levels, work rate and attitude inappropriate. Football dressing rooms can be quite unforgiving at times.

Dressing-room banter and 'taking the mickey'

In professional football, dressing-room culture is viewed as a traditional working-class shop floor culture comprising strict male chauvinism, a manual production mentality and a coarse sexist humour that is manufactured around practical jokes and gestures with quite often racist or homophobic connotations (Collinson, 1988). Dressing-room 'banter' involves slagging, 'taking the mickey' or 'ripping' each other's clothes, physical appearance, partners, sexuality and accents. Homophobia, bigotry and sexual promiscuity are common topics of conversation and the source of much banter. Because players have to give as good as they get (Parker, 2006), in terms of identity construction and peer group credibility, they quickly learn not to 'bite' or respond when subjected to slagging in the dressing room.

Banter tends to focus on specific aspects of a player's performance or physical appearance. In this regard, a key part of this process concerns the construction of nicknames for fellow team-mates; the funnier the nickname, the greater the laughter and credibility within the group. Implicit in this humorous process, for a young migrant player in particular, is a form of identity construction. Language and terminology have a particular place, much of which resembles cockney rhyming slang where everything has an abbreviation or double entendre. Nicknames can involve simple explicit additions (Mooney becomes Moonsy, Hawks is Hawkins, etc.) or they may have more implicit connotations, such as 'Daisy' (his passes cut daisy heads as they skim across the pitch at speed),

'Two-touch Johnny' (his second touch is a tackle), 'Glass ankle Willie' (always injured). Some nicknames are a combination of both, for example 'Pufter Pads' (Irish players' dislike of 50/50 tackles or tough play in general). Nicknames can also relate to physical characteristics such as 'Honker' (big nose), Fat Head (large shaved head), Chewbacca (excess bodily hair) or Mant (half man, half ant). In practice, players look for every possible avenue to rip players, and *every* dressing room has a 'Mutton Head' in reference to a player's perceived lack of intellectual ability. In the confines of the dressing room in general and shower room in particular, male genitalia are the subject of much ripping and banter. Common nicknames exist for players such as king-ding-a-ling (well endowed), king donger (promiscuity) and mushroom dick (not so well endowed). In the context of the latter, it is not uncommon for younger, less developed players to shower after training when everyone has left the dressing room. This is an important point because while many young players will have previously experienced some form of banter, professional football dressing-room banter is considerably more cut-throat, ruthless and crude.

Some of the more uncouth and crude dressing-room practices, initiation ceremonies and jokes quite often involve masturbation and bodily excretions. Moreover, because banter can be quite personal and intimidating and lack any sentimentality, it is often construed as a form of bullying. In this regard, implicit in dressing-room banter is an underlying theme of competitiveness and ruthlessness. For example, banter can relate to individual performances in training and competitive matches. Sometimes comments such as 'You've just had a Macedonia' (in reference to the Ireland team's poor performance against Macedonia) are passed in the dressing room. In addition, players may cast votes for the worst performance in training, with the winner being allocated a yellow bib. Banter can have a darker, more alienating dimension. The devastating impact on a player's identity and sense of self when dropped from the starting team can be intensified when players form cliques and openly laugh at and ridicule their replacement player's mistakes in the stand, dugout and subsequent training matches.

Many practical jokes and types of banter incorporate bets and forfeits that involve some form of initiation ceremony for the losers. For example, former Leeds keeper Paddy Kenny bent over and pulled his shorts down to show the Liverpool fans at the Kop end his behind. Forfeits and ceremonies may involve picking up the training kit or performing a demeaning and humiliating act in front of the senior professionals and/or coaching staff. Initiation ceremonies quite often involve the shaving of some part of a player's facial hair such as an eyebrow. In this regard, no dispensations exist, as experienced by the son of Argentine star Diego Simeone, who was subjected to an embarrassing semi-head shaving initiation by his team-mates at River Plate. The traditional practice of urinating in the senior professional's tea pot still exists. Banter and jokes can operate as a medium whereby collective solidarity is utilised to resist managerial control (Collinson, 1988). For example, a manager's pre-match and half-time speeches are a common focus of player sweepstakes, where bets are taken on the number of times the manager says 'Fuck' or praises one of his favourite players. For players, impression management plays a key role here as the slightest smile can warrant a managerial backlash; unless of course the manager has been 'tipped off' and appears to play along with the bet in an attempt to gel with the players. Managers and coaches (dress, mannerisms, accents, etc.) are the subject of much 'piss taking' in the dressing room and in more public domains. In this regard, players can attain legendary status within the game. For example, Jimmy Bullard's goal celebration involved a replication of his then Hull manager Phil Brown giving his players a dressing down at half time on the pitch. No holds are barred in the dressing room and quite often players overstep the mark, as when a pig's head was left in Kenwyne Jones dressing-room locker at Stoke. In this regard, the general public's knowledge of such jokes, pranks and initiation ceremonies is rare because, in professional football, 'what goes on in the dressing room, tends to stay in the dressing room'. For professional footballers, the dressing room is a sacred place, closed to outsiders, and those who break the omerta of silence are severely reprimanded and ostracised by their fellow players.

For players, nicknames, practical jokes and banter are seen as an ice breaker for new team-mates in general and one of the many ways of circumventing the stress and pressures associated with the repetitive and physically demanding nature of footballers' daily training routines. However, the point of drawing attention to this aspect of professional football culture is twofold. Firstly, some players do overstep the mark in general and in relation to homophobic and racist comments in particular. In the context of the latter, outside the confines of the dressing room, references to work colleagues as 'Paddy', 'Taffy' or 'Jock' would certainly be frowned upon, yet within the closed world of professional football they are considered the norm. In the world of professional football, references to black players with orange hair as 'jaffa cake' seem acceptable, due in part to the lack of any racial intent (Taylor, 2013). Consider the recent furore following England manager Roy Hodgson's 'feed the monkey' joke or Alan Hansen's reference to black players as 'coloured' on *Match of the Day*, and you realise the increased sensitivity of language and the context in which it is expressed. Context is everything, and in the confines of the dressing room such comments are viewed as an acceptable aspect of football culture. In addition, during training sessions tackles fly, players get crunched and punched and heated exchanges do occur in which comments such as 'black bastard, 'Irish twat' or 'Welsh wanker' are made. Most players take no offence, unless of course the racial or homophobic comments are made by a player that you have a particular distaste towards. Then, it can be construed as being more personal than racial and taken together the racial content takes precedence and its meaning is construed in a different manner. This is an important point because, within the confines of the dressing room, the meaning contained in racial or homophobic comments is heightened when there is a particular dislike towards the player making them. Outside the closed world of professional football such comments are totally unacceptable and anti-racist campaigns such as 'Kick It Out' are designed to educate players that such language is indeed unacceptable.

Secondly, many young players take offence at and have considerable difficulty in coping with banter and piss-taking in general and the more uncouth and crude dressing-room practices in particular. Most players find masturbating or excreting in a fellow player's sock funny, and everyone laughs along publicly, but privately they detach themselves completely from such acts. However, failure to conform to such practices in the confines of the dressing room may demonstrate to others a lack of commitment or engagement that may lead to rejection or exclusion from the cultural setting. In addition, public displays that reflect your distaste towards certain acts tend to be kept private for fear of further rip-taking. It is important to note that dressing-room banter is one aspect of professional football that many players miss following their retirement.

Education

Within the confines of the hyper-masculine dressing room, player preferences for reading 'the red tops' and the *Daily Sport* over the *Guardian* reflect a deeper underlying culture of anti-intellectualism in professional football. Young players are solely focused on sporting performances and are engulfed in the social world of football, which can cultivate a one-dimensional identity that results in diminished involvement in academic and social activities (Brown & Potrac, 2009). Thus, many footballers get 'caught up in and by the beautiful game', and the perceived prestige associated with being a professional footballer means that football is the only thing they have ever done and the only thing they know how to do (McGillivray *et al.*, 2005, p.102). Because the vast majority of young Irish football players leave Ireland without completing their secondary level education (Curran, 2013), youth training schemes are viewed as an attempt to redress this and ensure the majority of youth players possess educational and vocational skills that may be utilised in the wider labour market. In addition, both Charity X-pro and the PFA cater for the educational needs of all players by providing numerous educational opportunities and support funding to undertake educational and vocational courses. However, for many players any interest in, or engagement with, educational discourse is viewed as having little if any relationship with the process of attaining a professional football identity (Cushion & Jones, 2006; see also Weedon's chapter). Moreover, dressing-room culture can marginalise players interested in engaging with educational discourse (Gearing, 1999; McGillivray & McIntosh, 2006), and in many cases this is explicitly communicated by some clubs and coaches as actually threatening their prospects of becoming professional footballers (McGillivary *et al.*, 2005; McGillivray & McIntosh, 2006; Parker, 2000, 2006; Platts & Smith, 2009). It is worth noting that in Germany, Holland and Spain a more holistic philosophy is adopted that encompasses educational and vocational skills (Potrac & Jones, 2009).

The ugly

Entry into professional football in general, and at youth level in particular, involves increased levels of commitment, sacrifice, dedication, discipline and an ever-increasing affinity with the role of football (Potrac & Jones, 2009). In professional football, the induction period for a young trainee can be quite intimidating and revolves primarily around a strict diet of authoritarian attitudes, physicality, domination, ruthlessness, and hyper-masculine workplace practice (Parker, 1996, p.199) where players need to be able to "look after themselves" (Magee, 1998, p.29). One aspect of the culture of professional football in the UK is its highly authoritarian style of coaching and management (Parker, 1996; Cushion & Jones, 2006).

Professional football is an aggressive, tough, masculine and at times violent industry, and these values are reflected in workplace behaviours and in the socialisation of young players in particular (Kelly & Waddington, 2006; Kelly, 2010). While the ability of players to accept these deeply rooted cultural values is questionable, many would argue that such styles of management and coaching are viewed as a necessary aspect of preparing young players for the rigours of the professional game (Cushion & Jones, 2006; Roderick, 2006). The acceptance of abuse and intimidation is directly related to a player's demonstration of appropriate behaviours and attitudes to their managers and coaches. Failure to accept such abuse and adopt appropriate behaviours can, for young players especially, threaten their career prospects. These values and behaviours are embedded in professional football culture and for players they are unavoidable. While some players may experience fear, conformity to the informal but institutionalised norms may prevent them from displaying their emotional response to such experiences.

While there is a general acceptance in all occupations that newcomers will experience uncertainty and anxiety, there is evidence to suggest that players' preconceptions concerning workplace behaviours in professional football are somewhat misplaced. For example, Parker (1995, p.120) identifies how players' "enthusiasm for the game had waned since their arrival at the club". For many, the first few months in a professional club are viewed as a culture shock. Research currently under way attempts to examine arguments that authoritarian styles of coaching and management at academy level are changing, which is reflective of a wider shift in coaching style at academy level in general (Richardson *et al.*, 2012). It is important to note though that when outsiders (e.g. visiting coaches, members of the press, etc.) visit academies, coaches adopt less authoritarian, more humane styles of coaching because, as one English Premier League academy player recently confided in me, "the coaches like to put on a show".

Curly fingers and shepherd's hooks

In the UK, all young players face considerable difficulties making the transition from youth to the senior professional ranks, a trend that is replicated in Belgium, Finland and Germany (Richardson *et al.*, 2004; Vaeyens *et al.*, 2008; Brown & Potrac, 2009; Relvas *et al.*, 2010; Weedon, 2012). Youth player progression is considerably influenced by players' experience of, and socialisation into, professional football culture in general (Maguire & Pearton, 2000; Richardson *et al.*, 2004; Brady *et al.*, 2008; Henriksen *et al.*, 2010) and by many aspects of professional football culture discussed previously. Other factors, such as a player's willingness to learn, mental strength, discipline, dedication, character, professional attitude and work ethic (Stead & Maguire, 2000; Bourke, 2002, 2003; Holt & Dunn, 2004; Roderick, 2006; Christensen, 2009; Elliott & Weedon, 2010), also play a role, as well as an ability to cope with the physical demands of the game (Williams, 2013), the quality and provision of coaching, and support from families, agents and existing migrant players (Nesti, 2010; Richardson *et al.*, 2012). More importantly, a player's off-field behaviour, for example an overly active social life or excessive gambling and alcohol consumption in particular, is considered by managers and coaches as far more important than any innate talent (Kelly, 2010). It is worth noting that the vast majority of Irish migrant players never play in the English Premiership or at senior international level, and the average length of their careers in professional football in the UK is less than six seasons (Curran, 2014). In recognition of the high failure rate for young players and in an attempt to facilitate their re-entry into Irish football, perhaps the Football Association of Ireland and Professional Football Association of Ireland should be more proactive in providing services for Irish players following their deselection and subsequent return to Ireland.

All young players fear the day when they are informed by their coaches whether or not they will be granted a professional contract. Being told that the 'Gaffer wants a word with you in his office' strikes fear into every player's mind. For many players, deselection and rejection can be a devastating experience, while for others they serve as a motivational opportunity to prove their previous employers and coaches wrong, which may, in time, assist in the (re)confirmation and (re)establishment of their footballing identities. Following rejection, some players do 'get a second bite at the cherry'. However, for many players whose self-concept does not extend beyond the limits of their sport (Brown & Potrac, 2009) deselection may lead to questions surrounding their footballing identity in general and result in feelings of anxiety, depression, anger, humiliation and a diminished sense of self, self-efficacy and self-esteem. Following rejection, players, like all elite athletes, lose what has been the focus of their being for most of their lives and the primary source of their identities: the physical prowess, the adulation and fame, the camaraderie with team-mates and the intense highs of competition (Drahota & Eitzen, 1998). Because most young players have not planned for an alternative career, deselection can be quite traumatic. As Potrac and Jones (2009, p.149) stated, "the creation of such a one-dimensional and unbalanced sense of self based around the athletic identity can lead to traumatic experiences when this identity is lost or relinquished". Thus, for young players deselection shatters their previously taken-for-granted assumption that they will realise their dream of playing professional football. Considering the high failure rate in professional football, perhaps a more holistic approach to player development in general and greater provision of counselling and psychological support are required (Potrac & Jones, 2009; Nesti, 2010). In this regard, many have argued that clubs have not only an obligation but also a duty of care in terms of providing academic counselling and support following deselection.

In the context of the many aspects of professional football discussed previously and in terms of player rejection in particular, one important point needs to be made. Recent high-profile cases of player depression and suicide have drawn attention to the loneliness, isolation and depression that some current and former professional footballers experience (see Elliott's chapter). A culture of 'keeping quiet', 'bottling it up' or 'hiding your emotions' is a prominent aspect of young male adolescents in general and especially within the ranks of young professional football players. Seeking help is viewed by many players as a source of weakness, which is probably more reflective of the inability of young males in general to openly speak to practitioners about their feelings. Speak-up campaigns now in situ attempt to alleviate these barriers and facilitate, anonymously, the option of consulting with expert medical and counselling personnel. Historically though, the tough, physical and masculine nature of the industry has been resistant to the role of psychology in general and counselling in particular (Nesti, 2010).

Conclusion

When a young migrant player signs a contract with a professional club, he learns as part of a process of occupational socialisation to accept what, in football, are considered appropriate values and attitudes in the context of the 'ruthlessness and hyper-masculine' culture of the professional game. These values are deeply embedded in the culture of professional football and are internalised by players. Young migrant players, in particular, are vulnerable and relatively powerless in relation to the manager, and they quickly learn that it is important for them to develop a 'good professional attitude', not least because this will affect the way in which they are perceived and evaluated by their manager, upon whom they are heavily dependent for career advancement. In this regard, the manager is a very powerful figure. He is the gatekeeper who controls access to the desired goal: for young apprentices, the offer of a full-time professional contract. Moreover, players who do not accept and behave appropriately in terms of these values are likely to be perceived by their managers as 'troublemakers', or as people who do not have the 'right attitude', and their careers are likely to suffer as a consequence.

Because most young Irish players fail to make the grade and end up returning to Ireland, it is suggested that these players are better served by continuing their academic and football education in Ireland (e.g. Curran, 2014). In this regard, numerous player development structures and pathways exist for young Irish footballers in terms of both football and educational development. For example, the FAI's High Performance and Emerging Talent Programme is facilitated by a national network of regional development officers and twelve regional centres of excellence (FAI, 2012). To date, 28 Emerging Talent Programme players have signed with professional clubs in England and Scotland. The success of this network is evident not only in terms of Irish teams' qualification for elite phases of European competition but also in terms of the progression of players from the more non-traditional football towns and cities. Like many other countries' national youth development structures and coach education programmes, these are currently being revised, with plans for a National Academy already under way. In addition, FAI/FAS football academies, now in their ninth year, provide young Irish players with the opportunity to receive full-time football training combined with formal education in the area of health and fitness and an opportunity to progress to tertiary level education. Further research is required to examine the argument that players recruited via the League of Ireland such as, Noel Hunt, Conor Sammon, Stephen Ward, Kevin Doyle, Dave Mooney and Wes Houlihan seem to progress better than those recruited at an earlier age.

References

Bauer, T., Morrison, E. and Callister, R. (1998) Organizational Socialization: A Review and Directions for Future Research. In G. Ferris (Ed.) *Research in Personnel and Human Resource Management.* Greenwich, CT: JAI (149–214).

Bourke, A. (2002) The Road to Fame and Fortune: Insights on the Career Paths of Young Irish Professional Footballers in England. *Journal of Youth Studies* 5(4): 375–89.

Bourke, A. (2003) The Dream of Being a Professional Soccer Player: Insights on Career Development Options of Young Irish Players. *Journal of Sport and Social Issues* 27: 399–419.

Bourke, A. (2007) Marketing Football in the Republic of Ireland. In M. Desbordes (Ed.) *Marketing and Football: An International Review.* Oxford: Elsevier Publications (237–72).

Brady, C., Bolchover, D. and Sturgess, B. (2008) Managing in the Talent Economy: The Football Model for Business. *California Management Review* 50(4): 224–46.

Brown, G. and Potrac, P. (2009) You've Not Made the Grade, Son: De-selection and Identity Disruption in Elite Level Youth Football. *Soccer & Society* 10(2): 143–59.

Buckley, W. (2004) *The Man Who Hated Football.* London and New York: Fourth Estate.

Cable, D. and Parsons, C. (2001) Socialisation Tactics and Person–Organisation Fit. *Personnel Psychology* 54: 1–23.

Cashmore, E. (2010) *Making Sense of Sports.* London: Routledge.

Christensen, M.K. (2009) 'An Eye for Talent': Talent Identification and the 'Practical Sense' of Top-Level Soccer Coaches. *Sociology of Sport Journal* 26(3): 365–82.

Christensen, M. and Sørensen, J. (2009) Sport or School? Dreams and Dilemmas for Talented Young Danish Football Players. *European Physical Education Review* 5(1): 115–33.

Collinson, D. (1988) Engineering Humour: Masculinity, Joking and Conflict in Shop-Floor Relations. *Organization Studies* 9(2): 181–99.

Curran, C. (2013) Irish Born Players in Britain's Football Leagues, 1945–2010: A Geographical Assessment. Presentation at the Sports History Ireland Conference, University of Ulster Magee, University of Ulster.

Curran, C. (2014) Professionals on the Move: Irish Born Footballers in Britain, 1945–2010: An Historical and Contemporary Assessment. Unpublished FIFA Havelange Research Scholarship.

Cushion, C. and Jones, R. (2006) Power, Discourse, and Symbolic Violence in Elite Youth Soccer: The Case of Albion F.C. *Sociology of Sport Journal* 23(2): 142–61.

Darby, P., Akindes, G. and Kirwin, M. (2007) Football Academies and the Migration of African Football Labor to Europe. *Journal of Sport and Social Issues* 31: 143–61.

Donnelly, P. and Young, K. (1988) The Construction and Confirmation of Identity in Sport Subcultures. *Sociology of Sport Journal* 5(3): 223–40.

Drahota, J.T. and Eitzen, S.D. (1998) The Role Exit of Professional Athletes. *Sociology of Sport Journal* 15(3): 263–78.

Elliott, R. (2014) Football's Irish Exodus: Examining the Factors Influencing Irish Player Migration to English Professional Leagues. *International Review for the Sociology of Sport*. Published online 11 February 2014: DOI 10.1177/1012690213519786.

Elliott, R. and Weedon, G. (2010) Foreign Players in the Premier Academy League: 'Feet-Drain' or 'Feet-Exchange'? *International Review for the Sociology of Sport* 46(1): 61–75.

Ezzy, D. (2001) A Simulacrum of Workplace Community: Individualism and Engineered Culture. *Sociology* 35(3): 631–50.

FAI (2012) Football Association of Ireland Annual Report. Dublin: FAI.

Gearing, B. (1997) More Than a Game: The Experience of Being a Professional Footballer in Britain. *Journal of the Oral History Society* 25(1): 63–70.

Gearing, B. (1999) Narratives of Identity among Former Professional Footballers in the United Kingdom. *Journal of Aging Studies* 13(1): 43–58.

Gilmore, S. and Gilson, C. (2007) Finding Form: Elite Sports and the Business of Change. *Journal of Organizational Change Management* 20(3): 409–28.

Goffman, E. (1959) *The Presentation of Self in Everyday Life.* New York: Anchor.

Henriksen, K., Stambulova, N. and Roessler, K.K. (2010) Holistic Approach to Athletic Talent Development Environments: A Successful Sailing Milieu. *Psychology of Sport and Exercise* 11(3): 212–22.

Holt, N.L. and Dunn, J.G.H. (2004) Toward a Grounded Theory of the Psychosocial Competencies and Environmental Conditions Associated with Soccer Success. *Journal of Applied Sport Psychology* 16(3): 199–219.

Kelly, S. (2010) The Role of the Contemporary Professional Football Manager in the UK and Ireland. Unpublished PhD thesis, University College Dublin.

Kelly, S. and Waddington, I. (2006) Abuse, Intimidation and Violence as Aspects of Managerial Control in Professional Soccer in Britain and Ireland. *International Review for the Sociology of Sport* 41(2): 147–64.

McCall, G. and Simmons, J. (1978) *Identities and Interactions.* New York: The Free Press.

McGillivray, D., Fearn, R. and McIntosh, A. (2005) Caught up in and by the Beautiful Game: A Case Study of Scottish Professional Footballers. *Journal of Sport and Social Issues* 29(1): 102–23.

McGillivray, D. and McIntosh, A. (2006) Football Is My Life: Theorizing Social Practice in the Scottish Professional. *Sport in Society* 9(3): 224–48.

McGovern, P. (2000) The Irish Brawn Drain: English League Clubs and Irish Footballers, 1946–1995. *British Journal of Sociology* 51: 401–18.

Magee, J.D. (1998) International Labour Migration in English League Football. Unpublished PhD thesis, University of Brighton.

Magee, J. and Sugden, J. (2002) 'The World at Their Feet': Professional Football and International Labor Migration. *Journal of Sport and Social Issues* 26(4): 421–37.

Maguire, J. and Pearton, R. (2000) The Impact of Elite Labour Migration on the Identification, Selection and Development of European Soccer Players. *Journal of Sports Sciences* 18: 759–69.

Maguire, J. and Stead, D. (1998) Border Crossings: Soccer Labour Migration and the European Union. *International Review for the Sociology of Sport* 33(1): 59–73.

Nesti, M. (2010) *Psychology in Football: Working with Elite and Professional Players.* London: Routledge.

Parker, A. (1995) Great Expectations: Grimness or Glamour? The Football Apprentice in the 1990s. *Sports Historian* 15: 107–26.

Parker, A. (1996) Chasing the Big-Time: Football Apprenticeships in the 1990s. Unpublished PhD thesis, University of Warwick.

Parker, A. (2000) Training for 'Glory', Schooling for 'Failure'? English Professional Football, Traineeship and Educational Provision. *Journal of Education and Work* 13(1): 61–80.

Parker, A. (2001) Soccer, Servitude and Sub-cultural Identity: Football Traineeship and Masculine Construction. *Soccer and Society* 2(1): 59–80.

Parker, A. (2006) Lifelong Learning to Labour: Apprenticeship, Masculinity and Communities of Practice. *British Educational Research Journal* 32(5): 687–701.

Platts, C. and Smith, A. (2009) The Education and Welfare of Young People in Professional Football Academies in England: Some Implications of the White Paper on Sport. *International Journal of Sport Policy* 1: 323–39.

Potrac, P. and Jones, R. (2009) Micro-political Workings in Semi-professional Soccer Coaching. *Sociology of Sport Journal* 26: 557–77.

Potrac, P., Jones, R.L. and Armour, K.M. (2002) It's About Getting Respect: The Coaching Behaviours of a Top-Level English Football Coach. *Sport, Education and Society* 7(2): 183–202.

Reilly, T., Williams, A. and Richardson, D. (2008) Talent Identification and Development in Football. In R. Fisher and R. Bailey (Eds.) *Talent Identification and Development: The Search for Sporting Excellence*, vol. 9 of Perspectives series. Germany: ICSSPE (183–99).

Relvas, H., Littlewood, M., Nesti, M., Gilbourne, D. and Richardson, D. (2010) Organisational Structures and Working Practices in Elite European Professional Football Clubs: Understanding the Relationship between Youth and Professional Domains. *European Sport Management Quarterly* 10(2): 165–87.

Richardson, D., Gilbourne, D. and Littlewood, M. (2004) Developing Support Mechanisms for Elite Young Players in a Professional Soccer Academy: Creative Reflections in Action Research. *European Sport Management Quarterly* 4(4): 195–214.

Richardson, D., Littlewood, M., Nesti, M. and Benstead, L. (2012) An Examination of the Migratory Transition of Elite Young European Soccer Players to the English Premier League. *Journal of Sports Sciences* 30(15): 1605–18.

Roderick, M. (2006) *The Work of Professional Football: A Labour of Love.* London: Routledge.

Roderick, M. (2013) Domestic Moves: An Exploration of Intra-national Labour Mobility in the Working Lives of Professional Footballers. *International Review for the Sociology of Sport* 48(4): 387–404.

Sam, D. and Berry, J. (2006) *Cambridge Handbook of Acculturation Psychology.* Cambridge: Cambridge University Press.

Stead, D. and Maguire, J. (2000) 'Rite de Passage or Passage to Riches'? The Motivation and Objectives of Nordic/Scandinavian Players in English League Soccer. *Journal of Sport and Social Issues* 24: 36–60.

Stevenson, C. (1990) The Early Careers of International Athletes. *Sociology of Sport Journal* 7(3): 238–53.

Taylor, D. (2013) Roy Hodgson Guilty of Being a Plum, Not a Racist, over Monkey Remark. *Guardian*, 19 October.

Taylor, M. (2001) Beyond the Maximum Wage: The Earnings of Football Professionals in England, 1900–39. *Soccer and Society* 2(3): 101–18.

Vaeyens, R., Matthieu, L., Williams, A. and Renaat, P. (2008) Talent Identification and Development Programmes in Sport Current Models and Future Directions. *Sports Medicine* 38(9): 703–14.

Van Maanen, J. and Schein, E. (1979) Towards a Theory of Organisational Socialisation. In B. Staw (Ed.) *Research in Organizational Behavior*. Greenwich, CT: JAI (209–64).

Walters, G. and Rossi, G. (2009) (Eds.) *Labour Market Migration in European Football: Key Issues and Challenges*. Conference proceedings from Feet-Drain Conference, Birkbeck Sports Business Centre, London, Research Paper Series 2(2): 224–48.

Weedon, G. (2012) 'Glocal Boys': Exploring Experiences of Acculturation amongst Migrant Youth Footballers in Premier League Academies. *International Review for the Sociology of Sport* 47(2): 200–16.

Whannel, G. (2002) *Media Sport Stars: Masculinities and Moralities*. London: Routledge.

Williams, A.M. (2013) *Science and Soccer: Developing Elite Performers*. London: Routledge.

Williams, J. (2006) 'Protect Me from What I Want': Football Fandom, Celebrity Cultures and 'New' Football in England. *Soccer & Society* 7(1): 96–114.

7 Football and migration

An analysis of South Korean football

Jung Woo Lee

The global flow of people, including the migration of highly skilled workers, accounts for one of the major features of globalisation (Castells, 2010; Ritzer, 2010). The forms of migration vary and can include colonial conquest, labour migration, international student movements, and the migrations of religious missionaries, asylum seekers, political refugees and holidaymakers. In this respect, Ritzer (2010) categorises two types of migratory pattern, namely tourists and vagabonds. As metaphorical expressions, the former indicates those who choose to move because they want to be a migrant. The latter, by contrast, means those who have no choice but to move because of unfavourable political and/or economic circumstances and/or living conditions in their home countries.

The movement of people is both a cause and a consequence of globalisation (Cohen & Kennedy, 2013). For instance, the structure of the global economic system gives rise to a series of unequal relations between the advanced north, such as the United States of America and some members of the European Union, and the less developed south, which comprises nations in Africa and Latin America. Under these circumstances, the citizens of the north are more likely to be 'tourists' when they travel and the migrants from the south 'vagabonds'. In addition, those migrants, regardless of their intention to move, have a significant impact on host countries. The movement of people can promote multiculturalism in a host nation. At the same time, immigration can also cause segregation and conflict between the indigenous people and the foreign settlers. The consequences of the movements of global migrants can be framed through what Appadurai (1990) calls ethnoscapes, which contribute to the emergence of global culture.

Sport is arguably the most globalised and universal form of culture that transcends linguistic and cultural barriers between nation-states (Higham & Hinch, 2009). As sport becomes global, the migration of elite athletes also increases (Elliott & Maguire, 2008). In fact, in the sports industry today athletic workers are valuable assets that are sought after by professional teams and clubs (Castells, 2010; Poli, 2010) and contribute to the development of transnational trade circuits and networks between athletes, agencies and governing bodies (Cornelissen & Solberg, 2007; Carter, 2011b). Consequently, the performance of migrant athletes is increasingly visible in the global sport arena.

This chapter will investigate the globalisation of South Korean football and the migration of football labour in this specific context. Before examining the case of this particular country, it is necessary to consider the nature of global sport and the structure of the global football industry, as they offer a background to this study and a useful theoretical tool for analysing the patterns of football migration. Thus, the following two sections look at these issues.

Globalisation, football and migration

Sport today is increasingly globalised and three distinctive features of global sport can be identified. These are the establishment of global sport governing bodies, the organisation of mega sporting events, and the commercialisation of the sports industry (Andrews, 2004; Houlihan, 2004; Roche, 2006). The global governance of sport is exercised by an institution that sets out the rules and regulations of a particular sporting activity and that oversees the conduct and behaviour of individuals and groups who are officially involved in sport at all levels according to its code of practice (Miller *et al.*, 2001). In addition, it claims an authority over its sport which transcends the sovereignty of national governments, and few agencies and stakeholders are able to reject any decision made by the sport governing body (Houlihan, 2008). This organisation also controls the movement of international sport labour (Carter, 2011b). For instance, FIFA regularly publishes global rules regarding the status of migrant professional footballers and their eligibility to participate in the league sanctioned by the governing body (FIFA, 2010). In this respect, it can be argued that global sport governance establishes an institutional system within which a particular sport is organised and regulated.

Secondly, mega sporting events such as the Olympic Games and the FIFA World Cup constitute an integral part of global sporting culture (Robertson, 1992; Maguire, 1999). Such sporting events are often portrayed as a global ritual that 'celebrates humanity' and promotes the idea of international development through sports (Cornelissen, 2009; Lee & Maguire, 2009). Mega sporting events also facilitate both the short-term and the long-term migration of people (Higham & Hinch, 2009). With regard to short-term migration, the FIFA World Cup, for instance, attracts a large number of football fans from various countries. Also, the delegates of the participant nations, both athletes and staff, need to travel and stay in the host nation. A longer-term migration of football labour includes the recruitment of foreign coaches for national teams. At the 2002 FIFA World Cup, the English team was managed by Swede Sven-Göran Eriksson and Guss Hiddink from the Netherlands was manager of the South Korean squad. Another important aspect of the FIFA World Cup related to the migration of football players is that footballers from developing countries use the World Cup as a stepping stone to cultivate their professional careers abroad (Cornelissen & Solberg, 2007). By displaying their skills at the competition, some players can increase their chances of being recruited by football clubs in other countries.

The commercialisation and commodification of products and services associated with sport (including athletic labour) comprise the third characteristic of global sport (Andrews, 2004; Horne, 2006). From a neo-liberal perspective, the main factor that accelerates the globalisation of sport is the saturation of a domestic professional sport market that compels Western sports leagues and clubs to seek a new market abroad (Whitson, 1998). Such a tendency is particularly discernible in the European football industry. The major clubs' global marketing strategies include the recruitment of non-European players from China, South Korea and Japan, as these are perceived to be emerging markets for European football clubs (Giulianotti & Robertson, 2009). Under this strategy, selling broadcasting rights and attracting foreign tourists to the home stadium can generate profits. Also, elite football clubs such as Manchester United and Arsenal often tour around East Asian countries during the off-season, and the Asian players within these squads are one of the main attractions for the Asian fans. The presence of African footballers in European leagues is also closely related to the economy of the global football industry. As Darby *et al.* (2007) note, a number of football academies are in operation in African countries such as Ghana, Mali and Senegal. In those academies, young African footballers are trained and educated for their professional careers in more lucrative football markets abroad. In fact, the recruitment of African football workers is regarded as a cost-effective way to build a team because it is less costly and more convenient for European clubs to select a ready-made player from the pool of African talent than to train young footballers in their home nations (Darby, 2007; Poli, 2010). Thus, in the global football industry, talented African players are regarded as commodities that contain good commercial value (Poli, 2006). In this view, the recruitment of East Asian and African footballers is a good investment for the clubs that can be understood as a result of the international division of football labour.

The world system of football

So far, I have discussed the three characteristics of global sport and how they are related to the migration of football talents. However, it should be noted that globalisation is an uneven process that engenders unequal relationships between the various stakeholders involved in it (Sklair, 2002; Ritzer, 2010; Cohen & Kennedy, 2013). The globalisation of sport is no exception, and the pattern and direction of labour migration clearly show the unbalanced nature of global sport. In this respect, Wallerstein's world system theory (1974) offers a useful theoretical tool for understanding the contemporary global flow of sports workers. Put simply, world systems theory attempts to explain the emergence and transformation of the international division of labour, and the world can be divided into three areas according to the role each region plays within the division, namely core, semi-peripheral and peripheral areas (Wallerstein, 1974; Sklair, 2002). The core area includes North American and Western European countries, as they are defined as being located at the financial and cultural centre of the current global order. The peripheral area consists of African, South American and South East Asian countries, which tend to supply raw materials and natural resources to the rest of the world. Transnational corporations' manufacturing plants are also located in these peripheral countries, largely due to the cheap labour forces that can be recruited there. The economy of this region is heavily dependent on the core countries. The newly emerging economic powers such as Taiwan, Singapore and South Korea are the countries located in the semi-peripheral area. The economy of these countries does not completely rely on the global core, and they make an effort to develop advanced technologies and to produce technology-centred products. However, their economies are weaker than those of the global core countries because, without capital investment from the core, the semi-periphery's high-tech industry could be unsustainable in the long term.

In this respect, Magee and Sugden (2002) note that relationships based on world system theory can also be identified in the flows that are evident when analysing global football migration. They suggested that the top European football leagues such as the English Premier League, Bundesliga and La Liga have become the global core of professional football in terms of organisational structure, attendance, salaries, marketing activities, facilities and the skills of players. African countries fall into the peripheral category because a limited number of domestic professional leagues exists in the region and many young football players wish to move to the core footballing nations (Cornelissen & Solberg, 2007). This gives rise to a situation in which the peripheral countries, regardless of their will, continually supply young talented players to the European leagues (Darby, 2007). The North East Asian countries are regarded as semi-peripheral areas within the international division of football labour (Akindes, 2013). These countries have more established football leagues, good football facilities and sustainable domestic football markets (Lee, 2002; Ichiro, 2004). Also, many football clubs in this region, especially those in the South Korean and Japanese professional leagues, recruit footballers from African, East European and South American countries. At the same time, some talented football players in the semi-peripheral countries continuously seek to develop their professional careers in the leagues in the global core. Therefore, in terms of the international division of football labour, North East Asian football markets are positioned between the core and the periphery.

The world system of football offers a valuable theoretical framework that explains the structural and economic dimensions of the migration of workers. However, it is also necessary to examine individual motivations and other non-economic push and pull factors that facilitate the global flow of sport migrants so that more comprehensive characteristics of international football labour migration can be discerned (Elliott & Maguire, 2008, Elliott, 2013, 2014). The seven types of migrants outlined in the work of Maguire (1999) and Magee and Sugden (2002) certainly provide a useful analytical tool for examining different push and pull factors that influence the migratory patterns of sport workers. When the migration typologies are considered in combination with the theory of the world system of football, a more accurate picture of the flow of football migration can be painted. With this in mind, the next part of the chapter will investigate the movement of football workers in the South Korean context.

The development of the K-League and migration

Until the 1980s the state played a crucial role in developing sport in South Korea (Chung, 2004). The government frequently exploited sport as a political tool and thereby subsidised its elite sport system from the 1960s to the 1980s in order to foster internationally competitive athletes (Ahn, 2002). Football was one of the main beneficiaries of this policy, and the government even established a number of 'shamateur' football clubs (Kang, 2006). When North Korea, the enemy state of South Korea during the Cold War, displayed a remarkable performance at the 1966 FIFA World Cup in England, the South Korean government's investment in football increased so that the South would outperform the North in the future (Kang, 2006). As part of this, the state constructed a national athletic training centre and organised an annual international football competition named the Presidential Cup in Seoul. Through this strategy not only was the national team able to be trained under a more systematic programme, but the players could also gain international experience more regularly (Hwang, 2002). As a result, the visibility of South Koreans in international football began to increase.

The Presidential Cup was regarded as a minor competition from a European perspective, but to some extent it functioned as a platform for Korean players to display their skill and talent to international audiences. In fact, a number of European clubs showed an interest in many talented footballers during the competition and eventually recruited them. In relation to this, the most notable Korean footballer is Cha Bum-kun, who started his European career in the Bundesliga in 1978. He stayed in the German league for 12 years (1978–89) and during his career appeared in 308 matches and scored 98 goals. Another Korean player, Huh Jung-moo, followed Cha's route to Europe and migrated to the Netherlands in 1980. Huh spent three seasons at PSV Eindhoven and developed a reasonably successful career in Holland. Yet he had to return to South Korea because his family was unable to assimilate into the foreign culture.

In 1983 Korean football became professional, which led to the organisation of the Super League. Initially, five clubs joined the league, but it had a somewhat odd structure because only three clubs consisted of professionals and the other two teams were made up of amateur players (Ravenel & Durand, 2004). The following year an additional amateur club took part, and matches between three professional and three amateur clubs continued until 1987, when the league turned into an all professional competition (K-League, 2013). It is true that professionalisation to some extent facilitated the growth of the football industry in South Korea (Lee, 2002). Nevertheless, facilities, attendances and the quality of the performances were relatively poor throughout the 1980s and the early 1990s compared with many European leagues (Ravenel & Durand, 2004). This indicates that Korean football was still positioned on the margins of the global football system.

From the mid-1990s the circumstances surrounding the Korean football industry began to change, the most notable development being its rapid commercialisation. Until 1993 the league was organised and administered by the Korea Football Association (KFA). In 1994 the Korea Professional Football Federation (KPFF) was founded, and since then this commercially oriented institution has been in charge of organising the league (K-League, 2013). The KPFF adopted a more aggressive marketing approach that included selling a title sponsorship. Moreover, five additional clubs, which received corporate sponsorship, joined the league. The transformation of South Korean football gained further momentum when a successful bid was made in 1996 to co-host the World Cup with Japan (Ravenel & Durand, 2004). The South Korean government invested more money into the Korean football industry and decided to build ten world-class stadiums in preparation for the mega event. Co-hosting the 2002 World Cup resulted in improvements in football facilities and infrastructure that would be felt in the coming years. In 1998 the Korean professional league was officially rebranded as the K-League in an effort to enhance the marketability of Korean football. Such developments gave rise to a significant increase in football attendance in the late 1990s and the early 2000s (K-League, 2013).

The founding of the Japanese professional 'J-League' in 1993 also influenced the Korean football industry. Among other things, the most important factor would be its impact on Korean football's migratory pattern. As noted earlier, most South Korean footballers played only in their home country until the early 1990s. The launch of the J-League changed that. From the beginning, the J-League adopted commercialist logic, and therefore the flow of monies into the Japanese football market was larger than that into the Korean one (Ichiro, 2004). With its economic strength, the J-League attracted many footballers from neighbouring countries, including Korean nationals (Dolles & Soderman, 2013). A total of 86 Koreans registered in the J-League from its inception to 2012, and currently 31 Korean migrants are playing for Japanese football clubs. Also, some of the key members of the Korean squad for the 2002 World Cup, such as Ahn Jung-hwan, Choi Yong-soo, Hong-Myung-bo, Lee Chun-Soo and Park Ji-Sung played in the J-League before or after the 2002 World Cup. This shows that a relatively large number of Korean footballers have been moving to Japan since the start of the J-League. In an Asian football landscape, Japan was portrayed as a land of opportunity primarily because of the large salaries that Japanese clubs were offering (Dolles & Soderman, 2013). While lucrative financial rewards entice many footballers into seeking playing opportunities abroad, Stead and Maguire (2000) and Elliott (2013, 2014) note that there also exist cultural and political reasons that profoundly affect athletes' decisions to enter foreign playing fields. Likewise, it is considered that geographical proximity and a cultural similarity between the two states are influential pull factors for the Korean footballers' migration to Japan.

Another important aspect of football migration is the influx of foreign players into the Korean professional league. Korean clubs have recruited foreign-born players since the launch of the Super League. When the Super League started, it imposed a quota system that allowed each club to employ only two foreign players (K-League, 2013). The first foreign footballers who landed on Korean soil were Jose Roberto Alves and Sergio Luis Cogo from Brazil. However, their contribution was minimal and they returned home after the first season. More memorable footballers in the early period of the Super League included Piyapong Pue-on

(LG Hwangso FC, 1984–6) from Thailand and Rob Landsbergen (Hyundai Horang FC, 1984–5) from the Netherlands. Korean players were overwhelmed by Landsbergen's European style football, and Pue-on, with his skilful performance, significantly helped the team to win the league. In recognition of their performances, they both won player of the year awards. Over the first ten years, those footballers who played in the Korean league were mainly from South American and Eastern European countries. In consideration of the trajectory that the football migrants took and the reputation of Korean football in the 1980s and the early 1990s, the influx of foreign players seemed to follow what Akindes (2013) calls 'South to South routes'.

With the commercialisation of Korean football, the K-League introduced a new quota system in 1996 that allowed each football club to employ up to five non-Korean players (K-League, 2013). According to the new regulation, three players could appear on the pitch simultaneously. This relaxation of the quota system facilitated the migration of foreign players to South Korea and eventually made the presence of migrant players more visible. For instance, the number of foreign players registered in the K-League increased from 24 in 1995 to 48 in 1996. In addition, of the top ten goal scorers in the 1996 season, four players were non-Koreans (K-League, 2013). These figures clearly indicate that the percentage of foreign players in the K-League was growing. In 1999 the K-League introduced an additional regulation to prohibit the recruitment of foreign goalkeepers in order to prevent the deskilling of indigenous goalkeepers. Before this restriction was introduced, a large number of Korean football clubs had wanted to have at least one foreign goalkeeper because of the reliable defending skill that many non-Korean players displayed. Given that a relatively small number of positions are available for goalkeepers in a club, the employment of foreign goalkeepers had a direct impact upon the career development of local goalkeepers. In effect, the K-League has completely banned the use of non-Korean goalkeepers.

The 2002 FIFA World Cup and migration

The most memorable year in South Korean football history would be 2002. This is the year the country co-hosted the FIFA World Cup Finals and its national team advanced to the semi-finals. This was recorded as the most outstanding performance in the history of Korean football. It was also a moment in which South Korean football could be described as moving from the periphery to the semi-periphery of football's world system (Petrov, 2002; Close & Askew, 2004). Before 2002, the country was located in a marginal area in football's global geography. The South Korean team was regarded as one of the weakest teams at the major international football competitions. For instance, although South Korea had participated in the World Cup Finals five times (1954, 1986, 1990, 1994 and 1998) prior to the country co-hosting the championships, the national squad had not won any of their World Cup matches. While a few individual players displayed impressive performances, the South Koreans had always been an underdog at the FIFA World Cup in the 1980s and the 1990s. Yet, through this international experience, some players grabbed a chance to enter European leagues. For instance, Seo Jung-won and Kim Joo-sung were able to develop their careers in France and Germany respectively in the 1990s.

When South Korea and Japan were awarded the 2002 FIFA World Cup finals, one of the key tasks for the KFA was to improve its national team's performance at the competition. In order to foster a better equipped team for the World Cup to be held on its home soil, the KFA decided to invite European coaching staff to train Korean footballers. The managerial position was offered to the former Netherlands manager Guss Hiddink, and he agreed to coach the team for the World Cup. The KFA considered him a suitable individual because he had experience of coaching some of the top European clubs, including Real Madrid, and he had managed the Netherlands team to the semi-finals at the 1998 World Cup in France. The fact that the Dutch team beat South Korea 5–0 at the same competition was also an important factor.

South Korea's performance in the 2002 World Cup contributed to improving the country's profile in the international football industry. Subsequently international football agencies started to pay more attention to Korean footballers. In fact, for South Korean players, the 2002 World Cup opened a new path to European football leagues. It should be noted that international football competitions often function to develop and secure footballers' career routes to more lucrative leagues, ideally the big five leagues in Europe (Cornelissen & Solberg, 2007; Lee *et al.*, 2007; Akindes, 2013). Because the Korean side did not show any impressive performances before 2002, it was uncommon to see a Korean footballer recruited by a European club after the championships. But after the 2002 World Cup in which the Korean team reached the semi-finals, beating the Italian and Spanish teams on the way, seven players from the Korean squad were offered contracts by European clubs. This shows that a correlation may exist between performances at major football competitions and career opportunities abroad. Additionally, within the process of the South Korean players' migration to Europe the role of Guss Hiddink must not be underestimated. As Carter (2011a) highlights, the web of human networks is a significant factor that lubricates the process of international sport labour migration. The fact that four of the seven players signed for Dutch football clubs after the World Cup clearly demonstrates the importance of networks in the global sport labour market. Since 2002, European clubs have continuously recruited South Korean players. For instance, the South Korean squad for the 2002 World Cup consisted of only two players at European clubs. By contrast, the number increased to five in 2006 and six in 2010. A total of 15 Korean footballers played in European leagues in 2013.

In relation to sport labour migration, another significant legacy Guss Hiddink left to Korean football is the increased dependency on foreign coaching staff for its national team. In fact, the Dutch manager was not the first foreign manager of the Korean squad; there were two foreign coaches who led the Korean team before him – the German Dettmar Cramer and the Russian Anatoliy Byshovets. These managers coached the Korean Olympic football team in 1990–2 and 1994–6 respectively. However, they did not produce any remarkable results and consequently left the country before the end of their contracts (K-League, 2013). By contrast, Hiddink's achievements meant that the KFA wished to extend his contract at the end of its term. Ultimately, the Dutchman refused the deal and returned to his home country. Pointing out Korean coaches' inexperience and inability to lead the team at the World Cup Finals, the KFA had continually nominated foreign nationals as the Korean team's manager until 2007 (Lee *et al.*, 2007). Those who coached the Korean team after Guss Hiddink included Humberto Coelho (2003–4), Jo Bonfrere (2004–5), Dick Advocaat (2005–6) and Pim Verbeek (2006–7). This indicates that Korean football's dependency upon foreign managers increased in the 2000s, a further significant consequence of the migration of football workers into the country.

The pattern of football migration in South Korea

So far, this chapter has examined the development of Korean football and various forms of football labour migration associated with it. On this basis, four distinct stages can be identified, and each stage shows different migratory patterns. In the first stage, which covers the 1970s to the early 1980s, South Korea was located on the margins of international football (Chung, 2004). This was also a period in which the government heavily subsidised the sport in order to enhance the visibility of Korean football at an international level (Kang, 2006). In spite of such support, however, only limited career opportunities were available for the talented elite players in the country because South Korea did not have an organised football league during this period. As a result, some footballers such as Cha Bum-kun had to seek to develop their football careers abroad, with Cha finding his place in Germany. Such movements are good examples of intercontinental migration from the periphery to the core.

The second stage, which stretches from the mid-1980s to the early 1990s, is the period of professionalisation. The environment of domestic football was significantly improved because of the launch of the Super League (Ravenel & Durand, 2004). Throughout this stage, South Korean football became more visible as its national team participated in the 1986 and 1990 FIFA World Cup Finals in Mexico and Italy. In spite of such an effort, South Korean football still remained on the periphery of the global football system (Petrov, 2002). Nevertheless, these international experiences gave Korean players a chance to display their skills to international audiences, and subsequently a few notable Koreans found their way to Europe after the competitions.

Another significant migratory pattern found in this stage was the influx of South American and Eastern European footballers to South Korea. This can be characterised as South to South migration (Akindes, 2013). During this period, the Korean professional league was in its incipient stage; objectively speaking, the Super League was an almost unknown football league (Petrov, 2002). In this respect, it is difficult to believe that those footballers who came to South Korea at this time had a desire to develop their careers in a peripheral footballing country.

LIVERPOOL JOHN MOORES UNIVERSITY
LEARNING SERVICES

Instead, economic considerations were more likely to be a factor that led Eastern European and South American footballers to the league.

The third stage, which lasted from the mid-1990s to 2001, is the period of commercialisation. This should be seen as part of the wider process of the globalisation of Korean football in which a neo-liberal logic dominated the way football was organised in the country (Giulianotti & Robertson, 2009). This was also a period in which South Korea's power increased at FIFA through both the South Korean sponsorship of the governing body and the election of a South Korean vice-president of the organisation (Close & Askew, 2004). These developments indicate that Korean football was gradually moving from the periphery to the semi-periphery of the global football system. The fact that South Korea was selected to co-host the 2002 FIFA World Cup also enhanced the country's reputation. Such an improved reputation attracted footballers from more diverse countries to the K-League. Additionally, this period also witnessed the migration of South Korean players to Japan, an international migration within the same continent and between two semi-peripheral countries. Japanese football clubs recruited a number of experienced Korean footballers such as Hong Myung-bo and Hwang Sun-hong, and the appearance of these Koreans in the J-League attracted attention from Japanese football fans. It should be noted that, at that time, the South Korean team was ranked higher than the Japanese team in FIFA's rankings, and the J-League was not seen as being particularly superior to the K-League (Ichiro, 2004). In this sense, it is hard to argue that Korean players moved to Japan purely for economic reasons. It may be that the cultural similarity between the two countries and the emerging football culture in Japan also motivated them to migrate to the neighbouring country.

The fourth stage is defined as a post-World Cup period that covers from 2002 to the present day. This is the time in which South Korea consolidated its position as a semi-peripheral country in football's world system (Close & Askew, 2004). The magnitude of the Korean football industry has expanded and the quality of football performance has improved since the 2002 World Cup (Chung, 2004). In terms of football migration, the remarkable success at the World Cup paved a new path to the core European football leagues for talented players. This movement is characterised as intercontinental sport labour migration between the semi-periphery and the core. Unlike in the initial two stages of football migration, the European clubs did not recruit Korean footballers simply because they were cheap. These East Asian footballers tended to receive better salaries than their predecessors in the 1980s and the 1990s. In return, the European leagues and clubs attempted to sell products and broadcasting rights to South Korea and, through these commercial transactions, the core football countries could make more profits (Andrews, 2004; Giulianotti & Robertson, 2009). The former Manchester United midfielder Park Ji-sung is a good example of a player that followed this newly established route. In addition, the influx of foreign coaches is another distinctive feature of this stage. From 2002 to 2009 a number of Europeans managed the Korean national team. The recruitment of a Western coaching staff can be seen as the Asian semi-peripheral country's strategy to emulate the European core (Maguire, 2005).

Concluding remarks

Sport labour migration is one of the key features of global sport (Maguire, 1999). This chapter has examined the structure and pattern of labour migration in South Korean football, and clearly shows that South Korean football players and the South Korean professional league are interlinked with the global football system and global capitalism underpinned by a neo-liberalist logic (Andrews, 2004; Giulianotti & Robertson, 2009). In fact, as discussed, Korean footballers are now continuously on the move at international and intercontinental levels, and the K-League attracts foreign nationals. More importantly, as the country relocated its position from the periphery to the semi-periphery within football's world system, different migratory patterns have emerged. South Korea co-hosted the 2002 World Cup, and this event also facilitated the globalisation of Korean football with regard to the size of the football industry and the flow of football workers with more diverse ethnic and cultural backgrounds (Close & Askew, 2004). These developments clearly indicate that, as a semi-peripheral country, South Korea is actively engaged with the global football economy and, more specifically, the global movement of football labour.

Regarding research into South Korean football, it should be noted that relatively little attention has been paid to the motivation and experiences of foreign players in the K-League. While this study attempts to investigate this area, only a partial explanation was provided from the author's perspective, relying largely on secondary sources. Given that non-Korean-born footballers have played in the league for more than 20 years, and that their number is continuously increasing, the question of why these migrants decide to enter the Korean league would, I believe, meaningfully enhance our understanding of football migration today. This is a topic on which future research should focus.

References

Ahn, M. (2002) The Political Economy of the World Cup in South Korea. In W. Manzenreiter and J. Horne (Eds.) *Japan, Korea, and the 2002 World Cup*. London: Routledge (162–73).

Akindes, G.A. (2013) South Asia and South East Asia: New Paths of African Footballer Migration. *Soccer and Society* 14: 684–701.

Andrews, D.L. (2004) Sport in the Late Capitalist Moment. In T. Slack (Ed.) *The Commercialisation of Sport*. Abingdon: Routledge (2–28).

Appadurai, A. (1990) Disjuncture and Difference in the Global Cultural Economy. In M. Featherstone (Ed.) *Global Culture: Nationalism, Globalization and Modernity*. London: Sage (295–310).

Carter, T.F. (2011a) *In Foreign Fields: The Politics and Experiences of Transnational Sport Migrations*. London: Pluto Press.

Carter, T.F. (2011b) Re-placing Sport Migrants: Moving beyond the Institutional Structures Informing International Sport Migration. *International Review for the Sociology of Sport* 48: 66–82.

Castells, M. (2010) *The Rise of the Network Society* (2nd edn). Oxford: Wiley-Blackwell.

Chung, H. (2004) Government Involvement in Football in Korea. In W. Manzenreiter and J. Horne (Eds.) *Football Goes East: Business, Culture and the People's Game in China, Japan and South Korea.* Abingdon: Routledge (117–30).

Close, P. and Askew, D. (2004) Globalisation and Football in East Asia. In W. Manzenreiter and J. Horne (Eds.) *Football Goes East: Business, Culture and the People's Game in China, Japan and South Korea.* Abingdon: Routledge (243–56).

Cohen, R. and Kennedy, P. (2013) *Global Sociology* (3rd edn). London: Palgrave Macmillan.

Cornelissen, S. (2009) A Delicate Balance: Major Sport Events and Development. In R. Levermore and A. Beacom (Eds.) *Sport and International Development.* Basingstoke: Palgrave (76–97).

Cornelissen, S. and Solberg, E. (2007) Sport Mobility and Circuits of Power: The Dynamics of Football Migration in Africa and the 2010 World Cup. *Politikon* 34: 295–314.

Darby, P. (2007) African Football Labour Migration to Portugal: Colonial and Neo-colonial Resources. *Soccer & Society* 8: 495–509.

Darby, P., Akindes, G. and Kirwin, M. (2007) Football Academies and the Migration of African Football Labor to Europe. *Journal of Sport and Social Issues* 31: 143–61.

Dolles, H. and Soderman, S. (2013) Twenty Years of Development of the J-League: Analysing the Business Parameters of Professional Football in Japan. *Soccer and Society* 14: 702–21.

Elliott, R. (2013) New Europe, New Chances? The Migration of Professional Footballers to Poland's Ekstraklasa. *International Review for the Sociology of Sport* 48(6): 736–50.

Elliott, R. (2014) Football's Irish Exodus: Examining the Factors Influencing Irish Player Migration to English Professional Leagues. *International Review for the Sociology of Sport.* Published online 11 February 2014: DOI 10.1177/1012690213519786.

Elliott, R. and Maguire, J. (2008) Thinking Outside of the Box: Exploring a Conceptual Synthesis for Research in the Area of Athletic Labor Migration. *Sociology of Sport Journal* 25: 482–97.

FIFA (2010) *Regulations on the Status and Transfer of Players.* Retrieved 1 November 2013 from: http://www.fifa.com/mm/document/affederation/administration/01/95/83/85/regulationsstatusandtransfer_e.pdf.

Giulianotti, R. and Robertson, R. (2009) *Globlization and Football.* London: Sage.

Held, D., McGrew, A., Goldblatt, D. and Perraton, J. (1999) *Global Transformations: Politics, Economics and Culture.* Cambridge: Polity.

Higham, J. and Hinch, T. (2009) *Sport and Tourism: Globalization, Mobility and Identity.* Oxford: Butterworth-Heinemann.

Horne, J. (2006) *Sport in Consumer Culture.* Basingstoke: Palgrave.

Houlihan, B. (2004) Sports Globalisation, the State and the Problem of Governance. In T. Slack (Ed.) *The Commercialisation of Sport.* Abingdon: Routledge (52–71).

Houlihan, B. (2008) Politics, Power, Policy and Sport. In B. Houlihan (Ed.) *Sport and Society: A Student Introduction.* London: Sage (33–55).

Hwang, B. (2002) Soccer and Nationalism in Park Chung Hee's Era. *Dangdaebipyung (Contemporary Criticism)* 15: 145–87.

Ichiro, H. (2004) The Making of a Professional Football League: The Design of the J-League System. In W. Manzenreiter and J. Horne (Eds.) *Football Goes East: Business, Culture, and the People's Game in China, Japan and South Korea.* Abingdon: Routledge (38–53).

Kang, J. (2006) *The Korean Football: The 124 Years History of Korean Football (1882–2006).* Seoul: Inmul.

K-League (2013) *K-League 30th Anniversary.* Seoul: K-League.

Klein, A.M. (1991) *Sugarball: American Game, Dominican Dream.* New Haven, CT: Yale University Press.

Lee, J. (2002) The Development of Football in Korea. In W. Manzenreiter and J. Horne (Eds.) *Japan, Korea and the 2002 World Cup.* London: Routledge (73–88).

Lee, J.W. and Maguire, J. (2009) Global Festivals through a National Prism: The Global–National Nexus in South Korean Media Coverage of the 2004 Athens Olympic Games. *International Review for the Sociology of Sport* 44: 5–24.

Lee, N., Jackson, S.J. and Lee, K. (2007) South Korea's 'Glocal' Hero: The Hiddink Syndrome and the Rearticulation of National Citizenship and Identity. *Sociology of Sport Journal* 24: 283–301.

Magee, J. and Sugden, J. (2002) 'The World at Their Feet': Professional Football and International Labor Migration. *Journal of Sport and Social Issues* 26: 421–37.

Maguire, J. (1999) *Global Sport: Identities, Societies, Civilizations.* Cambridge: Polity.

Maguire, J. (2005) Introduction: Power and Global Sport. In J. Maguire (Ed.) *Power and Global Sport: Zones of Prestige, Emulation and Resistance.* Abingdon: Routledge (1–20).

Maguire, J., Jarvie, G., Mansfield, L. and Bradley, J. (2002) *Sport Worlds: A Sociological Perspective.* Champaign, IL: Human Kinetics.

Miller, T., Lawrence, G., McKay, J. and Rowe, D. (2001) *Globalization of Sport: Playing the World.* London: Sage.

Petrov, L.A. (2002) Korean Football at the Crossroads: A View from Inside. In W. Manzenreiter and J. Horne (Eds.) *Japan, Korea and the 2002 World Cup.* London: Routledge (106–20).

Poli, R. (2006) Africans' Status in the European Football Players' Labour Market. *Soccer and Society* 2–3: 278–91.

Poli, R. (2010) Understanding Globalization through Football: The New International Division of Labour, Migatory Channels and Transnational Trade Circuits. *International Review for the Sociology of Sport* 45: 491–506.

Ravenel, L. and Durand, C. (2004) Strategies for Locating Professional Sports Leagues: A Comparison between France and Korea. In W. Manzenreiter & J. Horne (Eds.) *Football Goes East: Business, Culture and the People's Game in China, Japan and South Korea.* Abingdon: Routledge (21–37).

Ritzer, G. (2010) *Globalization: A Basic Text.* Chichester: Wiley-Blackwell.

Robertson, R. (1992) *Globalization: Social Theory and Global Culture.* London: Sage.

Roche, M. (2006) Mega-events and Modernity Revisited: Globalization and the Case of the Olympics. In J. Horne and W. Manzenreiter (Eds.) *Sports Mega-events: Social Scientific Analysis of a Global Phenomenon.* Oxford: Blackwell (27–40).

Sklair, L. (2002) *Globalization: Capitalism and Its Alternatives* (3rd edn). Oxford: Oxford University Press.

Stead, D. and Maguire, J. (2000) 'Rite de Passage or Passage to Riches'? The Motivations and Objectives of Nordic/Scandinavian Players in English League Soccer. *Journal of Sport and Social Issues* 24: 36–60.

Wallerstein, I. (1974) The Rise and Future Demise of the World Capitalist System. In F.J. Lechner and J. Boli (Eds.) *The Globalization Reader.* Oxford: Blackwell (63–9).

Whitson, D. (1998) Circuits of Promotion: Media, Marketing, and Globalisation of Sport. In L.A. Wenner (Ed.) *Media Sport.* London: Routledge (pp. 57–72).

Yang, E.K. (2012) The Transnational Movement of Athletes and the Formation of Flexible National Identity: Discourse Analysis on Ji-Sung Park as National Competitiveness. *Korean Journal of Journalism and Communication Studies* 56: 80–104.

8 League of retirees

Foreigners in Hungarian professional football

Gyozo Molnar

Athletic talent migration has attracted growing and notable academic attention over the last two decades. The emerging presence of new areas of study could be perceived as a shift in focus in the field of migratory research, which includes giving more attention to countries and leagues that may not be associated with the core/metropolitan states. For example, there is a significant and increasing body of literature focusing on Africa (Darby, 2011, 2013), New Zealand (Bruce & Wheaton, 2011; Obel & Austin, 2011) and the Pacific (Grainger, 2011; Horton, 2012; Kanemasu & Molnar, 2013a, 2013b), and their engagement with regional and global migratory structures. What appears to be the chief message of this corpus of research is the importance of understanding local engagement with global structures through which units of migration move from country to country and league to league via the constant interplay between structure (macro) and agency (micro).

Despite the increasing scope of sport-specific migration research examining economically and politically core as well as peripheral countries, there is still limited attention given to semi-peripheral areas that also form part of migratory structures and experiences (see Elliott, 2014). For instance, some of the ex-communist states of Central and Eastern Europe, with limited purchasing powers, have been actively involved internationally in directly sending and transiting migrant athletes since the collapse of the iron curtain (Duke, 1994; Maguire *et al.*, 2002; Molnar, 2006, 2011). There is, however, another function which almost completely lacks scholarly note: post-communist states' role in sport migration as host environments (for an exception see Elliott, 2014). Here, this migratory role will be considered via the case of Hungary, which displayed significant host country features shortly after the velvet revolution in relation to general migrations (Dövényi, 1995) as well as football migrations (Molnar *et al.*, 2011). Molnar *et al.* (2011, p.262) specifically acknowledged Hungary's host country function and noted that, "in the past two decades, nearly 700 foreign-born footballers have plied their trade in the Hungarian leagues". In considering these observations, and filling a small part of the existing gap in the literature, this chapter focuses on Hungary from a host environment perspective through exploring the migratory experiences of foreign players in its professional football league (called OTP Bank Liga since 2011).[1] With this in mind, the chapter has two interlinking aims: to explore the reasons for having foreign players in the Hungarian professional football league and to understand Hungary as a host environment through migrants' experience of plying their trade in the land of the Magyars. As the study is informed by both primary and secondary evidence, in the next section the empirical aspects of the study will be considered; this is followed by a discussion driven by interview data collected in Hungary.

Method and participants

To uncover football-specific migratory experiences, this research adopted a qualitative approach. Data was gathered via semi-structured interviews as they "yield rich insight into people's biographies, experiences, opinions, values, aspirations, attitudes and feelings" (May, 2001, p.120). Interviewing is an active data collection technique that gathers information about social relations/attitudes through interaction between an interviewer and an interviewee. Here, a version of semi-structured interview, the long interview (see McCracken, 1988), was employed as the preferred data collecting technique to provide an in-depth account of foreign players' perception of Hungarian football.

Interviews took place in three Hungarian cities (Budapest, Debrecen and Sopron) at various venues which were mutually agreed upon between participants and the interviewer. Participants were identified and recruited via a snowball sampling method (Patton, 1990) and included three managers, three head coaches and four foreign players. Participants were volunteers and individually agreed to take part in the research and to allow their interviews to be voice recorded. For reasons of safeguarding anonymity and confidentiality, information collected via interviews that might have revealed the identity of the participants and their football associations was omitted from the discussion. All migrant football players interviewed had spent at least one full season in the Hungarian professional league and had had experience of at least two other countries' football leagues. Although it would have been desirable to include more migrant players in the sample, it was a challenging exercise to secure interviews with foreign footballers as most of them did not appear to have an appropriate command of the Hungarian or English language. Generally, in addition to their own native tongue, they spoke a so-called *football Hungarian* which was sufficient to get by on the football field and to understand short instructions, but inadequate to take part in more complex everyday dialogue. For instance, one of the foreign players who had a good level of Hungarian, and thus was interviewed, revealed that most of his fellow migrant players had hardly spoken to the media whilst in Hungary due to the fact that they only spoke their native tongue. This issue was also mentioned by one of the coaches, who highlighted the fact that most of the players who transferred from ex-communist countries had only a limited understanding of Hungarian and thus faced serious difficulties when communicating with their coach and team-mates.

The data collection and analysis included three key phases: "recording the data, editing the data (transcription) and construction of a 'new' reality in and by the produced text" (Flick, 2002, p.166). Accordingly, data was recorded with the participants' permission via a digital voice recorder. The interviews were conducted predominantly in Hungarian (one interview was conducted in English), which was the language of the verbatim transcriptions. The transcripts were thematically coded on the basis of the research questions (see also Butt & Molnar, 2009; Kanemasu & Molnar, 2013a) with a view to arriving at a rich, in-depth understanding of the ways in which foreign players perceive their football-related experience in Hungary. The thematically selected parts of the transcripts were then translated into English. Great care was taken during the translation of interview data as "it is not simply the formal language that must be understood [but] . . . it is also very often the 'argot' – the special uses of words and slang that are important to penetrate that culture" (Bryman, 2001, p.328). That is, it is crucial for the translator to be familiar with not only the written/formal expressions of the languages in use but also the colloquial forms. This aspect of translating data was carefully observed in order to retain meaning.

In the following sections, three key themes that emerged from the qualitative data analysis will be discussed. These are: 1) the reasons for employing migrants, 2) why migrants choose Hungary, and 3) foreigners' perception of the Hungarian professional football league.

Reasons for employing migrants

Three main reasons emerged for hiring migrant players: the lack of available domestic talent, clubs' financial incentives, and the 'fashion' for having *the want* for foreigners in professional clubs. The managers and coaches interviewed admitted that it was a necessity for all Hungarian professional clubs to employ foreign players because there is a lack of available, good quality domestic footballers, for which the sub-standard talent development system was held chiefly responsible. A coach explained this as follows: "There isn't enough good quality footballers in Hungary . . . [and] this is why they [foreigners] come here." A manager reinforced this view:

> Today, there aren't many good Hungarian footballers. When we take a look at the [professional] teams, I think, it is not possible to build up three or four full teams only with Hungarian footballers which could achieve a moderate level of recognition at the international stage.

The view that Hungarian football suffered from a lack of available domestic talent was shared by all managers and coaches, indicating a widespread concern regarding contemporary Hungarian football, which could only be remedied by investing additional financial and human capital into talent development. For example, a manager described the conditions of his team: "Here we have four football pitches for 700 kids and adult footballers to play on. Coaches just cannot do good quality work [with limited resources]!" A coach added that "facilities are very low quality . . . I think that talented kids do not even get to the pitch to play ball." In line with participants' views and given football's social significance in

Hungary (see Hadas, 2000; Molnar, 2007), Vincze (2009) also noted that in the post-communist era inadequate attention was paid to the development of young footballers. In other words, clubs seem to have barely adequate facilities to cater for the multiple needs of grassroots development and talent identification, and neither do they have the financial resources to effectively augment their existing circumstances. Participants suggested that in order to improve current conditions more extensive state and/or private investment would be required. This is something that is challenging to secure in Hungary (Molnar *et al.*, 2011). Therefore, providing the much needed boost to grassroots football, and general football, development has been problematic given the post-communist legacy and more recent struggles with economic (re)development (Molnar, 2011).

Due to the domestic football conditions, foreigners are viewed as a quick and affordable solution (see also Poli, 2005) through which the football culture and level can be maintained, but not necessarily improved. Purchasing foreign players offers a swift, temporary solution that, to some extent, addresses the issue of financial instability and ineffective youth development. The practice of implementing predominantly short-term measures to address existing football-related issues illustrates the longitudinal effect of the degree to which Hungarian football was chaotic in the post-communist transition (see Molnar, 2007; Molnar *et al.*, 2011). During this period, the management of professional football clubs was frequently replaced, as was the ownership, creating an unstable and uncertain environment that did not lend itself to developing and implementing long-term strategies. Bocsák (2001) observed that between 1986 and 2004 the Hungarian national team had 17 different managers and the FA ten presidents. The phenomenon of frequently replacing management was experienced during the empirical phase of this project. In one instance, two months after arrangements for interviews had been made, I travelled to the participating club's location to begin data collection. Only then was I faced with a recently appointed, entirely new management that had no knowledge of the research and the agreement that had been made with the previous administration. Thus, it can be argued that, owing to the high degree of instability in the football sector triggered mostly by post-communist (pre-EU and, later, post-EU accession) transition(s), most management teams did not anticipate running the same club for a prolonged period and thus tended not to implement long-term strategies (see also Duke, 1994).[2] Instead, they preferred short-term, immediate solutions which, in most cases, meant filling existing football gaps with affordable foreign players.

The financial struggles of Hungarian football began prior to the collapse of the communist state but its effects came fully to light in the 1990s (see Hammond, 1999). Under the communist regime, sports, including football, were financed through the state budget, local council budgets and state-owned businesses and were given tax allowances (Földesi, 1993). When these sources ceased to provide financial stability after the 1980s, all sport organisations, including those of football, began facing challenging times. In their quest for survival, sport organisations and clubs initiated the implementation of novel structures and practices (Bukta, 2004). In the case of football, one of the money saving provisions that began to emerge was contracting an affordable foreign labour force. The financial incentive behind employing migrant players was indicated by both managers and coaches, who stated that foreign players are generally more affordable than Hungarians who would normally have higher monetary demands. A manager explained:

Lots of clubs struggle with financial difficulties and many of them try to bring in cheaper foreigners instead of buying more expensive Hungarians. They save money this way . . . Hungarian players seem to have a certain level of financial expectation. Clubs don't want to meet their demands unless it is absolutely necessary. This situation especially concerns the smaller teams where money is so tight that they can hardly buy balls and pay utility bills. To them it really matters if they can find a 23–24-year-old Bulgarian, Ukrainian, Bosnian or Georgian player who can replace one of the 18-year-old Hungarian players and is willing to sign for less money, and can provide almost the same performance.

This phenomenon was also mentioned by participants who recalled clubs where valuable players, in Hungarian terms, were sold under new management and their places then filled with less expensive migrant footballers. The following case was recollected during an interview:

It happened to . . . [a Hungarian pro team] not long ago that the team's performance became weak . . . The club was then relegated to a lower division and someone bought the club cheaply as it was on the verge of bankruptcy . . . The players still held some of their original market value and got quickly sold. But the team had to have players to qualify for playing in that lower division. At that point, to fill the need, the team management bought in concerningly low quality foreign players.

This quotation and the practice of 'quick fixes' demonstrate a short-term profit oriented attitude that emerged as part of post-communist privatisation tendencies, leading to deliberate exploitation in football in particular and, perhaps, industrial production in general (see Szalai, 1995). Employing foreign players appears to have become a cost-reducing practice into which clubs are forced by poor financial circumstances and short-term profit oriented attitudes. By virtue of the above, we can observe that the existing migratory pipelines between Hungary and most of its donor countries (see Molnar, 2006, 2011) channel players of average or below average skills to the professional football league. In most cases, these players are purchased with the main purpose of providing short-term financial solutions to existing money shortages and preserving the current state of Hungarian football.

Aside from the financial need for foreign players, some of the participants noted that the early years of post-communist transformation saw the emergence of a football trend regarding migrations and explained that in those years it became somewhat fashionable amongst professional clubs to employ foreign footballers. This might have been an attempt to copy Western practices, where the presence of good quality foreign players is often associated with raising media attention and attracting fans (Maguire *et al.*, 2002; Andreff, 2009). One of the coaches made this observation: "I would say this in inverted commas that 'fashion' was also playing a part regarding this phenomenon [recruiting foreign players]." A manager recalled the case of a Brazilian player who had been contracted to play in Hungary and had been initially glamorised by the media:

> There was this case with a Brazilian footballer . . . His arrival was celebrated by the media because according to his pedigree he had played for impressive teams. So there were great expectations for his Hungarian debut. He scored one goal in his first game but that was a stroke of luck and was due to his positioning on the pitch. Later, he managed to score goals here and there, but his overall personal performance was appalling. He could not be part of team tactics due to his poor physical condition. He was grossly out of shape. Then the shit really hit the fan and covered the whole club as the media and the fans began to question his transfer and the reason why the club had bought such a worn out player.

This quotation illustrates the *fashion* for purchasing foreign 'stars' to boost public interest. However, this aspect of migration did not seem to function well in the Hungarian football environment, as domestic football clubs were (are) not financial powerhouses that could compete with their Western European counterparts and, thus, they could only afford second class or already 'worn out' players. So, due to limited financial resources and some backfired transfer attempts, the *fashion* for purchasing foreign players gradually vanished from Hungarian football and the employing of foreign players became a pure necessity. One of the managers explained this:

> Elsewhere the primary reason for recruiting foreign players is to have stars in the first division who improve and popularise football. If I think about this then I must say that in the Hungarian championship such players can hardly be found. If so, it is very rare. There have only been one or two [foreign] players who could become stars in Hungary. The rest are just average, filling the gap.

As this quotation explains, foreign players are considered an affordable, temporary solution to some of the financial issues that have plagued Hungarian football.[3] However, regardless of the financial uncertainties in domestic football (Hammond, 1999; Elliott, 2014), there is still a significant inflow of foreign players to Hungary (see Molnar, 2006, 2011) which will be discussed below.

Hungary: the last shelter

The foreign players interviewed explicitly stated that Hungary was not their primary destination country. In fact, they highlighted that it was the only place where they could secure a contract. That is, in their quest for Western riches they were limited by both push and pull factors and switched to the only available option. Push factors directing certain migrant players here could include: domestic football conditions with limited potential for development and/or financial security and the (lack of or already declining) football talent of foreign players. On the other hand, pull factors can relate to the demand of the football industry for players of various prices and qualities (Molnar & Maguire, 2008). The way migrant athletes are "'pushed' from one location and 'pulled' to another will affect the way in which they experience that particular sojourn" (Elliott, 2014, p.4). Push and pull factors are interrelated and jointly responsible for the formation of migratory macro structures. In this case, two general scenarios have been detected regarding push–pull influences on migrant players in the professional football league. The skills of migrant players in Hungary are either of average quality or already at the stage of decline. As they are not sought after by prestigious Western European clubs or are at the stage of reaching retirement, the majority of football migrants appear to have had no other option but to be 'pushed' towards the Hungarian professional league. One of the players admitted that he was not happy with his previous employment, but he could not sign for another Western European club and his only option was Hungary:

> I initially went to Stuttgart to play football, but I had to 'warm the bench' after half a year because of the coach . . . So I did not play and just had to sit on the sidelines and then I decided to try to move on [to another team]. But then the main problem was that . . . there weren't many places for me to go to, but Hungary . . . As I did not want to retire just yet but couldn't go anywhere else . . . I ended up here [Hungary].

Another player suggested that footballers have a relatively short career span, the threshold of which he had already exceeded, and thus he perceived his move to Hungary in light of that as a pre-retirement destination:

> In sport, but not only in sport, in life too, there are two avenues: for a while you go up and then you go down. I always went up and up and then the time came when I noticed that I started going slowly-slowly down. This was the time when I moved here [Hungary].

While declining abilities seem to be pushing players out of more demanding leagues towards Hungary, so does a lack of skills. One foreign player expressed the difficulty of finding a host club as his abilities were not outstanding or internationally recognised: "I tried to go to other places [Western clubs], but the best offer came from here [Hungary]. When you are not selected for the national team then it is very difficult to get into those big [Western] clubs." That is, due to his average football skills and his de-selection from the national team, this player received limited opportunities to launch his career abroad and was 'pushed' towards Hungary as the best (or only possible) option.

Nevertheless, sometimes the careers of migrant players with above average abilities are influenced by unpredicted external factors (see Molnar & Maguire, 2008), in which case they may be directed to less desirable leagues. One of the players reflected on some problems prior to signing for a Hungarian club:

> I had a place promised to me in Greece. I went there but did not sign a contract. I was almost 100% sure that I was going to play there. Then in the last minute a problem appeared between the president and the coach. The president fired the coach and the new coach took other players. He had another vision and other players. I was without a club for one and a half months. So, after a while I had to take the only option available [which was Hungary].

This player indicated that he was 'pushed' towards his current position and decided to accept a place in Hungarian football as he had been without a contract for a significant period and been desperately searching for opportunities. A manager also disclosed a situation with regard to a foreign player in his team whose contract negotiations had failed in Germany and, due to a lack of other options, had signed for a Hungarian club:

> We are very happy that he [migrant player] came here. He could not work out a contract with that German team and, thus, he was without a team for a while and he decided to come here to our advantage. He belongs in the pool of better players who could hold their place in a Western European club. But to secure a player of this quality is quite rare.

Another player revealed an additional push factor: the domestic football circumstances of his home country. Regardless of the previous observation concerning the unstable economic conditions in Hungary, the circumstances that some foreign players endure in their home countries are often inferior even to those they experience in the Hungarian league. To these migrant players, Hungary represents a better working environment and a more modern and Western lifestyle. One of the migrant players admitted: "It is more peaceful here. In my home country my salary could be six–seven months late and it then becomes a problem when you can't pay your bills … In my home country, there were serious problems with finances and I became stressed." This perception was further strengthened by managers and coaches, who all agreed that, to most migrant footballers coming from the East, Hungary still represents a higher level of security, with a more developed and Western-type social life, and, as a consequence, they are motivated to take a chance on Hungarian football, irrespective of the general conditions discussed above. For example, a coach stated that "these [migrant] players can hardly make a living there [in their home country] … [and] we are the West to them". A manager reinforced this: "Players basically and predominantly come from Eastern Europe. In Hungary, the life is a bit better compared to those countries. As far as I know, they can earn a bit more here as well." Aside from the differences in living standards between Hungary and some of the Eastern European donor countries (see Molnar, 2006), there is another attractive aspect to Hungarian football, which is the country's geographical location and its perceived transitory status.

Hungary is believed to be a *gateway* to Western European football. Dövényi (1995, p.17) observed that "Hungary lies in an exposed geographical situation in Europe. Some of the most important pan-European routes cross the country. These routes support cargo and 'normal' passenger transport, and waves of refugees . . . as well." This observation appeared conterminous with general migration patterns in the post-communist transition period (see Wallace & Stola, 2001), but participants in this study did not support the idea of Hungary as a well-established transit country for football migrants. Nevertheless, newcomer migrant players seem to initially embrace this image of Hungary and aim to use their position as a springboard to Western Europe. They soon realise, however, that their chances of gaining access to Western riches are limited.

Interviewees clearly indicated that Hungary is not a transit country for football migrants, and it is considered unusual for migrant players to move on to more prestigious Western clubs. For instance, a migrant player noted: "I hoped it would be easier to move on from here [Hungary] but I feel I am stuck and can go nowhere [in Western Europe]." One of the managers made the following observation:

> They [migrant footballers] mostly come from countries where they do not have good chances to move forward [to Western Europe]. Hungary is closer to Austria and to Germany and they believe that they will be able to move towards those countries . . . Aside from one or two exceptions, this does not work this way.

Another manager also indicated that players regularly come to Hungary with great hopes, but "after a while they simply move back to their country of origin or move to lower divisions as they can't get to those glamorous Western clubs". A coach asserted that: "Most of the foreigners stay here [Hungary] for a few years and then they go back to their home countries or maybe move to Germany or Austria, but play only in the second or third divisions."

That is, the myth of Hungary being the 'football gateway' to Western riches derives mainly from Hungary's location, which projects the idea of an obvious geographic proximity to some of the Western European countries. However, geographical location evidently does not guarantee football contracts, and foreign footballers have the tendency to miscalculate the opportunities that are open to them once in Hungary. This phenomenon is present as foreign players are frequently bound to rely on information provided to them mainly by their agents and what the latter lead them to believe (see Poli, 2005). However, after their arrival foreign footballers tend to learn that Hungary does not represent a significant international football market and that its clubs, and their players, are not in the ambit of Western European football. When they become conscious of the current status of Hungarian football and their life chances in it, they may pursue football further in Hungary, move back to their country of origin or, in a few cases, attempt to seek out moderately profitable jobs in the lower divisions of some Western countries.

Poli (2005) made a similar observation regarding African players and their 'downward mobility', leading to the exploitation of foreign players who are often victimised by speculative transfer networks. As Poli (2005, p.229) explains: "African players, at the beginning of their career, lend themselves perfectly to the role of a flexible and easily exploitable force, of which European clubs and players' agents do not hesitate to take advantage." One of the interview participants in Poli's research (2005) indicated that African players often come to France in search of contracts, but these endeavours regularly end in players cruising the streets of a foreign country without a visa, contract or money. In Hungary a somewhat similar situation can be observed, the difference being that most of the players come from neighbouring countries so that when their professional situation becomes problematic they can simply move back home. These circumstances can be explained by the fact that the majority of migrant footballers arriving in Hungary are not highly sought-after commodities and that the effective units of migration are not the individuals but sets of people linked by acquaintances or work experiences (Tilly, 1990). These units are important, mainly in the case of cross-country migrations, because migrating from one state to another usually entails many risks, ranging from personal security to cultural awareness. Most individuals do not dare to take those risks by themselves and tend to let their migratory intentions be directed by various units of migration (e.g. agents) with pre-existing links to and familiarity with the host culture. These units have already established good and reliable contacts with possible destinations and work opportunities, and thus people with migratory desires, but with a lack of cultural and language knowledge, depend on established interpersonal networks for information that minimises the risks that migration may involve (Tilly, 1990). This network of units of migration develops pipelines between host and donor countries, forming simultaneously a binding and a supervising agency that often protects as well as constrains migrants' life chances (Molnar & Maguire, 2008). This observation is evidently applicable to the majority of football-related immigrations to Hungary, which are driven by established agent connections predominantly between Hungary and other post-communist countries. Players arriving in Hungary through these pipelines form views of their host country, which are the focus of the next section.

Hungarian football: 'today we take it easy'

Migrants generally viewed Hungarian football, in comparison to the football standards of other countries, as a sporting environment characterised by a limited degree of professionalism, training sessions of mediocre intensity and an overall relaxed atmosphere. One of the players, who had experience of other leagues, compared Hungary to Western Europe: "Italy, Germany and Austria are a different world . . . I think that when good quality Hungarian teams . . . take part in the UEFA Cup [Europa League], then you can see the obvious difference." Another expressed one of the disparities between Hungarian and German football:

"It [Hungarian football] is more relaxed. Not like in Germany . . . There you must always work hard. Here [in Hungary] we say: 'Ok. Today we take it easy.' And then we do!" The relaxed nature of Hungarian football was further emphasised by another migrant: "The game is different here [Hungary]. It is much more relaxed . . . Training sessions are longer but relaxed. In other leagues, training sessions are shorter but much harder and more disciplined." These quotations indicate that foreign players perceive Hungarian football, in comparison to other European football environments, as a less physically demanding and challenging setting. Hungarian football represents a site where players of declining skills can come to retire, or second class players can reside, because they can meet the required standards.

Foreign players also indicated that in Western European leagues there is always a high degree of competition and pressure on players to perform because that is the only way to get selected for and remain in the first team. Therefore, there is an endless, intensive competition amongst players at the same club to preserve their position or to shift to a new, more profitable one. One player described this pressure:

> It is different there [in Western Europe]. Here [in Hungary] it is much more relaxed. For example, in Germany, players would have to strongly hold onto their position in the team . . . Everybody wants to play in the first team as everybody wants more money and more visibility [public exposure]. If you do not play [in the first team] you do not get that much [exposure].

Contrary to Western football pressures, Hungarian football culture appears to have adopted a more relaxed approach to training and team selection. In line with the participants' observations, Bocsák (2001) notes that footballers often possess contracts that are not greatly concerned with their on-field performance and, thus, they are not motivated to win. Bocsák and Imre (2003) emphasise that footballers in Hungary are not sufficiently motivated by contractually driven monetary factors to perform.[4]

Whether as a result of a lack of contractual pressures and/or dominant cultural attitudes to football performance, foreign players noted that domestic players are not as aggressive and motivated to win as one would expect an elite athlete to be. For instance, one interviewee noted:

> I always want to win. I do not like to lose even if it is only a training session. When there is a two-on-two game, I do not like to lose. It is in my blood to win . . . This mental difference [wanting to win] exists between me, players of [my home country], and Hungarian players.

Another migrant player experienced similar footballing attitudes:

> I hate to lose even if it is only training . . . This is not the case here [Hungarian football]. Training sessions aren't taken very seriously. They don't seem to matter as much as elsewhere I played before. I don't understand why, as

training is the basis of football. I don't understand why they [domestic players] have this attitude to training and hard work.

It has, however, been noticed that not all Hungarian players have these attributes. Some Hungarian players with foreign experience tend to represent different attitudes and display a more professional approach:

> Here [Hungary] . . . there are lots of players who have played outside of Hungary. I came from aboard, so did many others. We have 8–9 experienced players [in this team] who have played abroad or have come from abroad. They represent another way of thinking but for how long?

This observation indicates that migrations could have an impact on Hungarian football development in a way that foreign experiences could contribute to changing the dominant cultural practices underpinning Hungarian football. On the other hand, the above quotation also suggests that there is an issue with holding onto that Western-acquired football attitude in the long term. It has been noted by interviewees that their knowledge, skills and experience were never directly utilised in the Hungarian context and that they (and other migrants too) accepted the dominant domestic practices. An interviewee with extensive migratory experience admitted:

> I have never been asked [to use my foreign experience]. I am not going to volunteer. There are things I remember such as training programmes. I have accurately written down what we did and on which day we did it. But I am not going to knock on anybody's door to say 'Hey I have got these ideas!' These are just not needed here [in Hungary].

A somewhat disgruntled player expressed his opinion:

> It [experience/knowledge accumulated in foreign leagues] could be used, but you are not allowed to. There is a certain playing style here and you have to get used to that. There are players who try but they usually fail . . . We have to come to terms with that there is a way of doing things here [in Hungary] . . . There is a way [of football] everywhere, although this way is crap because Hungarian football is crap(!), but still we have to live in it and learn to get used to it.

These quotations show that migrant players believe they are not in a position to effectively use or transmit their international experience. Indeed, it was frequently expressed that they had to get used to the Hungarian environment and were not required, allowed or asked to apply their expertise gained abroad. One player explained:

> There are many players in Hungary who are mentally strong. Wanting to win is typical of them and it is a good thing, but after a while they sink into this

Hungarian environment and lose this plus, because this is a plus. Not all players in Hungary have this desire.

Another of the players reinforced the above:

They [Hungarian players] come back home from abroad and they get into a Hungarian environment from, let's say, a German one. And after a while their Western[-acquired] attitude to training fades away. I, personally, cannot comprehend this. I suspect that the problem has to be in the environment, which simply allows a more relaxed approach to football.

A coach made a similar observation regarding returnee Hungarian players:

[My] experience shows that when they come back you can see the difference for about 1 or 2 months, then they get used to the [domestic] environment. That is, they get back to a previous stage. They say: 'What [should I work hard] for?' . . . 'I don't need any extra. I do not need to do 130% when I can get by with 80%!'

This issue is arguably recognised by most involved in football in Hungary. The 'relaxed mentality' of Hungarian footballers has become a stereotype and part of the football culture. This label has even been used to motivate footballers. One of the players recalled a provocative situation that demonstrates the general mentality of Hungarian players, the status of Hungarian football and existence of this 'relaxed-mentality' stereotype:

We have got a coach here who is forward thinking and I think he wants to achieve and change something. He tries to reform training sessions and match strategies. He tries to make us work harder and tries to make us believe that we can achieve something. I feel that he understands this [situation of Hungarian football] because he sometimes says: 'Do not be Hungarians! Be professionals!' I think that he wants to push us to achieve what is fundamentally required abroad.

These quotations demonstrate a value conflict between domestic and foreign attitudes to football in Hungary. Foreign players (and returnees as well) have become aware of the cultural conflict inherent in contemporary Hungarian football, which is also evident in the way the above-mentioned coach encouraged his players '*not to be Hungarians*' but to '*be professionals*'. This 'request' (or advice) suggests a clear distinction between the value system of a Hungarian footballer and that of a 'professional' one and reveals the cultural struggle that migrant (and returnee) players may face in Hungary due to the dominance of specific football-related – *archaic* – cultural practices that emerged during the communist era. *Dominant* values are established political and cultural practices which exist throughout a civil society, and a series of sporting, cultural, political and ideological practices to cement a society into relative unity (Bennett *et al.*, 1979). Ingham and Hardy (1993) argue that the dominant is never complete and that it always exists in relation to alternative social ideas. That is, in order to see the dominant one needs to be familiar with other forms of social practices (Ingham & Hardy, 1993). This, perhaps, is the main reason why migrant players are in a position to identify the dominance of a relaxed atmosphere in the domestic football environment. The dominant 'relaxed'/unprofessional football-related cultural practices are also *residual* ones as they tie the past to the present. As Williams (1977, p.122) noted: "The residual, by definition, has been effectively formed in the past, but it is still active in the cultural process, not only and often not at all as an element of the past, but as an effective element of the present." Interviewees clearly identified the effective presence of the residual as part of the dominant, a process which Williams (1977, p.122) explained as the "active manifestation of the residual". In this sense, the dominance of residual communist football attitudes is still characteristic of Hungarian football, together with sporadic emergent practices which tie the present to the future (see Ingham & Hardy, 1993). These emergent practices or alternative voices, which were represented and recognised by the migrant players, may themselves become incorporated in the dominant cultural formation (Ingham & Hardy, 1993) in the process of further transitions. Given that the dominant discourse is never completely successful in silencing dissident voices (Kanemasu & Molnar, 2013b), it is possible (and perhaps desirable) that the normative cultural power – which may be jointly implemented by a range of managers, coaches and players in Hungarian football to preserve the dominance of the residual – will be effectively challenged by alternative voices, leading to the emergence and solidification of counter-hegemonic, alternative cultural practices. As Williams (1977, pp.113–14) puts it succinctly: "The reality of any hegemony . . . is that, while by definition it is always dominant, it is never either total or exclusive. At any time, forms of alternative or directly oppositional politics and culture exist as significant elements in the society." Therefore, dominant cultural practices have to be continually "renewed, recreated, defended and modified" (Williams, 1977, p.112). Although residual communist cultural attitudes still appear to dominate in Hungarian football, there can be observed sporadically emerging alternative voices directly linked to migrations, which, though present and arguably slowly gaining momentum (see Molnar, 2002; Collins, 2004), are still, by and large, muted by mutually consenting to the *active residual*. That is, migrant (and returnee) players may attempt to resist the currently established relaxed attitude to football in Hungary, but after some resistance they seem to accept and consent to the cultural 'common sense' (Williams, 1977) approach to football, thereby submitting to still powerful established cultural practices at the expense of their own life chances and domestic football development.

Conclusion

This chapter has focused on the presence of migrant players in the Hungarian professional football league and their perception of the domestic football culture.

The current domestic conditions making foreign athletes' presence necessary, attractive and, to some extent, profitable were briefly discussed – and linked to the post-communist transitory circumstances. Three reasons for employing migrant players were identified: the lack of available domestic talent, clubs' financial incentives, and the now in decline 'fashion' aspect. It has been observed that, due mainly to the underdeveloped football grassroots system, the pool of available domestic talent is limited and there is a real need to employ migrant players. It was also observed that foreign players tend to be less expensive than domestic players, which is of great significance for clubs struggling to balance their books. Hence, the presence of foreign players in Hungary can be seen as a predominantly momentary, cost reducing solution to some of the contemporary issues of domestic football.

It was then established that Hungary was not the primary choice of host country for foreign footballers. In fact, in most cases, Hungary was the only hope, 'the last shelter' for these players to launch or continue their football careers as migrants. Players sought out contracts in Hungary as they became superfluous commodities in more advanced Western leagues or were out of contract for some time and, thus, became desperate to secure some form of football income. They were also pushed towards Hungary by their host country's unstable social and economic conditions. Additionally, the lure of Hungary's geographic proximity to Western Europe and the distant, often unrealistic, chance to transfer to one of the lucrative Western leagues encouraged a significant number of footballers, especially from the countries of the post-communist bloc, to transfer (see Molnar, 2006). It was observed that the majority of migrant players aim to make an attempt to pursue more lucrative football avenues outside of Hungary. However, many foreign footballers appeared to miscalculate Hungarian football conditions and the opportunities that would be open to them once in Hungary. Bound by agent networks and their life chances in the given milieu, migrants may decide to prolong their careers in Hungary, move back to their country of origin, or attempt to seek out moderately profitable jobs in the lower divisions of Western countries.

In the last section, foreign players' perceptions of Hungarian football were discussed. These players unequivocally stated that Hungarian football and footballers display a more relaxed, less professional and less motivated attitude in comparison to their Western counterparts. Interviewees also stated that they were not given opportunities to utilise their experience gained in other leagues and had to assimilate to the dominant domestic football expectations. The observations of migrant players regarding the culture of Hungarian football can be perceived as the active engagement of the residual with the dominant which fundamentally drives current football-specific cultural practices and attitudes in the professional domestic football league. Although migrant players (and, arguably, returnee Hungarians as well) may represent an alternative, Western-type emergent cultural practice and for a short while seem to be able to hold onto their Western-acquired cultural values, eventually they all seem to acquiesce in or to the dominant cultural practice. Due to the effective hegemonic naturalisation of *the way* of football in Hungary, migrant players all seem to accept the dominance of the residual, which clearly links contemporary Hungarian football with its communist past. To shed the cultural burden of the *residual*, migrants and migrations could play a key role in breaking the mould of *the way* of football and helping much needed cultural change to emerge in the form of *a new way* of football. A cultural transformation of this nature could significantly enhance Hungary's current international football performance and reputation, much to the appreciation of those devoted fans of the sport who have been exposed to its decline since the 1970s.

Notes

1 The name of the Hungarian profession football league changes as a new sponsoring organisation is appointed. For instance, the league was named the Sorproni Liga between 2007 and 2010 as the main sponsor was the Soproni beer brewery. Currently, OTP (Országos Takarék Pénztár – the National Savings Bank) is the main sponsor.
2 There are exceptions to this observation regarding instability in long-term football club leadership. The Debreceni Vasutas Sport Club (DVSC) – one of Hungary's professional football clubs – has had the same CEO since 2002 and has been one of the most successful clubs in Hungary. DVSC won the Hungarian professional championship six times between 2002 and 2012, which is currently unmatched by other teams in the league.
3 The high and constant supply of players from neighbouring countries and the limited demand – number of professional clubs – further devalue foreign players in Hungary, i.e. "if the supply overshoots the demand wages sink" (Marx, 1976: 25). As long as this situation exists, club owners and managers, who are mostly interested in short-term financial gains, will be unlikely to invest significant money in youth development.
4 It is to be noted that contracts between clubs and players have been subject to considerable media and public speculation in Hungary; thus, the views of Bocsák (2001) and Bocsák and Imre (2003) should be treated with some degree of caution.

References

Andreff, W. (2009) The Economic Effect of 'Muscle-Drain' in Sport. In G. Walters and G. Rossi (Eds.) *Labour Market Migration in European Football: Issues and Challenges.* London: Birkbeck Sports Business Centre.

Bennett, T., Martin, G., Mercer, C. and Woollacott, J. (1979) (Eds.) *Culture, Ideology and Social Process.* Milton Keynes: Open University Press.

Bocsák, M. (2001) *Miert haldoklik a magyar futball?* [Why is Hungarian Football Dying?]. Dabas: Dabasi Nyomda Rt.

Bocsák, M., and Imre, M. (2003) *Megelhetesi Foci* [Cost of Living in Footy]. Dabas: Dabasi Nyomda Rt.

Bruce, T. and Wheaton, B. (2011) Diaspora and Global Sports Migrations: A Case Study in the English and New Zealand Contexts. In J. Maguire and M. Falcous (Eds.) *Sport and Migration.* London: Routledge (189–99).

Bryman, A. (2001) *Social Research Methods.* Oxford: Oxford University Press.

Bukta, Z. (2004) Sport in Hungary: The Relationship between the Governmental and the Civil Sphere in Sport on a Local Level. In G. Anders, J. Mrazek, G. Norden and O. Weiss (Eds.) *European Integration and Sport.* Munster: LIT Verlag (29–38).

Butt, J. and Molnar, G. (2009) Involuntary Career Termination in Sport: A Case Study of the Process of Structurally Induced Failure. *Sport in Society* 12(2): 240–57.

Collins, M. (2004) Epilogue: Eastern European Sport – Which Ways from the Current Crossroads? *International Journal of the History of Sport* 21(5): 833–43.

Darby, P. (2011) Out of Africa: The Exodus of Elite African Football Talent to Europe. In J. Maguire and M. Falcous (Eds.) *Sport and Migration*. London: Routledge (245–58).

Darby, P. (2013) Moving Players, Traversing Perspectives: Global Value Chains, Production Networks and Ghanaian Football Labour Migration. *Geoforum* 50: 43–53.

Dövényi, Z. (1995) Spatial Aspects of the Refugee Issue in Hungary. In M. Fullerton, E. Sik and J. Tóth (Eds.) *Refugees and Migrants: Hungary at the Crossroads*. Budapest: Institute for Political Science of the Hungarian Academy of Science (17–26).

Duke, V. (1994) The Flood from the East? Perestroika and the Migration of Sports Talent from Eastern Europe. In J. Bale and J. Maguire (Eds.) *The Global Sport Arena: Athletic Talent Migration in an Independent World*. London: Frank Cass (153–67).

Elliott, R. (2014) Brits Abroad: A Case Study Analysis of Three British Footballers Migrating to the Hungarian Soproni Liga. *Soccer and Society* 15(4): 517–34.

Flick, U. (2002) *An Introduction to Qualitative Research*. London: Sage Publications.

Földesi, G. (1993) The Transformation of Sport in Eastern Europe: The Hungarian Case. *Journal of Comparative Physical Education and Sport* 15(1): 5–21.

Grainger, A. (2011) Migrants, Mercenaries and Overstayers: Talent Migration in Pacific Island Rugby. In J. Maguire and M. Falcous (Eds.) *Sport and Migration*. London: Routledge (129–40).

Hadas, M. (2000) Football and Social Identity: The Case of Hungary in the Twentieth Century. *Sports Historian* 20(2): 43–66.

Hammond, M. (1999) *The European Football Yearbook*. Warley: Sports Projects Ltd.

Horton, P. (2012) Pacific Islanders in Global Rugby: The Changing Current of Sport Migration. *International Journal of the History of Sport* 29(17): 2388–404.

Ingham, A. and Hardy, S. (1993) Introduction: Sport Studies through the Lens of Raymond Williams. In A. Ingham and J. Loy (Eds.) *Sport in Social Development: Traditions, Transitions and Transformations*. Champaign, IL: Human Kinetics (1–19).

Kanemasu, Y. and Molnar, G. (2013a) Collective Identity and Contested Allegiance: A Case of Migrant Professional Fijian Rugby Players. *Sport in Society* 16(7): 863–82.

Kanemasu, Y. and Molnar, G. (2013b) Problematizing the Dominant: The Emergence of Alternative Cultural Voices in Fiji Rugby. *Asia Pacific Journal of Sport and Social Science* 2(1): 14–30.

McCracken, G. (1988) *The Long Interview* (Vol. 13). London: Sage Publications.

Maguire, J., Jarvie, G., Mansfield, L. and Bradley, J. (2002) *Sport Worlds: A Sociological Perspective*. Champaign, IL: Human Kinetics.

Marx, K. (1976) *Value, Price and Profit*. New York: International Publishers.

May, T. (2001) *Social Research: Issues, Methods and Process* (3rd edn). Buckingham: Open University Press.

Molnar, G. (2002) Globalization: The Structural Changes of the Hungarian Sport Life after the Communist Regime. Unpublished Master's Thesis, Miami University, OH.

Molnar, G. (2006) Mapping Migrations: Hungary Related Migrations of Professional Footballers after the Collapse of Communism. *Soccer & Society* 7(4): 463–85.

Molnar, G. (2007) Hungarian Football: A Socio-historical Perspective. *Sport in History* 27(2): 293–318.

Molnar, G. (2011) From the Soviet Bloc to the European Community: Migrating Professional Footballers in and out of Hungary. In J. Maguire and M. Falcous (Eds.) *Sport and Migration*. London: Routledge (56–70).

Molnar, G., Doczi, T. and Gal, A. (2011) A Socio-structural Overview of Hungarian Football. In H. Gammelsæter and B. Senaux (Eds.) *The Organisation and Governance of Top Football across Europe: An Institutional Perspective*. London: Routledge (253–67).

Molnar, G. and Maguire, J. (2008) Hungarian Footballers on the Move: Issues of and Observations on the First Migratory Phase. *Sport in Society* 11(1): 74–89.

Obel, C. and Austin, T. (2011) Touring, Travelling and Accelerated Mobilities: Team and Player Mobilities in New Zealand Rugby Union. In J. Maguire and M. Falcous (Eds.) *Sport and Migration*. London: Routledge (259–73).

Patton, M. (1990) *Qualitative Evaluation and Research Methods*. Newbury Park, CA: Sage.

Poli, R. (2005) Football players' Migration in Europe: A Geo-economic Approach to Africans' Mobility. In J. Magee, A. Bairner and A. Tomlinson (Eds.) *The Bountiful Game? Football Identities and Finances*. Aachen: Meyer and Meyer Sport (217–32).

Szalai, E. (1995) Political and Social Conflicts Arising from the Transformation of Property Relations in Hungary. In T. Cox and A. Furlong (Eds.) *Hungary: The Politics of Transition*. London: Frank Cass (57–78).

Tilly, C. (1990) Transplanted Networks. In V. Yans-McLaughlin (Ed.) *Immigration Reconsidered: History, Sociology, and Politics*. Oxford: Oxford University Press (79–95).

Vincze, G. (2009) Football Talent Care after the 1989–1990 Political Transformation in Hungary. *Physical Culture and Sport: Studies and Research* 46: 167–76.

Wallace, C. and Stola, D. (2001) Introduction: Patterns of Migration in Central Europe. In C. Wallace and D. Stola (Eds.) *Patterns of Migration in Central Europe*. Basingstoke: Palgrave (3–44).

Williams, R. (1977) *Marxism and Literature*. New York: Oxford University Press.

Players

9 Current patterns and tendencies in women's football migration

Outsourcing or national protectionism as the way forward?

Sine Agergaard

Football for girls and women is one of the fastest growing sports in the world, in terms of both participation and organisation. The number of registered players has more than doubled since 2000 and has long surpassed 25 million girls and women playing football worldwide (FIFA, 2007). Besides this, the game has also experienced a growth in economic support, an expansion of professional leagues in several countries, and an increase in media coverage, advertising and sponsorship (Kjær & Agergaard, 2013; Pfister *et al.*, 2014). Still, according to Tiesler (2012b) women's football is only established as a professional league in 23 out of 136 FIFA-listed countries. This means that talented and skilled female football players in 84% of these countries need to leave their home in order to become professionals.

Studies suggest that the international mobility of female football players has increased substantially in recent years; for instance, the percentage of national team players playing in clubs abroad grew from 13% among the squads participating at the 2008 Olympic Games (Tiesler, 2012a) to 26.6% at the 2012 Olympic Games.[1] Very little, however, is known about the main trends and patterns in the international mobility of female football players. Why do different areas come to appear as centres and peripheries? What is specific in the patterns and trends of women's football migration that may contribute to new insights on sports labour migration? Even if numerically smaller than the streams of male football players who migrate, case studies of women's football migration[2] may prove particularly useful when inquiring into the evolving dimensions of the globalisation of sports and sports labour migration.

So far, studies of women's football migration have helped to identify that athletic migrants continue to engage in cross-border activities through regular communication and travel (Botelho & Agergaard, 2011; Agergaard & Botelho, 2013). Hence, studies have pointed to the importance of comprehending the ways in which athletic migrants may maintain and develop a transnational embeddedness in various communities and countries simultaneously (Agergaard & Tiesler, 2014). In setting out to look into general patterns in football migration, this chapter will tend to describe streams of migration as one-directional flows from one location to another. Seen in a transnational perspective, it is worth bearing in mind that when athletes migrate, they also maintain links to their country of origin and/or countries they have passed through. Several aspects of transnational exchanges can be identified, ranging from sending remittances back home to regular travel and visits through participation in the national team and a possible return to take up a position in the country of origin. Thus the discussion of migration leading to inevitable loss for the country of origin and gains for the country of destination needs to be nuanced, as in the case of the study of the skills exchange following young football players' migration to English football academies (Elliott and Weedon, 2010).

State of the art: patterns identified in men's football migration

Studies of women's football migration may be based not only in the literature on sports labour migration but also in other research on women's migration (e.g. Haugaa Engh, 2014). Studies of highly skilled migrants also offer relevant research perspectives that may inspire sports researchers to think outside of the box (Elliott & Maguire, 2008b). As noted in the Introduction to this volume, much of the research to date has focused on trends and patterns in elite male football migration. This chapter sets out to make use of, but also contribute to, research in football migration by adding information from empirical studies of women's football migration, and pointing to trends and patterns that may be of use for research in sports and migration more broadly.

A predominant pattern of migration termed linguistic and cultural proximity is richly described in, among others, Maguire and Stead's (1998) study of Nordic and Scandinavian players moving into the English Premier League. The study points to the fact that the preference for these players in English clubs is based not only on the tendency for Danish players to speak the English language but also on the ascribed and achieved status of this group as a particularly hardworking and easily accommodating one (Maguire & Stead, 1998). Even closer cultural and linguistic proximity is described by Lanfranchi and Taylor (2001) in their historical account of Britain's splendid isolation. Further, Taylor (2006) and McGovern (2002) describe how until the late 1970s the options for migrating to the English leagues were restricted largely to British players, while the period following the Bosman ruling in 1995 still revealed a tendency to recruit from a limited number of countries sharing language and common ancestries.

A second predominant pattern in the literature on football migration is migration from the Global South (South America and Africa) to the North (in the case of men's football migration, primarily Europe). Lanfranchi and Taylor (2001) describe the movement of male footballers from Argentina, Brazil and Uruguay to southern European countries at the start of the 1900s and later more broadly to other European leagues. Here, linguistic and cultural similarity was also important and can be used to explain, in part, the movements of Argentinian players to the Spanish league and Brazilian players to the Portuguese league. Another prevalent stream in the migration from the Global South to North is the migration from African countries to Europe. This has been explained as a flux reinforcing colonial relations (Lanfranchi & Taylor, 2001; Bale, 2004). Paul Darby has contributed substantially to the understanding of neo-colonial patterns in men's (boys') football migration by describing the relations between football academies in Ghana and Nigeria, in particular, and European clubs (Darby 2000, 2007, 2009, 2011; Darby *et al.*, 2007). Raffaele Poli (2005, 2006, 2010a, 2010b) has also contributed to this area with demographic data and theorisation on the migration from South to North in describing that African players appear as a cheaper labour force and tend, for the most part, to migrate to less well-performing leagues (see also Poli & Besson, 2011).

A third pattern in male football migration (even if described less) is the migration from East (particularly Asia) to West (Europe). Takahashi and Horne (2004) mention the tendency for Japanese (and Chinese) players to migrate to Europe, as well as a significant migration of Japanese players to South America, particularly the Brazilian league (Rial, 2008). The pattern of East–West migration may also refer to the migration of players from Eastern European countries (former Soviet Bloc countries) to Western Europe. Molnar describes this in the case of Hungarian football players moving west in the post-communist period (Molnar 2006, 2011; Molnar & Maguire, 2008), a migratory route that has also been termed as part of the identification of a new talent pipeline after the removal of the political division between Eastern and Western Europe. Case studies of Western European players moving into Eastern Europe have also been described (e.g. Elliott 2013, 2014; Elliott & Bania, 2013).

Last but not least, a fourth pattern in the shape of internal migration within the southern hemisphere has also started to attract researchers' attention. Players migrate within and between African nations, where countries like South Africa seem to function as an intermediary for obtaining access to intercontinental migration (Cornelissen & Solberg, 2007; Darby & Solberg, 2010).

Method and material

This chapter is based on a secondary analysis of the club affiliation of players at the leading national women's football teams according to FIFA's ranking (as of 2 August 2013). The selection has been limited to the first 54 teams on the ranking based on the need to include an adequate number of players in the survey (that is, above 1,000) and prior knowledge of the countries where one can detect migration, including Equatorial Guinea (FIFA ranked 52 and emigration ranked 3) and Northern Ireland (FIFA ranked 54 and emigration ranked 25). For four of the countries, namely Costa Rica (FIFA ranked 40), Myanmar (FIFA ranked 43), Uzbekistan (FIFA ranked 45) and Papua New Guinea (FIFA ranked 47), it was not possible to find the relevant information, so these countries appear with missing values in the survey. Still, the sample consists of 50 national squads and 1,046 players.

Websites, supplemented with official lists on women's national football teams from FIFA, provide the sources of this data. All material was collected in October and November 2013 and is based on information from seasons 2012 and 2013. In one case (Switzerland) the information dated back to 2011, while in other cases the national team was just listed as the current squad without referring to a specific point in time. In all these cases the information given was sourced from a website that was updated at some point in 2013. On the websites a small number of players (eight) were not listed with a club affiliation, probably due to the fact that at the point of registration (often in connection with regional or international tournaments during summertime) transfers were ongoing. The number of players listed in the national squads varies, ranging from 13 to 27 and thereby making the percentage (rather than the number) of players abroad the criterion for sorting the list. Thus, there are some limitations to our estimate of the current percentage of national squad players affiliated to clubs abroad, which are also related to the fact that the numbers were not found at the same point in time or for squads of the same size participating in the same event.

Still, the sample here provides a substantial amount of material on the current status of migration among not only the very top women's national teams but also a larger group of national teams, not all of which participate in international tournaments such as the Women's World Cup (limited to 16 teams) and the Olympic Games (limited to 12 countries). However, it is not only in the national teams managing to qualify for these international tournaments that you find emigration. The fact that the sample is made up of national-team players rather than club players in selected countries means that we do not cover all aspects of the phenomenon of women's football migration, which also involves younger talents and senior players who are not, or have formerly been, national squad players. This sample provides a selection of national squad players who have a high visibility in international women's football, given that public attention for women's football is usually focused on international tournaments rather than national league matches (outside of the US and Germany, and some European Champions League matches, spectator numbers are limited). Visibility is intimately linked with the option of producing mobility (Carter, 2011). Thus, it has been demonstrated that access to the national squad and possible participation in an international tournament are crucial in producing visibility for players who wish to move abroad (Haugaa Engh & Agergaard, 2013).

General patterns

When working with this sample, it should be remembered that several of the national squads do not (at present) have players affiliated to clubs abroad. The number of players affiliated to clubs abroad stands at 27.8% in total and 29.4% for the national squad players from European countries. Considering the wide diversity in the national squads included in the sample, this proportion is considerable and reinforces the observation that the migration of women football players is growing. For instance, in a more strategically selected sample covering migratory fluxes for players in 40 national squads in 2008, Tiesler (2010) found that 23% of national squad players were playing abroad. Table 9.1 provides a more detailed list of the findings from the current survey.

The national squads are listed according to the percentage of players emigrating. The percentages rise to 88.9%. The two highest levels of emigration are found

Table 9.1 Emigration from national squads in women's football

EMI	Country	Listed Players	%	Abroad	Clubless	Destination Countries	Squad Data	FIFA RANK (2/813)
1	Canada	18	88.9	16		US 15, SE 1	2013	7
2	Mexico	18	77.8	14		US 13, ES 1	2013	24
3	Wales	20	75.0	15		ENG 11, US 3, SE 1	2013	37
4	Equ. Guinea	21	71.4	15	2	BR 10, PL 2, D 1, KAZ 1, ES 1	2012	52
5	Slovakia	18	66.7	12		AU 5, PL 3, CZ 2, WA 1, D 1,	2012	41
6	Switzerland	20	65.0	13		D 7, SE 2, FR 1, IT 1, NO 1, ES 1	2011	25
7	Triniad & Tobago	13	61.5	8		US 5, SE 2	2013	46
8	Rep. of Ireland	18	61.1	11	1	ENG 4, NO 3, US 2, SC 1, D 1	2012	34
9	New Zealand	18	61.1	11		D 6, SE 2, US 2, ENG 1	2012	18
10	Colombia	18	61.1	11		US 6, ES 2, SE 1, FI 1, ICE 1	2012	29
11	Iceland	23	52.2	12		SE 7, NO 4, ENG 1	2013	15
12	Ukraine	24	50.0	12	2	RUS 12	2013	23
13	Portugal	23	47.8	11		D 4, ES 3, US 3, FR 1	2013	42
14	Finland	23	43.5	10		SE 8, NO 2	2013	22
15	Cameroon	22	40.9	9		FR 2, RUS 2, NIR 1, PL 1, RO 1, SRB 1, SCH 1	2012	48
16	Serbia	20	40.0	8		ICE 3, AU 1, BE 1, D 1, KAZ 1, ES 1	2013	43
17	Scotland	18	33.3	6		ENG 2, SE 2, FR 1, D 1	2013	20
18	Netherlands	23	30.4	7		SE 4, D 2, US 1	2013	14
19	Romania	23	30.4	7	3	DK 2, TUR 2, IT 1, FR 1, RUS 1	2013	35
20	Belarus	27	29.6	8		RUS 5, UKR 2, KAZ 1	2013	38
21	Nigeria	21	28.6	6		SE 4, TUR 1, KAZ 1	2012	32
22	Hungary	21	28.6	6		D 4, AU 1, ICE 1	2013	36

(Continued)

Table 9.1 (Continued)

EMI	Country	Listed Players	%	Abroad	Clubless	Destination Countries	Squad Data	FIFA RANK (2/813)
23	Austria	25	28.0	7		D 7	2013	33
24	Brazil	18	27.8	5		RUS 4, SE 1	2012	4
25	Northen Ireland	18	27.8	5		ENG 4, NO 1	2013	54
26	Denmark	23	26.1	6		SE 5, NO 1	2013	12
27	Czech Republic	23	21.7	5		D 2, SE 2, AU 1	2012	26
28	Japan	21	19.0	4		D 2, FR 1, USA 1	2013	3
29	Sweden	23	17.4	4		FR 2, ENG 1, GR 1, D 1	2013	5
30	South Africa	18	16.7	3		US 2, RUS 1	2012	51
31	Germany	21	14.3	3		AUS 1, SE 1, US 1	2013	2
32	Spain	23	13.0	3		SE 2, US 1	2013	17
33	Italy	23	13.0	3		D 2, SCH 1	2013	12
34	Austrailia	21	9.5	2		USA 1, SE 1	2013	8
35	Poland	22	9.1	2		D 2	2011	30
36	Norway	23	8.7	2		D 2	2013	10
37	Jordan	23	8.7	2		TUR 2	2012	53
38	Belgium	24	8.3	2		D 1, NL 1	2013	27
39	Thailand	24	8.3	2		JAP 2	2013	31
40	Korea Republic	22	4.5	1		JAP 1,	2013	17
41	England	23	4.3	1		SE 1	2013	11
42	France	23	4.3	1		D 1	2013	6
43	China	12	–	0			2013	16
44	Ghana	18	–	0			2012	51
45	Korea DPR	18	–	0			2012	51
46	USA	21	–	0	1		2013	1

47	Russia	23	—	0	2013	21
48	India	23	—	0	2013	50
49	Vietnam	20	—	0	2012	28
50	Chinese Taipei	20	—	0	2013	39
51	Costa Rica	missing				40
52	Myanmar	missing				43
53	Uzbekistan	missing				45
54	Papua New Guinea	missing				47
	Europe	618	29.4	182		
	World	1046	27.8	291		

AU=Austria, AUS=Australia, BE=Belgium, BR=Brazil, CHI=Chile, CZ=Czech Republic, D=Germany, DK=Denmark, ENG=England, ES=Spain, FI=Finland, FR=France, GR=Greece, ICE=Iceland, IT=Italy, JAP=Japan, KAZ=Kazaksthan, MEX=Mexico, NIR=Nigeria, NL=Nederlands, NO=Norway, PL=Poland, RO=Romania, RUS=Russia, SC=Scotland, SCH=Switzerland, SE=Sweden, TUR=Turkey, UKR=Ukraine, US=USA, WA=Wales.

All figures from Wikipedia and FIFA's webpages.

among national squad players from Canada and Mexico, which is due to a particular collaboration between the American, Canadian and Mexican FAs, according to which up to 24 American, 16 Canadian and 12 Mexican national squad players are secured a position in the American league (see also the chapter by Harris in this collection). This is a new initiative that will be discussed in more detail below. Still, after taking away Canada and Mexico, the percentage of national squad players affiliated to clubs abroad rises above 70%, and 24 teams have more than 25% of their players affiliated to clubs abroad. The specific patterns in this substantial mobility of players will be examined below.

On analysing the material in relation to the patterns already identified in studies of men's football migration, a number of similarities appear. First of all, the pattern of linguistic and cultural proximity may account for the high percentage of players from Wales, the Republic of Ireland, Northern Ireland and Scotland playing in England. Also, a high percentage of migration can be found between the Nordic countries, particularly from Iceland, Finland and Denmark to Sweden (and, to a lesser extent, Norway). Similar patterns exist with players moving from Austria and Switzerland to clubs in Germany, and not least from Ukraine to clubs in Russia. Among the Eastern European countries there are also players affiliated to clubs in neighbouring countries, including other Eastern European as well as Western European countries. For instance, players from Slovakia play in clubs in Austria as well as in Poland and the Czech Republic (all neighbouring countries). Thus, in line with former studies of women's football migration, it is relevant to designate this pattern *geographical* and cultural proximity (Botelho & Agergaard, 2011; Tiesler, 2011).

When analysing the extent to which fluxes from East to West may appear as a central pattern in women's football migration, it appears that there are Eastern European countries sending players to Western European countries but rarely to the very top leagues such as those in Sweden and Germany. Instead, Serbian players can be found in Iceland and Romanian players at Danish clubs. There is also an emerging East–East migration within Eastern Europe, with players from Belarus going to Russia, Ukraine and Kazakhstan. As mentioned earlier, the pattern of migration from East to West may also take place between Asia and Europe. In the case of women's football migration, the Pacific is also included in the flux of players going from the East to the West. This is represented here by players from New Zealand and Australia going to Germany, Sweden and England (and the USA), and Japanese players playing in Germany, France and the USA. The latter flux has been described in detail and linked with a strategy on the part of the Japanese FA to send their best players abroad in order for them to improve and return as international players able to lead Japan to victory in the 2011 World Cup (Takahashi, 2014).

A third pattern is migration from the so-called Global South to the North. As is illustrated in the case of Cameroon, the North is diverse since Cameroonian players are found playing in Russia, Poland, Romania and Serbia, along with France and Switzerland. Nigerian players are also represented in clubs in Eastern European countries, which seems to reinforce the observation made by Poli and

Besson (2011) that African players are highly dependent on stepping stones to get into the central leagues in Europe. However, Brazilian players are also found in Russia, which indicates that Eastern European countries form a broader option for players from countries in the southern hemisphere who wish to enter Europe. In the case of Nigeria, we have evidence that Nigerian players have been using their presence in Eastern European and lower ranking countries as a position from which to gain further visibility and negotiate transfers into the Swedish league (Agergaard & Haugaa Engh, 2012). The particular case of Nigerian players going to clubs in the northernmost part of Sweden owes much to the role of more or less formal intermediaries and not least former players and coaches in paving the way for other players (Haugaa Engh & Agergaard, 2013). The tendency for acts of migration to develop through friends-of-friends networks and bridgeheads has also been described in the broader literature on sports labour migration (e.g. Bale, 1991; Elliott & Maguire, 2008a).

Last, but not least, the pattern of internal migration within the southern hemisphere which studies of men's football migration have started to take into account is not easily detected in this sample. This is also owing to the fact that there are a limited number of countries included in the sample from South America and Africa. Within Asia there are players from Thailand and Korea who are affiliated to clubs in Japan. A particularly interesting flux in the southern hemisphere is the percentage of national squad players from Equatorial Guinea (71.4%) playing in clubs in Brazil. Recent studies have drawn attention to the fact that Brazilian football players were nationalised to play for the national squad of Equatorial Guinea (Rial, 2014). So the migratory flux here may simply be a case of return migration – former Brazilian players playing in clubs at home or players from Equatorial Guinea coming to play in Brazil through networks developed between individuals involved in women's football in the two countries. Studies have also highlighted the particular case of the Portuguese national squad, where players of Portuguese descent have been brought to play for the national squad even if they were raised and still play abroad (Tiesler, 2010). Thus the tendency to make use of nationalisation and diaspora migration in emerging processes of sports globalisation is evident when studying women's football migration (Agergaard *et al.*, 2014).

Tendencies pertaining to women's football

A number of the tendencies described for men's football migration may also be found in women's football migration, even if on a smaller scale. However, there are also indications that the patterns diverge (e.g. in the case of Pacific countries such as New Zealand that are involved in East–West migration). Moreover, this sample also reveals tendencies in women's football migration that may be particular to the discipline. Given the sparse economy and limited career options, as well as the geographical dispersion, of women's football, there is a central flux into the US (professional league and colleges) along with migration to top leagues in northern Europe.

Table 9.2 Immigration destinations for national squad players in women's football

	Country	Immigrants	Immigrated from
1	USA	56	CA 15, MEX 13,CO 6, T&T 5, POR 3, WA 3, REP IRE 2, NZ 2, S.A 2, D 1, ES 1, NL 1, AUS 1, JP 1
2	Germany	49	AU 7, SCH 7, NZ 6, POR 4, HUN 4, NL 2, CZ 2, IT 2, PL 2, JP 2, NO 2, E.G 1, SLO 1, REP IRE 1, SRB 1, SC 1, SE 1, BE 1, FR 1
3	Sweden	47	FI 8, ICE 7, DK 5, NL 4, NIR 4, SC 2, CZ 2, SCH 2, ES 2, T&T 2, NZ 2, WA 1, CA 1, CO 1, BRA 1, D 1, ENG 1, AUS 1, S 1
4	Russia	25	UKR 12, BELA 5, BRA 4, CAM 2, RO 1, S.A 1
5	England	24	WA 11, REP IRE 4, N.I 4, NZ 1, ICE 1, SC 2, SE 1
6	Norway	12	ICE 4, REP IRE 3, FI 2, SCH 1, N.I 1, DK 1
7	Brazil	10	E.G 10
8	France	9	CAM 2, SE 2, SCH 1, POR 1, SC 1, RO 1, JP 1
9	Spain	9	POR 3, CO 2, E.G 1, MEX 1, SCH 1, SRB 1
10	Austria	8	SLO 5, SRB 1, 1 HUN, 1 CZ
11	Poland	6	E.G 2, SLO 3, CAM 1
12	Turkey	5	JOR 2, RO 2, NIR 1
13	Iceland	5	SRB 3, HUN 1, CO 1
14	Kazakhstan	4	E.G 1, SRB 1, BELA 1, NIR 1
15	Japan	3	THAI 2, K.R 1
16	Denmark	2	RO 2
17	Switzerland	2	CAM 1, IT 1
18	Italy	2	RO 1, SCH 1
19	Czech Republic	2	SLO 2
20	Ukraine	2	BELA 2
21	Netherlands	1	BE 1
22	Australia	1	D 1
23	Belgium	1	SRB 1
24	Serbia	1	CAM 1
25	Romania	1	CAM 1
26	Nigeria	1	CAM 1
27	Finland	1	CO 1
28	Scotland	1	REP IRE 1
29	Wales	1	SLO 1
	Total	291	

AU=Austria, AUS=Australia, BE=Belgium, BELA=Belarus, BRA=Brazil, CA=Canada, CAM=Cameroon,
CO=Colombia, CZ=Czech Republic, D=Germany, DK=Denmark, E.G=Equ. Guinea, ENG=England,
ES=Spain, FI=Finland, HUN=Hungary, ICE=Iceland, IT=Italy, JOR=Jordan, JP=Japan, K.R=Korea Republic, MEX=Mexico,
N.I=Northern Ireland, NIR=Nigeria, NL=Netherlands, NZ=New Zealand, PL=Poland, POR=Portugal, REP IRE=Republic of Ireland,
RO=Romania, S=Sweden, S.A=South Africa, SC=Scotland, SCH=Switzerland, SLO=Slovakia, SRB=Serbia, THAI=Thailand, T&T=Trinidad & Tobago, UKR=Ukraine,WA=Wales.

As indicated above, three preferred immigration countries host players from neighbouring countries, along with those from afar. Thus, clubs in the USA, Germany and Sweden host players from Africa, Asia/the Pacific and South America. On looking in more detail at the countries from where players move to the USA, it is evident that the neighbouring countries are prevalent (which is also the result of the new collaboration between the US, Mexican and Canadian FAs referred to above), followed by countries also within the Americas like Trinidad and Tobago and Colombia.

The fact that the USA emerges as the preferred destination may be explained partly by senior players migrating to the professional league of women's football in the USA. The development of professional women's football has had its ups and downs; numerous attempts have been made to bring in sponsors and to become a fully professionally run national league (see the chapter by Harris in this collection). The USA appears in qualitative studies as the most desirable league to play in for players of diverse nationalities (Agergaard & Botelho, 2013). As described by Booth and Liston (2014), the US forms a zone of prestige for players to migrate to. This status as a zone of prestige is responsible not only for some of the best national squad players being recruited to clubs in the USA but also for a considerable flow of players from all over the world migrating to American colleges to combine sports and education (see Bale, 1991). A scholarship at a college in the USA represents a unique opportunity to combine education, international experience and playing football in a country where women's football is highly popular and respected (Markovits & Hellerman, 2001).

Another prevalent flux in women's football migration is the tendency for players to seek out some of the top leagues in Europe, given the development of the game there and the duration of the season for almost an entire calendar year (unlike the American league). As indicated in Table 9.2, the players who seek employment in the Swedish and German leagues come not only from neighbouring countries but also from geographically distant countries (e.g. Nigerians in Sweden and New Zealanders in Germany). As mentioned, the Japanese FA has for some time been involved in supporting their top players' moves abroad, and this appears to be a deliberate strategy based on the rational calculation that the conditions for player development are better in Europe and the USA than in Japan (Takahashi, 2014). The same calculation, for both senior players' development and younger talent's development, seems to be the background also for national FAs to support showcases that help to get young female players from Trinidad and Tobago recruited to American colleges (McCree, 2014).

Discussion: outsourcing or national protectionism?

The extent to which national sports governing bodies may take advantage of or are challenged by sports labour migration and globalisation more broadly is discussed below. Here the range goes from supporting players' migration abroad, on the one hand, to applying national and regional protectionist approaches, on the other hand. The case of women's football migration exemplifies the diversity of strategies available in sports policy between applying national regulations and using the non-regulation of the global game to enhance national performance.

Recent studies of the policy of sports governing bodies in various countries show that national support for sport is rising, even if it is becoming more difficult to gain medals and countries must look out for (minor) sports disciplines where they may have a competitive advantage (Houlihan & Zheng, 2013). This has been designated the global sporting arms race (de Bosscher *et al.*, 2008).

Even if the professional organisation and financial resources of women's football are still limited, the development of migratory fluxes may illustrate an emerging systematisation within and competition between different nations. In relation to players' migration, there are deliberate strategies being developed on behalf of national governing bodies of women's football that may be described as an outsourcing of talent and player development to clubs abroad. The concept of outsourcing is defined as a practice in which an organisation contracts out one of its in-house processes or functions that the organisation does not or cannot focus on any more (Kumar & Eickhoff, 2006, cited in Lee, 2010). Using this definition, Lee (2010) describes the tendency for European football clubs to buy African players rather than develop local talents. In the case of women's football migration, a reverse migration is developing, where talent and player development is outsourced to take place outside of the borders of the nation-state. As described by Lee (2010), there may be three major reasons for outsourcing: 1) cost minimisation, 2) quality improvement, and 3) access to resources. So sending young talent and senior players abroad may reflect a desire to minimise costs and to improve the quality of these players at places with resources for women's football instead of building up a talent development system at home.

However, there are also risks for national sports governing bodies, as there are for all political institutions outsourcing some of their services. It is difficult to monitor and control the outsourced labour, even if numerous attempts are made to evaluate the outsourced funds in an 'audit society' (Power, 1999). In the case of women's football, relatively small sums are risked when the Japanese FA support their players' moves abroad. Similarly, limited efforts are required from national sports governing bodies in the Caribbean to set up showcases to exhibit their domestic talent to coaches from American colleges and thereby promote their migration abroad. Still, there is a risk in outsourcing your talent development to clubs abroad that some of your talented players may not continue to return to play for the national squad, and in some cases the players may decide to settle in and become citizens of their country of destination (Agergaard *et al.*, 2014).

Another strategy emerging from the migratory fluxes in women's football is the recent national or regional protectionist strategy that has developed around the revitalised US league of women's football. As already mentioned, the American, Canadian and Mexican FAs are respectively paying 24, 16 and 12 of their national squad players' salaries in the US league. Thus it is becoming more difficult for players from abroad to migrate into the league. This strategy can be described as an attempt to protect internal national resources in the shape of a professional league, educated coaches and not least the huge number of female players with football skills. According to the coach of the US women's national team, Tom Sermanni, this initiative will make it easier for him to gather the national squad and to ensure that all players are undergoing well-designed training.[3] However, Sermanni also points to the risk of isolation, referring to his experience that American squad members playing abroad develop new football skills and not least prepare themselves for international football competitions by encountering other playing styles. Thus, the advantages and disadvantages of migratory fluxes are to be weighed up in the further development of women's football.

Conclusion

Using research on men's football as a starting point, this chapter has identified a number of central patterns and trends in women's football migration. The most prevalent pattern reflects a series of fluxes that are appearing between countries that share not only cultural and linguistic relations but also geographic proximity. The prevalence of this pattern may also be related to the fact that the economy in women's football is small and therefore clubs seldom have the resources to undertake long-distance scouting trips or pay players from afar to come for trials (Agergaard & Botelho, 2011). In the second pattern of migration from the Global South to the North, particular migratory routes appear (e.g. between Nigeria and Sweden). Such routes are to a large extent related to bridgeheads and friends-to-friends networks that pave the way for these particular fluxes.

Also, the pattern of migratory fluxes between East and West can be identified in women's football migration, while we also see migration within Eastern European countries and migration from the Far East (including Pacific countries) to Europe and the US. The geographical dispersion of women's football migration is also prevalent in migratory fluxes between countries within the southern hemisphere, even if this pattern is difficult to estimate in our sample.

In the case of one particular flux pertaining to women's football, this chapter has highlighted migration to the so-called zone of prestige in the shape of the US professional league (and colleges). This, along with the fact that most migration is occurring in a small number of European leagues, indicates that top-level conditions for women's football still only exist in a limited number of countries. Related to this, the chapter has identified a tendency to outsource talent and player development to the US league or colleges and to leading leagues in Europe.

Given that women's football migration is a growing phenomenon and also a new topic for research, a number of studies are pending. These could follow up on the migratory fluxes by accounting not only for national squad players' club affiliation but also transfers between clubs. Also, qualitative studies are needed on the development of particular migratory routes and the role of intermediaries therein. There are reports of various more or less formal strategies being used to recruit female football players from abroad. These strategies and how they intermesh with gender and ethnicity, along with the agency of women's football migrants in gaining visibility and producing mobility, should be studied further.

Notes

1 Survey conducted by the author through accessing national squad lists on various internet sites in October 2013.
2 The concept of women's football migration is used here, even if it has been argued that migration may not be the most appropriate term for the intermittent and short-term mobility of highly skilled labour (Koser and Salt, 1997). In line with this, former studies show that sports labour migrants may not be primarily motivated to migrate for long periods (e.g. to settle) but are often temporary migrants who constitute a particular group of sought-after guest workers that are generally offered good socio-economic conditions (Agergaard, 2008; Agergaard and Botelho, 2011). Still, as in the case of other groups of migrants, sports labour migrants of various kinds undergo some degree of adaptation or adjustment in settling into work and everyday life in their country, and not least club, of destination (Agergaard *et al.*, 2014)
3 Personal interview with Tom Sermanni at the Algarve Cup, March 2013.

References

Agergaard, S. (2008) Elite Athletes as Migrants in Danish Women's Handball. *International Review for the Sociology of Sport* 43(1): 5–19.
Agergaard, S. and Botelho, V. (2011) Female Football Migration: Motivational Factors in Early Migratory Processes. In J. Maguire and M. Falcous (Eds.) *Sport and Migration: Borders, Boundaries and Crossings*. London: Routledge (157–72).
Agergaard, S. and Botelho, V. (2013) The Way Out? African Players' Migration into Scandinavian Women's Soccer. *Sport in Society: Cultures, Commerce, Media, Politics*. DOI: 10.1080/17430437.2013.815512.
Agergaard, S., Botelho, V. and Tiesler, N. (2014) The Typology of Athletic Migrants Revisited: Transnational Settlers, Sojourners and Mobiles. In S. Agergaard and N. Tiesler (Eds.) *Kicking the Globe: Women, Soccer and Transnational Migration.* London and New York: Routledge (191–215).
Agergaard, S. and Haugaa Engh, M. (2012) Producing Mobility through Networks and Localities: Developing a Transnational Perspective on Sports Labour Migration. Presented as conference paper at European Association for the Sociology of Sport Conference, 2012, Bern, Schwitzerland.
Agergaard, S. and Tiesler, N. (Eds.) (2014) *Kicking the Globe: Women, Soccer and Transnational Migration.* London and New York: Routledge.
Bale, J. (1991) *The Brawn Drain: Foreign Student-Athletes in American Universities.* Urbana: University of Illinois Press.
Bale, J. (2004) Three Geographies of African Footballer Migration: Patterns, Problems and Postcoloniality. In G. Armstrong and R. Giulianotti (Eds.) *Football in Africa: Conflict, Conciliation and Community*. New York: Palgrave (229–46).
Booth, S. and Liston, K. (2014) The Continental Drift to a Zone of Prestige: Women's Soccer Migration to the U.S. NCAA Division One 2000–2010. In S. Agergaard and N. Tiesler (Eds.) *Kicking the Globe: Women, Soccer and Transnational Migration.* London and New York: Routledge (53–72).
Bosscher, V.d., Bingham, J., Shibli, S., Bottenburg, M.v. and Knop, P.d. (2008) *The Global Sporting Arms Race: An International Comparative Study on Sports Policy Factors Leading to International Sporting Success*. Aachen: Meyer & Meyer.
Botelho, V. and Agergaard, S. (2011) Moving for the Love of the Game: International Migration of Female Footballers in Scandinavian Countries. *Soccer & Society* 12(6): 806–19.

Carter, T. (2011) *In Foreign Fields: The Politics and Experiences of Transnational Sports Migration.* London: Pluto Press.

Cornelissen, S. and Solberg, E. (2007) Sport Mobility and Circuits of Power: The Dynamics of Football Migration in Africa and the 2010 World Cup. *Politikon* 34(3): 295–314.

Darby, P. (2000) The New Scramble for Africa: African Football Labour Migration to Europe. *European Sports History Review* 3(2): 217–44.

Darby, P. (2007) Out of Africa: The Exodus of African Football Talent to Europe. *WorkingUSA: The Journal of Labour and Society* 10(4): 443–56.

Darby, P. (2009) Ghanaian Football Labour Migration to Europe: Preliminary Observations. In G. Walters and G. Rossi (Eds.) *Labour Market Migration in European Football: Key Issues and Challenges.* London: Birkbeck Sports Business Centre (149–63).

Darby, P. (2011) Out of Africa: The Exodus of Elite African Football Labour to Europe. In J. Maguire and M. Falcous (Eds.) *Sport and Migration: Border, Boundaries and Crossings.* London: Routledge (245–58).

Darby, P., Akindes, G. and Kirwin, M. (2007) Football Academies and the Migration of African Football Labour to Europe. *Journal of Sport and Social Issues* 31(2): 143–61.

Darby, P. and Solberg, E. (2010) Differing Trajectories: Football Development and Patterns of Player Migration in South Africa and Ghana. *Soccer and Society* 11(1–2): 11–130.

Elliott, R. (2013). New Europe, New Chances? The Migration of Professional Footballers to Poland's Ekstraklasa. *International Review for the Sociology of Sport* 48(6): 736–50.

Elliott, R. (2014) Brits Abroad: A Case Study Analysis of Three British Footballers Migrating to the Hungarian Soproni Liga. *Soccer and Society* 15(4): 517–34.

Elliott, R. and Bania, K. (2013) Poles Apart: Foreign Players, Polish Football and Euro 2012. *Soccer and Society.* Published online 29 October 2013: DOI 10.1080/14660970.2013.849190.

Elliott, R. and Maguire, J. (2008a) 'Getting Caught in the Net': Examining the Recruitment of Canadian Players in British Professional Ice Hockey. *Journal of Sport and Social Issues* 32: 158–76.

Elliott, R. and Maguire, J. (2008b) Thinking Outside of the Box: Exploring a Conceptual Synthesis for Research in the Area of Athletic Labour Migration. *Sociology of Sport Journal* 25(4): 482–97.

Elliott, R. and Weedon, G. (2010) Foreign Players in the English Academy League. *International Review for the Sociology of Sport* 46(1): 61–75.

FIFA (2007) *Big Count.* FIFA communications Division, Information Services. Retrieved from: http://www.fifa.com/mm/document/fifafacts/bcoffsurv/bigcount.summary report_7022.pdf.

Haugaa Engh, M. (2014) Bringing Gender into Sports Labour Migration Research: Gendered Geographies of Power in African Women's Soccer Migration. In S. Agergaard and N. Tiesler (Eds.) *Kicking the Globe: Women, Soccer and Transnational Migration.* London and New York: Routledge (175–90).

Haugaa Engh, M. and Agergaard, S. (2013) Producing Mobility through Locality and Visibility: Developing a Transnational Perspective on Sports Labour Migration. *International Review for the Sociology of Sport.* Published online 18 November 2013: DOI 10.1177/1012690213509994.

Houlihan, B. and Zheng, J. (2013) The Olympics and Elite Sport Policy: Where Will It All End? *International Journal of the History of Sport* 30(4): 338–55.

Kjær, J. and Agergaard, S. (2013) Understanding Women's Professional Soccer: The Case of Denmark and Sweden. *Soccer & Society.* DOI: 10.1080/14660970.2013.843915.

Koser, K. and Salt, J. (1997) The Geography of Highly Skilled International Migration. *International Journal of Population Geography* 3: 285–303.

Lanfranchi, P. and Taylor, M. (2001) *Moving with the Ball: The Migration of Professional Footballers.* Oxford: Berg.

Lee, S. (2010) Global Outsourcing: A Different Approach to an Understanding of Sport Labour Migration. *Global Business Review* 11: 153–65.

McCree, R. (2014) Student Athletic Migration from Trinidad and Tobago: The Case of Women's Soccer. In S. Agergaard and N. Tiesler (Eds.) *Kicking the Globe: Women, Soccer and Transnational Migration.* London and New York: Routledge (73–85).

McGovern, P. (2002) Globalization or Internationalization? Foreign Footballers in the English League, 1946–95. *Sociology* 36(1): 23–42.

Maguire, J. and Stead, D. (1998) Border Crossings: Soccer Labour Migration and the European Union. *International Review for the Sociology of Sport* 33(1): 59–73.

Markovits, A. and Hellerman, S. (2001) *Offside: Soccer and American Exceptionalism.* Princeton, NJ: Princeton University Press.

Molnar, G. (2006) Mapping Migrations: Hungary Related Migrations of Professional Footballers after the Collapse of Communism. *Soccer & Society* 7(4): 463–85.

Molnar, G. (2011) From the Soviet Bloc to the European Community: Migrating Professional Footballers in and out of Hungary. In J. Maguire and M. Falcous (Eds.) *Sport and Migration: Borders, Boundaries and Crossings.* London: Routledge (56–70).

Molnar, G. and Maguire, J. (2008) Hungarian Footballers on the Move: Issues of and Observations on the First Migratory Phase. *Sport in Society* 11(1): 74–89.

Pfister, G., Klein, M. and Tiesler, N. (2014) Momentous Spark or Enduring Enthusiasm? The 2011 FIFA Women's World Cup and Its Impact on Players' Mobility and on the Popularity of Women's Soccer in Germany. In S. Agergaard and N. Tiesler (Eds.) *Kicking the Globe: Women, Soccer and Transnational Migration.* London and New York: Routledge (140–58).

Poli, R. (2005) Football Players' Migration in Europe: A Geo-economic Approach to Africans' Mobility. In J. Magee, A. Bairner and A. Tomlinson (Eds.) *The Beautiful Game? Football Identities and Finances.* Aachen, Germany: Meyer and Mayer Sport (217–32).

Poli, R. (2006) Migrations and Trade of African Football Players: Historic, Geographical and Cultural Aspects. *Afrika Spectrum* 41(3): 393–414.

Poli, R. (2010a) Understanding Globalization through Football: The New International Division of Labour, Migratory Channels and Transnational Trade Circuits. *International Review for the Sociology of Sport* 45(4): 491–506.

Poli, R. (2010b) African Migrants in Asian and European Football: Hopes And Realities. *Sport in Society* 13(6): 1001–11.

Poli, R. and Besson, R. (2011) From the South to Europe: A Comparative Analysis of African and Latin American Football Migration. In J. Maguire and M. Falcous (Eds.) *Sport and Migration: Borders, Boundaries and Crossings.* London: Routledge (15–30).

Power, M. (1999) *Audit Society: Rituals of Verification.* Oxford: Oxford University Press.

Rial, C. (2008) Rodar: a circulação dos jogadores de futebol brasileiros no exterior. *Horizontes antropológicos* 14(30): 21–65.

Rial, C. (2014) New Frontiers: The Transnational Circulation of Brazil's Women Soccer Players. In S. Agergaard and N. Tiesler (Eds.) *Kicking the Globe: Women, Soccer and Transnational Migration.* London and New York: Routledge (86–101).

Takahashi, Y. (2014) International Migration of Japanese Women in World Soccer. In S. Agergaard and N. Tiesler (Eds.) *Kicking the Globe: Women, Soccer and Transnational Migration.* London and New York: Routledge (102–16).

Takahashi, Y. and Horne, J. (2004) Japanese Football Players and the Sports Talent Migration Business. In W. Manzenreiter and J. Horne (Eds.) *Football Goes East: Business, Culture and the People's Game in China, Japan and South Korea.* London and New York: Routledge (69–86).

Taylor, M. (2006) Global Players? Football, Migration and Globalization, c. 1930–2000. *Historical Social Research* 31(1): 7–30.

Tiesler, N. (2010) *Selected Data: Two Types of Women Football Migrants – Diaspora Player and Emigrants.* Retrieved from: http://sportmigration.au.dk/uploads/media/Tiesler-2010.pdf.

Tiesler, N. (2011) *Main Trends and Patterns in Women's Football Migration.* Retrieved from: http://sportmigration.au.dk/uploads/media/Tiesler-2011.pdf.

Tiesler, N. (2012a) Um grande salto para um país pequeno: O êxito das jogadoras portuguesas na migração futebolística internacional [A big move for a small country: Portuguese female players as international football migrants]. In N.C. Tiesler and N. Domingos (Eds.) *O Futebol Português: Política, Género e Movimento.* Porto: Afrontamento (221–46).

Tiesler, N. (2012b) Mobile Spielerinnen als Akteurinnen im Globalisierungsprozess des Frauenfußballs. In G. Sobiech und A. Ochsner (Eds.) *Spielen Frauen ein anderes Spiel? Geschichte, Organisation, Repräsentationen und kulturelle Praxen im Frauenfußball.* Berlin: VS-Verlag (97–122).

10 Youth migration in English professional football

Living, labouring and learning in Premier League academies

Gavin Weedon

After the England men's under-21 and under-20 football teams emerged winless from their respective European Championship and World Cup tournaments in the summer of 2013, the fallout was as predictable as it was familiar. Someone or something was to blame, and the range of culprits included the Football Association's lack of leadership and attentiveness to youth development, the overriding commercial interests of the Premier League, the tumultuous turnover of managers throughout English football's professional structure, antiquated coaching and managerial philosophies, the generalised moral and social codes and conduct of English players themselves, public expectations roused and amplified by sensationalist media, and other variations and combinations thereof. Looming large in many if not all of these perspectives, whether declared or intimated, was the presence of 'foreign' players in the English Premier League and 'their' apparent complicity in the relative shortcomings of England's senior and youth football teams.

Earlier that summer, Gary Neville had written in the *Daily Mail* (2013) in his dual role as national team coach and Sky television pundit that "it is time that we stood up to protect the soul of the English game" from the perceived ravages of a "globalised Premier League". Neville invoked at once the national collective 'we', the preemptive act of standing up and together in order to defend the 'soul' of the sport – its young, English players – and a wariness of foreign 'others' which has reverberated throughout the history of English professional football (Giulianotti, 1999). This narrative of preemptive protection echoes wider discourses on immigration in the UK and elsewhere (Charteris-Black, 2006), and while the *Daily Mail* is known for its right-wing conservative agenda and nationalistic scaremongering around immigration, Neville's views on the matter following the aforementioned tournament exits were also framed by the left-wing *Guardian* (2013) newspaper in relation to a Premier League now "flooded by foreign recruits".

The rhetoric invoked in debates surrounding labour immigration is a telling place to begin considering migratory experience, precisely because migrants' experiences take place within and can be active responses to this discursive field. Natural disasters (such as floods, swarms, tides and waves) and ostensibly secure 'containers' under threat of perforation and contamination (as in the borders programme were simply necessary sacrifices en route to the ultimate goal of attaining a professional contract.

Education and English language

While young player involvement in English professional football has been recognised and sanctioned by the Football Association since 1960, "the Modern Apprenticeship/Football Scholarship scheme introduced in 1998 represents football's latest and arguably most determined attempt to resolve a century-old problem" of labour overproduction, accusations of exploitation, and associated issues of career and identity disruption among aspiring young players (Monk & Russell, 2000, p.63). In response to these issues, the Football Scholarship includes both football-specific and academic/vocational components, thus appearing to address a legacy of concerns about the alternative career opportunities of those who commit to Scholarship programmes.

Including an educational component within a Football Scholarship is also a requisite of youth labour migration in FIFA's international transfer regulations for minors, which stipulate that players can only transfer between nations when aged over 18 years. This, however, is subject to three exceptional circumstances: the player living within 50 kilometres of the national border of the new club; the player's family moving to the country of the new club for non-footballing reasons; or the player moving within the European Union, in which case players over 16 years of age can be transferred. Moving from Holland placed Yohan, as well as most of the players I spoke with and most of the non-British players within the academy system, within this latter category. When a young player is recruited in accordance with these regulations, the host club is required to "guarantee the player an academic and/or vocational education, in addition to his footballing education and/or training, which will allow the player to pursue a career other than football should he cease playing professional football" (FIFA, 2010, p.57).

The delivery of academic/vocational education in academies is fraught with contradictions. As Hickey and Kelly (2008) observed in their research into educational provisions in Australian rules football, a sports training programme which includes an educational component "actively encourages elite level, professional footballers to undertake education and training in preparation not to be footballers" (p.481, original emphasis). Embracing education can be seen to represent an acknowledgement of the possibility, or even expectancy, of failure, which contravenes the attitude and behaviour expected of an elite athlete. After speaking with Yohan, I got the chance to sit down with his education and welfare officer and talk about such contradictions. These staff members are ominously tasked with encouraging players to contemplate and work towards alternative career opportunities where every other discourse, in language and practice, within the academy advocates absolute commitment to footballing excellence. To complicate matters, they must gain the trust of players who will, at least initially, see them simply as academy employees, and so be less likely to confide in them matters which suggest anything other than a focused, committed and uninhibited attitude.

Some education and welfare officers intentionally distanced themselves from the awarding of contracts to help alleviate these tensions in their job description, and some clubs make this decision on their behalf. Others, such as Yohan's officer, struggled to eschew those tensions and admitted the hierarchy of interests in the academy:

> We have three ambitions for all of the boys when they sign with this club. First ambition is a pro contract with [us], second one, if that doesn't work, is a pro contract somewhere else. If that doesn't work, third one is that they're employable, and can stand on their own two feet.

Of course the high ratio of Scholarships to professional contracts, awarded by academies, suggests that this hierarchy should be inverted. Later, the potential for tension between his role in the holistic development of adolescents and the aims, culture and philosophy of the academy was made clear:

> My priorities are the boys. I am employed by [this club] to make sure that we do the right thing by the boys. But, we are a football club. We are not a college. Our mission in life is to create first team footballers for [this club]. And once we lose sight of that, we're going down the wrong road.

The 'wrong road' is nevertheless the one travelled by the vast majority of youth players at the conclusion of their Scholarships; in Yohan's graduating cohort, only one player was awarded a professional contract, and this was only a twelve-month agreement – effectively an extension of his Scholarship – rather than a longer-term commitment.

While these issues and contradictions are difficult for all parties concerned, including those domestic players who have been trained within the academy system from a young age, they are often exacerbated for migrants and markedly affected by the insularity of the academy. For instance, the qualification undertaken in academies is the Apprenticeship in Sporting Excellence (ASE), a football-specific curriculum teaching and assessing physiological, psychological and nutritional aspects of their training programmes. This can be interpreted in a number of ways, such as providing players with a qualification which could help them to gain employment within football, should they cease playing (as per FIFA's aforementioned transfer regulations), or as homogenising their learning experience into an exclusively footballing pedagogy which allows little opportunity for diversifying interests or experiences. If one considers the opportunity to experience a new cultural environment to be one of the benefits of migration, then the extent to which migrant youth players are able to embrace that opportunity is questionable. It is also doubtful, and in my experience rare, that living and working in an academy cultivate any alternative interests, vocational or otherwise, among these players. On the one occasion I encountered where a migrant player had asked to register on a non-footballing qualification, his coach spoke in a later interview of how this was vetoed by the club as it would impede his football training programme:

> We had an issue with one of the boys, who wanted to do, I think it was an extra one, an extra course and it literally got in the way of the football . . . we couldn't really justify giving him the time that probably he wanted or needed to do some of the work . . . you know, you can't be in two places at the same time.

The exception to this notion that non-footballing education is in competition with the primary focus of the Scholarship is English language training. Players and staff agreed that a certain degree of English language competency is a prerequisite for undertaking the ASE qualification, and for otherwise living and labouring in the academy enclaves. The importance of developing English language skills was highlighted by this education and welfare officer, who, unlike those academies that 'outsource' their educational training, oversaw the education of academy players in-house:

> It's a bespoke service, to be honest with you, and first we have to look at the boy's level of English, English is the priority. You know, when they come here, they need to start interacting with conversational English because they can't become part of the group if they're not, so we saturate them with English lessons, you know, lots of intensive work there. I'll phone them every evening, make them talk on the phone, because that's a different level from face-to-face where you can sort of mime and everything, and we make sure the landladies only speak English with them, because English is the priority.

This bespoke service allows for the player, the academy and potentially other parties, such as agents and family members, to contribute to decisions about how or even whether to approach education. For instance, the priority given to English language is evidenced by the fact that several of the players in this study undertook English language tutelage as an alternative to the ASE programme. In one case, and after developing his language skills to the degree needed to communicate with players and staff on the field, a(nother) Dutch player I interviewed decided to discontinue his language course and any further educational training midway through his Scholarship, following discussions with his parents and his education and welfare officer, in order to 'focus on his football'.

Elsewhere (see Weedon, 2011) players spoke of elementary language skills and accented expression as a source of teasing and even humiliation, a marker of difference which led to ongoing friction or camaraderie and, in Yohan's experience, was a perceived barrier to career development: "My first year mission was learn English and that, 'cause my English wasn't consistent. So that's the reason why the coach put me on the bench and gave everyone else a chance." The bind is clear: migrant players are strongly encouraged to learn English to get the most out of their Scholarship, but doing so must precede – and can supersede – the ASE qualification. The acquisition of English language skills is clearly important for deriving the greatest value from players' migratory experiences, yet they do not tend to interact much outside of the academy and its extended circle of host families and perhaps college teachers during their tenures. Where they do, it is with people who know them primarily as footballers. In the formative years of adolescence, which in nearly all cases follows a lifetime of commitment to football where players have already developed strong football-oriented understandings of self, it is difficult to make the case for non-footballing education being anything more than 'something to fall back on', a distraction from the reason they moved in the first place, and something worth sacrificing if it adds to their chances of attaining a professional contract. This changes, of course, when that contract is not forthcoming.

Contractual and career uncertainty

I visited these academies in the spring, mostly for my own pragmatic reasons, but the timing of my research inadvertently came to shape my interactions with players and staff. Nearing the end of the season, players were being, or had recently been, informed as to whether they would remain at the club as professionals, or whether they should actively pursue other options. Of the players I interviewed, some still had a season of their Scholarships remaining, some had recently signed professional contracts of short duration, some had been told that they would not be offered a professional contract with the club, and most were awaiting imminent news of their career prospects. These were clearly crystallising experiences in the lives of these adolescent athletes, each akin to what Denzin (1992, p.83) has called an "epiphanic moment" which forms senses of self, perspectives of the past and projections to the future, and "leaves a mark on a person's life".

Yohan had been made aware about two weeks prior to our conversations that he would not be awarded a contract. Late in my visit, after speaking with other players and staff at the club stadium, I spent some more time with Yohan and asked whether he thought education was an important part of the Scholarship programme:

> Well obviously you think, uh, why am I sitting here [in the classroom]? I wanna be on the pitch kicking the ball, scoring goals, playing games, but um, yeah, it's, it's important, but I, I don't think most of the lads of my age realise how important [education] is until you get released and start thinking how will I [trails off]. I only got three weeks to get a club now, or I'm not getting a club, and what am I doing then? And that's when all the things, that's when I start thinking I'm happy about [having the ASE qualification].

For another player, born in Australasia, who was offered a contract and has since sustained a successful career in England, questions about education were dismissed and projections instead made to a secure future as a professional:

> Home is here, now. England . . . as soon as I got my contract here, I knew, this is where I'm gonna be, this is my home for, well, thirty years of my life,

hopefully. I'm happy to be here. I'd love to be in the Premiership until I'm thirty, thirty-five, if I can. Play full-time football until then. Yeah, and that's basically it, that's all I'm thinking about at the moment.

While the aim of the educational component of the Scholarship is to offer stability and opportunity to a player when a professional contract is not forthcoming, I found it to be paradoxically associated with the transience and the turbulence of the whole academy experience. Yohan's perspective on his qualification was instrumental, and defined differently over time in relation to his contractual status, culminating in his being pleased to have it only once his first choice of vocation was not forthcoming. For the Australasian player quoted above, the professional contract offered a sense of settlement, as well as achievement, that consigned the ASE qualification to the past.

The Premier League, its member clubs and all those involved in English professional football display an awareness of the personal and professional implications of early career disengagement, and there are various schemes and opportunities, such as exit trials, to afford players the opportunity to stay in English football. But the chances of success remain small, and examples of migrant youth players graduating through academies to establish themselves as professionals in the Premier and Football Leagues are few and far between. Consequently, the end-of-season period in which I conducted much of my research is a time of deep anxiety and trepidation for all concerned. Yet for one academy manager with whom I spoke, the circumstances of migrant player recruitment, adjustment and expectations served to heighten feelings of uncertainty and dislocation among migrant players, and these are exacerbated further for those who are not offered professional contracts and face leaving the academy:

Chances are they would have had advice which has cautioned against them going [to England] from some sections of their peer group or their family, or, you know, people in sport that they know. So they will potentially be going home to 'I told you so's'. So on one level, it must come in even harder than it is for a domestic player, because [foreign] individuals, I think, not only losing their contractual status, they made a massive commitment to come to a new country believing that to represent the sort of new horizon for them. And of course for that now to be shattered, I think that for the player it must be a real feeling of emptiness, of underachievement.

When I asked Yohan about how he had coped in the weeks and months leading up to finding out his fate as an Academy Scholar, he offered a glimpse into the kind of dissonance and despondency synonymous with disengagement from elite (youth) sport (Brown & Potrac, 2009), and, in accordance with the perspective above, amplified for migrant youth athletes:

I was thinking about getting a contract. That's right, I want a contract, okay, I want a contract. And then you start thinking about the contract, am I getting a contract or not, am I playing good enough, and then you start thinking, okay, um, do I wanna stay at this club? Or are you thinking that you're getting a contract but you're not playing at all, so are you going to another club or are you trying, looking for a long deal here? Or just, try to go to another club. And then after that, you start thinking, where do you wanna play? 'Cause for me, I started thinking, is this for me, or is Holland for me? And after that, I start thinking, okay, I'm not gonna play football my whole life, so what am I doing after football?

In many ways the academy is a kind of liminal space, and this uncertainty marks the entire experience for many youth players. Yohan even admitted that from the first day he was thinking about leaving, whether that meant returning home forlornly during, or at the conclusion of, his Scholarship, or graduating out of the academy and into the world of professional football. What makes all this especially difficult for all players is that these worlds are entwined; spatially and socially, the academy and the training ground are often the same location at most clubs, and our parting conversations were spent walking around the club's pitch in the empty stadium where Yohan acknowledged various senior players and staff over the course of the day. The labour and lifestyle of a professional are always on show, acting as a source of inspiration and aspiration to young Scholars. Professional football is part of the everyday present. Yet, despite this spatial intimacy, in career terms the Academy Scholarship is a passage en route to somewhere else.

The dissonance between the desire to be at home with one's family and friends and to feel at home in an unfamiliar and highly competitive environment places great strain on these players, who are becoming migrants, adolescents and elite athletes. The prospect of returning home without a contract only exacerbates this consternation. I had hoped to keep in touch with Yohan, to keep abreast of his life and career without giving the impression that I was in a position to help him attain the job he really wanted. Within a few weeks of our meeting his phone number was no longer in operation, and his name had been removed from the club's website. What I have been able to offer here is only a snapshot of a story, infused with a series of outtakes from neighbouring tales and told at or near the end of a fraught journey. To conclude the chapter, I reflect on what might be learned from his acculturation, experience and eventual departure from English youth football in relation to the established literature on sports labour migration.

Theorising migratory experience in (youth) football

Acculturation denotes the mutually transformative encounters resulting from migration. It affects all parties, the host culture and the migrant in transition, in myriad ways. It is at once the process and irreducible outcome of international mobility. In sports labour migration research, migratory experience has been predominantly theorised as occurring against the backdrop of globalisation processes (Bale & Maguire, 1994; Falcous & Maguire, 2011). Key debates have hinged on whether these experiences were reflective of the political-economic claims of Wallerstein's (1974) world systems theory (Magee & Sugden, 2002) or better understood as symptomatic of the political, cultural, social and economic processes said to characterise globalisation (Maguire, 1999). In each case, the overriding point of contention lies with what experiences of migration contribute to understandings of the 'bigger picture' of globalisation, and the globalisation of sports such as football. I favour acculturation due to its flexibility as a premise, rather than an explanatory framework or typology. That premise is simple: migration is an encounter between peoples, cultures, knowledges and so forth in which all parties are active, and all emerge from the process somehow changed. Understanding that encounter requires tracing the experiences of people, the circulation of policy, and so forth, to glimpse the consequences of their entanglements.

Acculturation is therefore not better or best suited for studying youth, athletes or any other population of migrants, but asks only that whatever or whomever forms the focus of study be traced anew across borders. Rather than prefigure power relations, or demonstrate how individual experiences of migration might help explain a wider theory or concept such as globalisation, the encounters between people, policy, commodities, knowledges and so forth are taken as important in their own right. This contention chimes with Thomas Carter's (2011) advocacy of ethnographically and experientially grounded approaches to understanding transnational labour movements. Carter's critique is that "the two pre-eminent works on the globalization of sport, Joseph Maguire's *Global Sport* (1999) and Toby Miller et al's *Globalization and Sport* (Miller et al, 2001), do not actually have any people acting in them . . . The only voices heard are from governing bodies and media outlets" (2011, p.7). More specifically, where the experiences of individual athletes are accounted for, Carter takes issue with the perceived tendency in the sociology of sport to seek out and treat lived experiences of migration as a means to understand something 'bigger', something structural or theoretical. He champions ethnography, undertaken in the anthropological tradition and, in his case, inflected with a neo-Marxist interpretation, on the basis that "the production of ethnographic knowledge is all about interaction and collaboration, not", as in typological accounts of labour migration, "Enlightenment-informed classification" (Carter, 2011, p.10).

I see Carter's (2011) contentions as a timely, if not belated, intervention, not least insofar as an approach grounded in the experiences of individual migrants is far less susceptible to, and can help to counter, the homogenising tendencies of immigration discourse within and outside of English football. Acculturation differs somewhat from Carter's chosen concept of 'transculturation', partly due to the influence of Marxian commodity fetishism in the latter and an associated emphasis on what is concealed or obscured by transnational labour mobility. Nevertheless, his definition of transculturation as "the processes by which the values and meanings of a commodity change when it moves from one locality to another" (Carter, 2011, p.17) clearly resonates with the notion of acculturation. Carter is also keen to develop more nuanced understandings of sports labour mobility than those communicated by assimilation, integration, resistance and related categories of migratory strategies, experiences and outcomes. Although I wouldn't hasten to dismiss the utility of these concepts, their potential for foreclosing rather than tracing anew sports labour migratory phenomena makes the consideration of alternatives a welcome development in the field. I have noted elsewhere (Weedon, 2011), for instance, that existing understandings of acculturation in sport have reached their limits when the process is described interchangeably with assimilation (Bourke, 2002), and that strategies of acculturation are less a case of autonomous, calculated decisions made my rational migrants and better understood as part of the complex political economy and socio-cultural surroundings in and through which migration takes place.

In this chapter I have attended to the acculturative encounters between migrant youth footballers and the academy staff with whom they have most contact. Those encounters have ramifications of course, and, since my study, English youth football has undergone significant changes through the Elite Player Performance Plan (EPPP). This plan, initiated in 2011 under the stewardship of the Premier League's then incoming Head of Youth Development, cites among its aims the intention to: "Increase the number and quality of Home Grown Players gaining professional contracts in the clubs and playing first-team football at the highest level" (Premier League, 2013). To achieve this, the Premier League has sought to free up the mobility of domestic youth players aged 16 years and under by rescinding the 90-minute rule (see note 2), classifying academies into a hierarchy based on financial outlay and the apparent quality of their training, and standardising compensation to clubs who lose youth players who transfer 'up' this hierarchy.

There is much to discuss in this controversial plan, which itself throws into question whether it is financially viable or worthwhile for some clubs to invest in youth development at all when they could lose precocious youth players for a fraction of what they might have later gained in the market for professional players. The aim, it seems, is to lubricate the movement of domestic youth footballers between academies and facilitate the concentration of that talent where resources are greatest. Richard Elliott and I have made recommendations of this ilk, insofar as we found academy coaches, managers and directors to believe the commingling of elite talent on a regular basis to be crucial to the mutual and maximal development of a collective (national) talent pool (Elliott & Weedon, 2011). From this perspective, the rescinding of the 90-minute rule is a positive move for footballing development in England. However, we were sure to stress that "[a]chieving a balance between the nurturing of elite talent and the holistic development of the player is a critical consideration" (Elliott & Weedon, 2011, p.73) in any revision of academy recruitment policy. It remains to be seen how the stability of child socialisation and formal education is affected by this removal of intra-national mobility regulations.

What is germane and needs emphasising in relation to this discussion is that the migration of players such as Yohan to Premier League academies is a partial driver of these changes in national recruitment policy. Moreover, such migrations were arguably made more likely by the initial implementation of the 90-minute rule, which effectively meant that clubs would have to look overseas if the talent available within their respective academy catchment areas was not deemed to be sufficient. Alongside these major policy changes, I have also drawn attention to some of the more mundane instances of acculturative encounters – concerning the dietary needs of youth players and the politics of further education when English language skills are rudimentary, for instance – producing changes in individual academy policies and in the behaviours and perspectives of academy staff, for better and worse. Life and labour in Premier League academies is not completely different for migrant players from their domestic counterparts, nor is it the same for all migrant players. But the differences are important, for countering pejorative discourses concerning labour migration in and beyond football by amplifying their stories of migration, for tracing how acculturation and individual encounters produce resonant effects that should not and cannot be severed from broader discussions of football's globalisation, and perhaps, if the Anglocentrism can be avoided, for contributing to future efforts towards the identification, education, retention and career trajectories of young people whose careers already span a decade, already include labour migration, and yet may never begin in earnest.

Notes

1 The Premier Academy League has since been restructured under the Premier League's Elite Player Performance Plan, which I discuss at the end of this chapter.
2 The '90-minute rule', which assigned academies a catchment area for recruitment, has since been rescinded (see the concluding comments of the chapter). Under this rule, academies could only recruit youth players who lived within 90 minutes' driving distance of the academy training facilities. This rule was initially developed in partial response to concerns that long commutes to and from training grounds were not in the best interests of the child's holistic development and formal education.

References

Andrews, D.L. and Ritzer, G. (2007) The Global in the Sporting Glocal. In R. Giulianotti and R. Robertson (Eds.) *Globalization and Sport*. Oxford: Blackwell Publishing (28–45).

Bale, J. and Maguire, J. (1994) *The Global Sports Arena: Athletic Talent Migration in an Interdependent World*. London: Cass.

Bourke, A. (2002) The Road to Fame and Fortune: Insights on the Career Paths of Young Irish Professional Footballers in England. *Journal of Youth Studies* 5(4): 375–89.

Brown, G. and Potrac, P. (2009) 'You've Not Made the Grade, Son': De-selection and Identity Disruption in Elite Level Youth Football. *Soccer and Society* 10(2): 143–59.

Carter, T. (2011) *In Foreign Fields: The Politics and Experiences of Transnational Sport Migration*. London: Pluto Press.

Charteris-Black, J. (2006) Britain as a Container: Immigration Metaphors in the 2005 Election Campaign. *Discourse & Society* 17(5): 563–81.

Daily Mail (2013) It's Time We Stood Up to Protect the Soul of the British Game. Retrieved 1 August 2013 from: http://www.dailymail.co.uk/sport/football/article-2301742/Gary-Neville-Its-time-stood-protect-soul-British-game.html.

Denzin, N. (1992) *Symbolic Interactionism and Cultural Studies: The Politics of Interpretation.* Chicago, IL: University of Chicago Press.

Elliott, R. and Weedon, G. (2011) Foreign Players in the English Premier Academy League: 'Feet-Drain' or 'Feet-Exchange'? *International Review for the Sociology of Sport* 46(1): 61–75.

Falcous, M. and Maguire, J. (2011) (Eds.) *Sport and Migration: Borders, Boundaries and Crossings.* London: Routledge.

FIFA (2010) Commentary on the Regulations for the Status and Transfer of Players, Retrieved 1 March 2011 from: http://www.fifa.com/mm/document/affederation/administration/51/56/07/transfer%5fcommentary%5f06%5fen%5f1843.pdf.

Giulianotti, R. (1999) *Football: A Sociology of the Global Game.* Oxford: Blackwell.

Guardian (2013) Gary Neville: Clubs' Desire for Instant Success Hindering English Talent. Retrieved 1 August 2013 from: http://www.theguardian.com/football/2013/jul/11/gary-neville-english-talent-academies.

Hickey, C. and Kelly, P. (2008) Preparing to Not Be a Footballer: Higher Education and Professional Sport. *Sport, Education and Society* 13(4): 477–94.

Magee, J. and Sugden, J. (2002) "The World at Their Feet": Professional Football and International Labor Migration. *Journal of Sport and Social Issues* 26(4): 421–37.

Maguire, J. (1999) *Global Sport: Identities, Societies, Civilizations.* Cambridge: Polity Press.

Miller, T., Lawrence, G., McKay, J. and Rowe, D. (2001) *Globalization and Sport: Playing the World.* Thousand Oaks, CA: Sage Publications.

Monk, D. and Russell, D. (2000) Training Apprentices: Tradition Versus Modernity in the Football Industry. *Soccer and Society* 1(2): 62–79.

Premier League Website (2013) Elite Player Performance Plan. Retrieved 10 August 2013 from: http://www.premierleague.com/content/premierleague/en-gb/youth/elite-player-performance-plan.html.

Roderick, M.J. (2006) *The Work of Professional Football: A Labour of Love?* London: Routledge.

Rowe, D. (2003) Sport and the Repudiation of the Global. *International Review for the Sociology of Sport* 38(3): 281–94.

Stead, D. and Maguire, J. (2000) 'Rite de Passage or Passage to Riches'? The Motivations and Objectives of Nordic/Scandinavian Players in English League Soccer. *Journal of Sport and Social Issues* 24(1): 36–60.

Wallerstein, I. (1974) *The Modern World-System, Volume I: Capitalist Agriculture and the Origins of the European World-Economy in the Sixteenth Century.* London: Academic Press.

Weedon, G. (2011) Glocal Boys: Exploring Experiences of Acculturation amongst Migrant Youth Footballers in Premier League Academies. *International Review for the Sociology of Sport* 47(2): 200–16.

11 "No one would burden the sea and then never get any benefit"

Family involvement in players' migration to football academies in Ghana

Nienke van der Meij and Paul Darby

"What is the objective of the academy?" The question is posed by Simon, a 17-year-old academy football player.[1] He is wearing a spotless, white, green and orange striped polo shirt. He sits in a noisy, white-tiled, Ghanaian eatery. Simon barely touches his food and instead gazes reflectively across the table. His demeanour, his posture and his deflated tone reveal that he is in low spirits. His question is surprising, not least because he has spent the last five years of his life at one of Ghana's established academies. The answer might appear obvious given the increasing journalistic and academic attention that has been paid to the place of academies in the African game. These facilities, in their various forms, are primarily concerned with the development of football talents in order to transfer them to Europe or further afield (Darby *et al.*, 2007). As he reflects on his own question, he is clearly disappointed. "I am not sure about the objective of the academy anymore", he explains. He continues that he always thought the aim was to transfer players abroad, to Europe preferably, and that his place at the academy, allied to hard work and ability, would inevitably lead to him fulfilling his ambitions. However, considering that only one player has been transferred to a European club during his time in the academy, he has serious doubts about where the experience will lead him.

For many young Ghanaian players, a place at an academy is deemed a privilege, one that they feel significantly enhances their prospects of becoming a professional footballer overseas. Simon remains fiercely ambitious and committed to this goal. Yet, at this juncture of his career, he finds himself at a crossroads. His contract at the academy has expired. He has been offered a one-year extension, but a number of Ghanaian Premier League teams have expressed an interest in signing him. There is also the option of going back to school to complete his secondary education. He speaks regularly with his father and manager in order to try to determine what option he should choose. This is not the first time Simon has experienced such a dilemma. His entry into the academy as a 13-year-old, and what he thought was the beginning of a journey that would end in the cathedrals of European football, was complicated. While he dreamt of emulating those African players who achieved illustrious careers in Europe, other significant actors in his life had different aspirations for his future. When he was young, his mother and uncle discouraged him from playing football, considering it as a wasteful use of time that could be better spent on his schooling. Occasionally he was beaten by his uncle for disobeying their wishes. His father, resident in the United States of America for over a decade where he worked as a truck driver, had a different perspective and encouraged Simon to pursue his passion. Closer to home, his sister was supportive, providing him with kit to play. His coach was also a significant influence on him and when an academy came calling, he, along with his father and sister, helped to persuade Simon's mother and uncle to allow him to become an academy player.

Simon's state of mind as he sits at this crossroads in his life and the way that he thinks carefully and strategically about his future tend to conflict with popular representations of young aspiring football players in Africa. The images that are often conjured are of poor, barefooted boys, legs caked in red dirt, playing the game with an old ball, or one made of recycled materials, on an uneven dirt pitch with pieces of rock as goalposts, wearing the tattered replica shirts of their favourite European football stars. Invariably, these boys are depicted as desperate to emulate their heroes and believing fervently that they can make it if only a European agent or club would discover them. Over the last five years or so, a number of documentaries, including Baff Akoto's *Football Fables* (2010), Vanguard's *Soccer's Lost Boys* (2010) and Pascale Lamche's *Black Diamond* (2010), as well as journalistic exposés of football-related trafficking, such as that by the *Guardian* journalist Dan McDougall (2008), have led to young African players being perceived through the prism of powerlessness, desperation and an 'escape from poverty' discourse. There is no doubting that there are aspects of the relationship between African youth and football that can be understood in these terms, and the exploitation that they often face from unscrupulous intermediaries and criminals as a consequence of their eagerness to pursue their dreams is very real. As much as this is reality for many young players, such representations conceal the agency enacted by them and, crucially for the purposes of this chapter, the agency exercised by their families. Instead, these players, and their relatives, are considered passive, powerless victims, shackled by the macro-economic context that they find themselves embedded in.

Simon's story briefly revealed above, and explored in more detail later, can in some senses be considered a counter-weight to this view. Superficially at least, observing Simon's fledgling football career might appear to confirm the archetypal image of young African players. However, the more one understands his story, the clearer it becomes that imagining him as a vulnerable individual who is merely driven by poverty, whose actions are constrained by economic context, who is ripe for cruel exploitation by profiteers, does little justice to his or his family's active role in and engagement with his football career, nor to their ongoing agency as it waxes and wanes. The brief vignette above and the further insights into his and other players' experiences and those of their families offered in this chapter make it obvious that those young boys who are recruited by academies, as well as their relatives, are significant actors in determining their life course and the development of their football career.

This analysis of the place of academies within a broader migration industry that increasingly defines football in Ghana (Darby, 2010) represents a departure from previous work on African football labour migration in two important senses. Firstly, while it acknowledges the importance of broader macro-structural constraints in influencing migration, the chapter foregrounds human agency in the decision-making processes around the movement of young, talented football players from their household to an academy. Secondly, and most importantly for the purposes of this chapter, it positions the family unit at the heart of migration decision-making by seeking to account for the ways in which Ghanaian families inform initial decisions around the migration (or otherwise) of football-playing family members to an academy. The focus on family allows this article to make a contribution to filling a significant lacuna in the literature on sport labour migration. Scholars in the field of migration studies have long recognised and sought to account for the role of the family in enabling or constraining the mobility of an individual migrant (Mabogunje, 1970). While there are some studies that acknowledge the influence of familial matters on sports migration, with the exception of Thomas Carter's work (2007, 2011) little light has been shed on the complex interplay between intra-family relations and migration decision-making and motivations.

This chapter begins by expanding on the neglect of family in studies of sports migration, before detailing the ways in which the role of the family in more general migration has been theorised. The discussion then moves on to consider the part played by the family in mediating child migration in the Ghanaian context. This is more than a mere ground-clearing exercise because it begins to sketch out a broad conceptual framework through which to make sense of the internal migration of young, highly skilled Ghanaian football players to a range of residential football academies within the country. The second half of the chapter is given over to 'thick' description of the experiences of two particular players, Simon and Ebo, and the role of their families in this process. The chapter draws to a close by considering how their narratives are reflective of diverging perspectives on football, education and intergenerational reciprocity.

The family in sports migration

As noted above, the neglect of family in studies of the mobility of athletic sojourners can be considered incongruous considering the attention paid to it within the broader migration studies literature. This is not to say that family has been completely neglected by those who write about sports migration. Some have at least flagged the importance of family in a range of processes associated with migration. In their research on the movement of football players from Nordic countries to England, Stead and Maguire (2000) revealed that partners and families of football migrants are generally closely involved in decision-making around career moves. In their study of the lived experiences of Hungarian football migrants, Molnar and Maguire (2008) briefly addressed the role of family in terms of how it has helped both to facilitate and also to hinder mobility. In his work on the transnational migration of Latin American baseball players to the

United States, Arbena (2003) has argued that, besides the political-economic factors that impinge on migration, family ties should also be taken into account. In a similar vein, Lanfranchi and Taylor (2001) hint at the importance of family by drawing attention to the fact that football migrants act in larger aggregates such as families and social networks and, consequently, their mobility should not be considered as solely influenced by the structural context in which they are embedded. This is explicitly teased out by De Vasconcellos Ribeiro and Dimeo in their study on Brazilian football migration, where they argue that a footballer's dream of migrating "is no straightforward selfish personal ambition: the financial rewards are seen as a long-term provision of the player's family" (2009, p.731).

While the role of remittances in the relationship between football migrants and their family members has been acknowledged in the existing studies on African football labour migration, this work has only considered the importance of family in this process to a limited extent. Broere and Van der Drift (1997) have illustrated the importance of remitting money home to their family for many African football migrants, even those who play for small European clubs. Darby (2002, p.171) adds to this by arguing that players perceive football in Europe "not just as a passport to fame and fortune but also as a means of supporting the families they leave behind". Poli (2006, 2010) has also touched on the importance of family in African football migration by including it in a list of intermediary actors or structures involved in facilitating migration and by exploring the expectations that families have of relatives pursuing an athletic career abroad. More recently, Esson (2013) has flagged the significance of the household as an influence on the value placed on education by Ghanaian youth vis-à-vis the 'allure' of football. Nevertheless, little detail is provided, and the specificities of the role played by family in the decisions of young players to become mobile (or not) are left unexplored.

As mentioned above, the notable exception to this neglect of family in sports migration is Thomas Carter (2007, 2011). He specifically argues for a redirection of the scholarly debate on sport labour migration away from a focus on the institutional structures within which it takes place to an anthropological approach that centres on "the people who actually engage in social action" (2011, p.7). He presents a compelling argument to consider family members as significant actors in the mobility of athletes and the family as a key unit of analysis in making sense of migration motivations and experiences. For example, in his study of Cuban baseball migrants, he demonstrates that sports migration is hardly ever a purely individual act and that families play a significant role in migration decision-making processes. Indeed, Carter observes that, in many instances, it is the family that permits the individual athlete to become mobile (Carter, 2007). Despite this, he highlights the fact that "the impact on and concerns over family, and their influence on migration strategies, are a vital aspect that has been hitherto ignored" (Carter, 2007, p.127). For Carter, this is a major anomaly in the scholarship on sports migration given "the centrality of family in so many investigations into transnational migration" (Carter, 2007, p.127).

The family in migration

As Carter notes, family has long featured as an important focus in studies on migration. This was partly a consequence of calls within this field for meso-level approaches that would allow scholars to circumvent what had become a preoccupation with debates and schisms between those who focused on micro-level agency and those who prioritised the macro structural context in their examination of migration (Hammar & Tamas, 1997). Concentrating on the meso-level and shifting attention to the role of intermediate units of analysis such as families, households or migrant networks have been considered invaluable in more fully understanding migration (Massey *et al.*, 1993; Faist, 1997; Fischer *et al.*, 1997). Of those meso-level approaches that foreground the role of the family, two are particularly prominent, namely the new economics of labour migration (NELM) models which emerged in the late 1980s and multi-disciplinary livelihood approaches which developed in the 1970s. In short, NELM and livelihood approaches argue that migration is essentially a risk-sharing strategy on the part of households to improve their livelihoods, and that household and/or family members of migrants play a key role in decision-making processes around migration (Massey, 1990; Stark, 1991; De Haan, 1997; McDowell & De Haan, 1997; De Haan *et al.*, 2002; Kuhn, 2002; Young & Ansell, 2003; Tiemoko, 2004; De Haas, 2010), especially in migration flows from rural areas in the Global South (Hugo, 1995, cited in Faist, 1997).

The central focus of NELM is on the role of economic remittances and the ways in which the migrant and their household share the material costs and rewards associated with migration (Stark, 1991; Taylor 1999). While its placement of family at the centre of the analysis of migration is welcome, it is important for the purposes of this chapter to raise two caveats. Firstly, NELM tends to conceptualise the household as a harmonious unit and neglects the presence of internal power struggles within families and how intra-family relations are contoured by factors such as gender, age and kinship (Desai, 1992). Secondly, it also fails to attribute sufficient significance to the non-economic, socio-cultural context of the household.

This latter limitation is specifically addressed in multi-disciplinary livelihood approaches to migration (De Haan, 1997, 1999; De Haan & Rogaly, 2002). These approaches define livelihood strategies as 'a strategic or deliberate choice of a combination of activities by households and their individual members to maintain, secure, and improve their livelihoods', wherein livelihood refers to "the capabilities, assets (including both material and social resources), and activities required for a means of living" (Carney, 1998, cited in De Haas, 2010, p.244). In livelihood approaches, migration is considered to be one of multiple strategies to secure and improve livelihoods and as such is deemed a deliberate decision to spread income risks, improve social and economic status and overcome local development constraints (Bebbington, 1999; De Haan *et al.*, 2002). What is significant here is the acknowledgement of agency among people operating in the context of global capitalist forces (De Haas, 2007) and the fact that livelihood approaches move beyond NELM's narrow focus on economic incentives in migration and incorporate socio-cultural factors (De Jong & Gardner, 1981; Castles, 2010). This more socio-cultural perspective on the role of family in migration is achieved by taking into account culturally defined intra-family arrangements and power relationships as well as the broader socio-cultural context in which the family is embedded. Of course, this is not to say that livelihood approaches ignore the significance of economics as a driver of migration. Indeed, those who subscribe to this perspective agree with advocates of NELM that expected financial remittances are at the centre of migration and that these are organised via reciprocal relationships, or what Stark (1991, p.25) called "intertemporal contractual arrangements" between family members.

Considering the value of both approaches and the overlapping of some of their central tenets, De Haas (2007, p.6) has suggested conceptualising migration "as part of a broader *household livelihood strategy* to diversify income sources and overcome social, economic and institutional development constraints in the place of origin" (italics in original). In doing so, he effectively frames livelihood approaches in a household perspective and acknowledges "that structural forces leave at least some room for agency, although at highly varying degrees" (De Haas, 2010, p.246). De Haas's approach allows for recognition of the fact that migration is informed by more than merely economic incentives and that the socio-cultural contexts in which migration decisions are made are hugely significant. While not specifically teased out earlier, this clearly resonates with the vignette that opened this chapter. Simon's aspirations to go abroad are undoubtedly influenced by economic motivations.[2] However, as was revealed, his decision to enter an academy in the first instance, and the way that he sought to navigate a path through the academy to his ultimate ambition of a professional contract in Europe, have also been contoured by the socio-cultural context in which he is embedded. Of particular concern for the purposes of this chapter are the complicated and contested intra-family relations that both constrained and enabled his internal migration to the academy. Simon is not alone in this regard and, as the second half of this chapter reveals, in order to fully understand the migration decision-making of young academy football players in Ghana, it is useful to consider the actions of these individuals within the context of the household. However, before moving to the empirical focus of this chapter, it is necessary to say something briefly about the nature of the family unit in Ghana. This is useful for three reasons. Firstly, it ensures that the subsequent analyses of internal migration to a football academy as being contoured by intra-family negotiation are appropriately situated in the local context. Secondly, it helps to account for the broad power relations and expectations that govern the actions of children and adolescents within Ghanaian families. Finally, it foregrounds a concept that informs, to varying degrees, the actions of young, migrant players, namely intergenerational reciprocity.

Family, migration and the Ghanaian context

Households in Ghana are diverse entities (Sjanek, 1982). As in many sub-Saharan African countries, two general compositions are common: the nuclear family and the extended family. Whereas the former typically consists of parents and their children, the latter is generally composed of family members further along the bloodline, often cross-generational. However, the concept of extended family is not always as narrowly defined as being linked to bloodline or genetics. Indeed, sometimes those who are not blood-related or bound together by marriage are considered to be part of the extended family. According to Adegoke (2001, p.27), the extended family is "a socio-cultural phenomenon that finds expression in mutual solicitousness about the welfare of one another, a quasi-communal approach to the supervision and the correction of younger ones, and a kind of social insurance that works". As such, the concept of family is rather fluid. As Hashim and Thorsen (2011, cited in Huijsmans, 2011, p.1310) argue about kin practices in West African contexts, "several adults may behave like fathers and mothers and have claims on and obligations to children".

Intra-family relations and expected roles and responsibilities also differ significantly depending on local cultural contexts. How these materialise in Ghana needs to be understood in order to facilitate an analysis of the role of Ghanaian families in migration decision-making processes in football. In Ghana, parents are expected to provide basic necessities such as food and shelter for their children. This is, of course, comparable to Western notions of parenting, though the involvement of other elders in the lineage is more commonplace than in the Western context (Langevang, 2008). However, whereas children in the West generally rely on what their parents provide for them and are not expected to do much in return in terms of an economic contribution to the household, in Ghana, as in many other developing countries, children are expected to contribute significantly to the household (Porter & Blaufuss, 2002; Hashim, 2006). From early childhood children know that they are expected to reciprocate for their parents' care by being obedient and doing household chores, and this reciprocal relationship develops as the child grows into adulthood (Hashim, 2006; Coe, 2012). As such, the most important feature that underlies most intra-familial relationships in sub-Saharan Africa is intergenerational reciprocity, which simply refers to a mutual agreement that parents will be taken care of by their offspring when they are old. As Coe (2011, p.105) put it: "For Ghanaians, like other West Africans, the reward of parenting is the lifelong ties of obligation among those one has raised." The existence of such reciprocal relationships not only supports the elderly, but also helps families through times of economic hardship, death or serious illness (Coe, 2012).

The intergenerational relationship described above is in effect a long-standing agreement between parents and their children, which has also been referred to as an intergenerational contract (Whitehead *et al.*, 2007). This is not a legally binding agreement, but is rather culturally embedded in social norms and values. As NELM and livelihood approaches to migration have demonstrated, the act of moving to another country and the sending of remittances home have been considered as one strategy, among others, to reciprocate to one's family and thereby live up to the expectations of the intergenerational contract (Adepoju, 2000). This agreement entails that dependency is transferred from the younger generation to the older generation, thus from children and adolescents to their parents. This implies that, within the family, children have a dependency relationship with their parents. Nonetheless, children tied to such social intergenerational obligations also make decisions concerning their future independently of their family, including those that involve migration.

The intergenerational transmission of values and knowledge via the family plays a critical role in terms of children's understanding of migration and whether they see it as part of a household livelihood strategy governed by intergenerational reciprocity. Parents are clearly involved in transmitting shared societal values and aspirations to their offspring, including those related to migration. This may substantially inform and influence the aspirations and decision-making of a potential migrant and socially reproduce a culture of migration. However, as demonstrated by Coe (2012) in her study on Ghanaian children's imagination of transnational migration, this cannot simply be assumed. Rather, she argues that it needs to be scrutinised in the local context by investigating "the extent to which children and adolescents adopt an adult culture of migration" (Coe, 2012, p.914). She further contends that children are active agents in how they are socialised into thinking about migration and will only internalise certain values if they consider them to be sufficiently important. Crucially, this is influenced by actors and institutions beyond the family, including peers, community leaders, schools, clubs, churches and various forms of media. As such, there are limits to the transmission of beliefs about migration via the family, and this draws attention to the agency of individual family members, including children, in developing and acting on social values and beliefs acquired through socialising experiences that occur outside the family unit. This does not underestimate the significance of the family in migration decision-making. It does, however, flag the fact that the family and its influence on a child's perspectives on migration should be considered in a wider social context that involves other actors.

The discussion above reveals migration to be a process that is heavily influenced by the socio-cultural context in which it takes place. An individual is placed within larger aggregates, particularly the family but also peer groups, communities and a whole host of social institutions, and these convey information to that individual that helps to shape their understanding of migration and the values and beliefs that they attach to it. With all of this in mind, this chapter draws on two specific case studies to illuminate the ways in which decision-making processes around the migration of young, talented Ghanaian boys to football academies within the country are negotiated in the context of the household. In particular, it assesses the extent to which this process can be understood as a household livelihood strategy, whether notions of intergenerational reciprocity are at play, and how intergenerational perspectives on football (and the possibility of migration through football) coalesce around and influence decisions to migrate to residential football academies in Ghana.

Ebo's football career: the supportive family

Ebo is a 15-year-old academy player. He was born in Accra and is the youngest of four brothers. His father is a trader in cement blocks and his mother is a market trader. While his eldest brother finished school and is working as an engineer, Ebo's other two brothers are still at school. Compared to his brothers, Ebo was in quite a comfortable position when he was growing up. Passionate about football, he found himself supported by his parents and three brothers, particularly Jacob, his older brother and manager of his former team, in his aspiration to pursue a football career, preferably outside of Ghana. Jacob and his other brothers, while interested in football, had been discouraged by their parents from playing, largely for economic reasons. His father explains why he and his wife did not want their three elder sons to play: "As for that time, things were not all that very good so that you can finance all the kids anything that they want to go and do. That is why we told them to stop."[3] Rather than play football, they preferred for them to focus on getting an education. But for Ebo it was different; with the support of his parents and his three older brothers, football was deemed to provide the most fruitful career path for him and one that would benefit his family. His brother Jacob explains:

[T]his time around, we have something like a division of labour . . . My brother has schooled, is working. I am also schooling, but I can play but then I never played and I am schooling now. And then my backbone is also schooling. So why don't we give him the chance for him to play . . . The whole family can at least push him to somewhere in football. Because he is talented in football and he really likes the game. He loves the game. Coming to academic perception too, he is very very sound, very good. Excellent in academics. But then we just told him "ok fine, here in Ghana here you can go to school, complete schooling and then even securing for a job is a very difficult thing . . . Why don't we leave you to play football, so that we can also support you in terms of finances, ritually, physically, anything we can support you." . . . Because, you know, for now, world wide, apart from football, what other job can you play to earn like football, you know.[4]

Encouraging Ebo to play football instead of solely focusing on his schooling was clearly a conscious decision on the part of family members to diversify the household income. Ebo's parents believed it wiser to have one son pursuing a route beyond education. As Jacob argues above, there were no guarantees that an education would provide a secure future for Ebo anyway, given the discrepancy between a senior secondary school education and economically attractive employment opportunities in Ghana (Esson, 2013). This explains why Ebo's family members were so supportive and encouraged him to work towards realising his ambitions. Jacob encapsulates this and is worth quoting at some length:

No one would burden the sea and then never get any benefit or something. It is a proverb. So then, in fact we are motivating this boy. You have to give him the motivational spirit. You have to back him physically, you have to back him spiritually, so he can make it. When he makes it in life, and then he is walking even, and people are pointing at him that this is the boy. Right now he says that his role model is Iniesta, Barcelona, and when he comes out to be a great player in Ghana now, I can walk sure this high . . . that this is my brother. He has made it. And there is no way you turn from the family. He knows what the family has done for him. That is the benefit we are gonna get from him. He can make it in life and then he can come out, buy car for daddy, buy car for mummy. In Ghana here too, with the Black Stars like this, you can see mummies with the players and calendars all around, with the cribs [houses] . . . so then, we are praying hard for him. We are giving him everything, every support that he needs, to make it what we want him to be in future. And we know that boy can make it in life.

What we see at play in the quotation above is the intergenerational contract and the notion of reciprocity writ large, at least in terms of the family members' perceptions of how their support for Ebo might benefit them in the future. Clearly, with such potential future benefits for the family in mind, Ebo's parents and siblings were closely involved in his football development and supported him as much as possible in the expectation that Ebo would reciprocate later on.

When academies started showing an interest in Ebo, Jacob became increasingly influential in helping to guide his brother. As for many players aspiring to go abroad to play football, Jacob deemed joining an academy to be a significant 'stepping stone' in his younger brother's career development, not least because, as he saw it, academies 'eat football, they drink football, everything is football'. None of this is to say that the family were eager to take up any opportunity that came Ebo's way. The Right to Dream academy, a charitable venture run by an English social entrepreneur, showed an interest in Ebo, but his parents and siblings were unimpressed and were unconvinced that Ebo should take up its offer of a place. As Jacob recounted;

I came home telling mummy and daddy that this is what happened. So they said "ok, we really have to investigate and know that they [the academy] are going to work for the boy". Not that the boy would just go somewhere and then the life would be a different thing all together.

Jacob assessed standards at the academy in terms of football, education, accommodation, food, facilities and hygiene. Based on his assessment and after careful consideration, the family decided not to take up an offer with this particular academy, nor with a subsequent offer from the Red Bull Ghana academy. The third academy to approach Ebo and express an interest in offering him a place was the Feyenoord Academy, one of Ghana's principal European academies. As Jacob explains, the family saw this offer as providing better opportunities for Ebo:

[The] reason why we made him go to the Feyenoord Academy is that Feyenoord can help your son to move outside of the country. To get outside exposure . . . Feyenoord Ghana is affiliated to outside Ghana. And I mean, the boy is also really playing very hard and as a more disciplined player, Feyenoord will definitely help him out. Because I know he has helped some people out. Harris now for number one. He played for Feyenoord, and he is now outside. He is doing well too. Every Feyenoord player is a very good player. That is what I know . . . Frankly speaking, talking about all academies, comparing the conduciveness of the environment, Red Bull is number one. If you go there . . . number one. And then they can also play. But then, comparing all the three academies, Feyenoord is the best when it comes to football.

This account of the decision-making process that preceded Ebo's move would seem to imply that it was straightforward and uncontested and that he played little role in deciding his short-term future. This was only partially true. The family did attempt to exclude Ebo from their deliberations. As Jacob elucidates: "We wanted to make a secret conversation with mum and dad. We were talking about he going or not going. We were all contemplating. Should this boy go or not?" However, suspicious about the fact that they had sent him away to take a bath in the compound where they lived with other families, and knowing that Feyenoord was interested in him, Ebo eavesdropped on the conversation. When Jacob found him out, Ebo expressed his frustration at the fact that his family had robbed him of his opportunity to go to the other two academies that were interested in him. Wanting his voice in the matter to be heard, he increased the pressure and said to Jacob: "If mummy and daddy don't allow me to go, I will kill myself." In attempting to calm Ebo down, Jacob made it abundantly clear that Ebo's future needed to be carefully considered against the backdrop of the interests of the whole family and that, as a consequence, they had his best interests at heart:

> You relax. We want the best for you. That is why we are doing all this. The academies are there, fine, but we want the best for you. You understand? Because right now, when you play and you make it in life, we are your family. There is no way you will turn your back against us. So we want the best for you.

For Jacob, his brothers and his father, Feyenoord was an attractive proposition and, after discussions with some of the coaches and former academy players, they were on the cusp of agreeing to Feyenoord's offer of a place. One hurdle remained, however: Ebo's mother. Even though she had actively supported her son by buying him football kit, she was unconvinced about the prospect of him joining an academy and remained concerned about his education. As Jacob explains: "Oh, you know, she is a mother. And then she doesn't really know more about football stuff. She also really liked education more. So she was also a little bit of a hard nut to crack. You know, very difficult to convince." As a result, the decision-making process required careful negotiation between Ebo's mother and other family members. In this negotiation, the academy's provision of education became a sensitive and crucial point. As Jacob elucidates:

> Since she really loves education so much [more] than the football, we had to convince her more with education stuff. So we made her know that all syllabus we are using here, it is the same thing over there. There is no difference. So then I made some examples to my mummy. Because I have two advanced boys in my area. So I called them and then they had to let mummy know that "oh, it is true. We are doing science here, we are doing English, we sit for the BECE, and then we write the WASSCE too". And mummy said "ok, fine, if there is education, my ward can go".[5]

After passing the selection process at the academy, which included football trials and a medical examination, Ebo moved to the academy.

Simon's football career: a challenging negotiation

Simon comes from a relatively well-off family in Kumasi. When he was six, his father moved to the United States and took up employment as a truck driver. As the primary breadwinner of the family, he has been able to support his wife and five children in Ghana, as well as provide for his own brothers and sisters. The house they live in is relatively luxurious and large. Simon is the third-born and has three brothers and an older sister. They all had the opportunity to go to school. While his older sister is a nurse in Ghana and wants to become a doctor, his older brother is studying medicine in the USA. His two younger brothers are currently still in school. Although all his brothers used to play football as they were growing up, only Simon and his *backbone* (his direct younger brother) cherished serious aspirations to become professional players. Simon had an interest in football from early childhood. At the age of eight, his parents and uncle, his mother's brother, unanimously agreed that it would be better for his future to concentrate on his schooling. Although his father had noticed his son's interest in football, while residing in the US, Simon recalls his father's view on football: "in this area football is not that good. Look at our older brothers in the top over there, that area. They play football, but nothing happened to them."[6] Beyond his parents' concerns that football would negatively impact on his education, Simon's mother's religious background (Seventh Day Adventist) and her perception that the game was a place where *juju* (black magic) was practised also created difficulties for his aspirations to play. These ideas featured prominently, along with fear of injury, in her perceptions of football. As Simon indicated:

> Because of my culture, my church, we don't like football. We don't like football. In the olden days they liked juju in football, so my mum said "ey, if you get injured, no one is going to take care of you. So don't try to be a footballer. You know football, they like juju. At the end of the day you are

going to be injured and you will be at home. No one is going to take care of you. They are not going to pay you."[7]

Despite his family members' view of football, Simon remained driven by his ambition to play and his belief that God had given him his talent for the game. To pursue his dream, he would sometimes sneak out to play football without his parents and uncle knowing. Simon explains: "I know that is my career. If God knows this, then I am going to make it. So I pushed myself and motivated myself and go and make it." He recalls that, before he turned ten, a local coach who trained young, talented children from the area approached him and asked him to join his team. Simon was clearly worried about how his parents and uncle would react, but nonetheless he decided to join the man's team. In every way possible, he tried to hide his football activities from his mother and uncle:

> I would just inform them I am going to play around, and she would tell me "hey, you have to come earlier". I would say "ok, I will come, I will come earlier. Don't worry, everything is under control." So I would move to the training pitch and we would train. When it is getting dark, I have to come back home. So I asked permission from the coach, the trainer, and I would come back. So if I am coming I have to wash my legs, I have to take a bath because if I am dirty, my mum will notice that I went to play football. So I have to clean my body and come back home from training . . . I would come here [home], but when I was about to play a match, I have to go. That time, I was not making any war here, so I would just pass this time and then move to the man's house.

However, his siblings were aware of his footballing activities. His older sister, for example, supported him and sometimes even bought kit, jerseys and boots for him to play. He used to hide them at his coach's house and every day before training he went there to change. However, whenever his uncle and mother found out about his football activities, he faced corporal punishment, administered by his uncle:

> My mum and my uncle, any time I go for football, ey, there is trouble! Yeah, because I can go to a football match, at the end of the day, no food for me, because they are telling me I have to stop playing football . . . anytime I go for football and I comes [sic] he [his uncle] would lock me up. He would lock all the doors. He would on the television, he would on the tape, and lower this thing [referring to shutters] . . . so when . . . if this man is beating me, no one would hear.

Despite the beatings he suffered and his mother and uncle's continued opposition to his involvement in football, Simon persevered and he clearly did not intend to give up the game. As he continues:

> I don't care. I know if I come back, he would beat me. And I pray to God . . . that time I had a dream that I am playing with a lot of crowd and people.

So I said "no, this is my talent, so I have to move on". So I don't care what people say. I don't care what people say. So I think that dream motivates me a lot.

It was the strength of his convictions that eventually gave Simon the courage to call his father in the US and tell him about his dream of pursuing a career in football. While his father initially shared the same perspective as Simon's mother and uncle, he gradually came to accept his son's wishes. From that moment onwards, Simon remembers, his father became actively involved and interested in his football development, albeit from afar. The clearest manifestation of this support was that he contacted the coach of a colts or youth team in the area where Simon lived to ask if his son could join.

At that moment, Simon was caught between two positions: his mother and uncle at home who discouraged him from playing, on the one hand, and, on the other, a father in the US and a youth team coach who recognised Simon's potential and supported him. What eventually resolved the matter was an acceptance on the part of all concerned of the power hierarchy within the context of Simon's family. In conversation with his father, Simon broached his mother and uncle's opposition. He asked his father, "Do you want my uncle and my mum to kill me, or what?", to which his father simply responded, "No, go there and tell them that I am the one who gave birth to you." Simon's father was clearly reinforcing his status as head of the family and hence his entitlement to decide on his son's future. The coach of the colts team that Simon was on the verge of signing for also played an important role in negotiating acceptance of his involvement in football. Realising that his mother had serious reservations, the coach accompanied Simon to his house to ask her for permission to let him play in his team after school, and she eventually relented. While her outlook on football had not changed particularly, she appreciated the approach of the coach. As Simon recounts: "She knows what the man thinks. Because he is old, for him to apologise to just my mum . . . So she took that respect and she allowed me to play for him . . . But she tell me, if I am injured, I should forget. She is not going to take charge of the injury." Three months later, Simon registered with the colts team.

From the outset, it became clear that the coach of the colts team aspired to move Simon on to an academy. He took him to tournaments and trials organised by particular academies in order to showcase his talent. This presented a further set of complications for Simon's relationship with his mother. Although she had acquiesced in her son joining a colts team, she was resistant to the idea of him joining an academy and did not give consent for Simon to be involved in trials. The reason for this is explained by Simon: "She thought I was going to suffer, I am not going to get any accommodation, anywhere to sleep, mosquitoes." The coach continued to pursue various avenues to facilitate Simon's relocation to an academy, but his mother proved immovable and on a number of occasions prevented him from taking part in trials and tournaments organised by academies. She was supported by another uncle from Simon's father's side of the family, who, while not averse to the idea of his nephew entering an academy, thought it best for him to complete his Junior High School education first. When another opportunity of a trial arose, however, Simon resorted to evasion, sneaking away from home to his coach's house and then onwards to the trial. To avoid being ordered to return home, he turned his mobile phone off for the two-week period required to travel to and complete the trial. When his mother eventually discovered his whereabouts and ordered him to return home, Simon turned again to his father, who recognised the potential value of an academy place for achieving a career in professional football. While he remained supportive, it took the intervention of the director of the academy to persuade Simon's mother about the wisdom of continuing with the trial. He visited her at home and sought to reassure her, indicating that Simon would be taken good care of and that he would be registered with a school just outside the academy where he could complete his Junior High School exams. She eventually relented and, on the successful completion of his trial, Simon's father returned from the US to sign a three-year contract with the academy.

Diverging intergenerational perspectives on football

The two cases of Ebo and Simon reveal differences and similarities in terms of the ways in which the ambition of young Ghanaian players to play professionally overseas coalesce around the broader aspirations and needs of the household. Both cases illuminate the active involvement of family members in their development and in decision-making processes linked to their career path. They also shed light on the ongoing and complicated process of intra-family negotiation that often underpins the relocation of young Ghanaian players to football academies. Despite Ebo's mother's more circumspect position on whether her son should pursue a place at the Feyenoord academy, given her concerns around his education, Ebo's story largely confirms the idea that young African players are supported and encouraged by family members because of the perceived potential future benefits that a professional career overseas might elicit for them. As such, his migration to an academy was relatively unproblematic and was contoured by the notion of intergenerational reciprocity. However, as the case of Simon reveals, it is not always the case that families enthusiastically embrace the prospect of one of their members relocating to a football academy.

In contrast to Ebo's situation, the extent to which reciprocal expectations played a part in Simon's move to an academy is at best unclear. According to Simon, his father assented to his move because he recognised that it would help him to become a professional footballer. However, whether this decision was part of a broader household livelihood strategy based on the idea that Simon would become a future provider for the family is doubtful. His family was relatively well off by Ghanaian standards, a consequence of the fact that his father had migrated to the US, obtained employment as a truck driver and remitted home on a regular basis to both his immediate and extended family. As a consequence, Simon did not feel that it was his responsibility to take care of his family, and it was not his ambition to do so. He rather hoped that each family member might move to Europe on the basis of their own individual talents and make a life for themselves.

We see in Ebo's and Simon's experiences that intra-family relations and expectations (or otherwise) of reciprocity act to either constrain or enable the migration of young, talented players to academies in Ghana. The extent to which reciprocal expectations feature in decision-making processes or negotiations around whether a young family member joins an academy differs from family to family and is often dependent on the perspectives that various family members have of football and football-related mobility. For many young boys in Ghana, the success of Ghanaian football players in Europe, such as Michael Essien, Abedi Pele and Asamoah Gyan, influences their understanding of football and what it can offer them. They often consider football as a feasible way to secure a lifestyle characterised by wealth, conspicuous consumption and considerable social status, one referred to by Ghanaian youth as the 'X-way' (Esson, 2013). But, a successful career in professional football overseas is also seen as a way to live up to reciprocal expectations from family members. This certainly featured in Ebo's case and reflects the fact that a lot of Ghanaian children, especially boys, feel a strong sense of responsibility towards their parents as they age. As one former football academy player formulates it: "Our parents helped us grow our teeth, we have to help our parents lose their teeth."[8] That said, this is not the case for all young Ghanaian footballers, as was evident in the case of Simon.

Even in those cases where aspiring players envisage a career in the game as the most feasible way to live up to reciprocal expectations, it is not always the case that all family members will share the same view. Despite the ubiquitous presence and popularity of the game in Ghana, many academy players are confronted with family members who see engagement in football and the pursuit of a professional career in the game as folly and a misdirection of energies that would be better off spent in acquiring an education. Strong social values about education are significant in this. As Esson (2013) has demonstrated, a series of post-independence state policies linked education directly to development in Ghana, and as a result education came to be considered crucial in terms of social mobility in the minds of parents and other older family members. To many parents, education is currently deemed a privilege that they view as important for becoming a 'somebody', defined as "a person of status and respect, somebody who is responsible, mature, independent, knowledgeable and capable of taking care of others" in the future (Langevang, 2008, p.2046). This helps to explain the value placed on education by members of both Ebo's and Simon's family and the reason why they were opposed to someone in their family pursuing an activity that they believed would detract from focusing sufficiently on education. Even though Simon wanted to pursue football, he recognised the value of education, stating that "there is a saying 'education is the key to success'". The friction between, and perceived incommensurability of, education and football has also developed because of a more general view that footballers lack interest in education. Indeed, footballers in Ghana are often referred to as *kobolo*, a term particularly used for children who drop out of school. It is a Ga word that has been adopted in most

Ghanaian languages and is routinely used to describe a vagrant or vagabond, someone who is lazy and lacks the skills or inclination to contribute anything positive to society and who is often unemployed and homeless. In Ghanaian parlance, to be a *kobolo* is to be considered a 'good-for-nothing' (Cobblah, 2011).[9] Given that football is considered an impediment to children's education and hence social mobility in some quarters, it is argued that devoting considerable time to the game will limit an individual's future prospects and will see them become a *kobolo*.

For older generations, this disapproving perspective on football as a fruitful career is substantiated by examples of former Ghanaian football stars who played football in Ghana's top leagues before the exodus of players to Europe. Many of them are said to have lacked an educational background due to their focus on football and have, as a result, ended up in penury, because they had little opportunity to take on a different career when they retired from football. Wary of such a prospect for their own children, Ebo's and Simon's respective mothers sought to discourage them from investing time and energy in the game. This idea of footballers as *kobolo* contrasts with the image of football that younger generations possess. Indeed, for both Ebo and Simon, much of the intra-family negotiations and discussions around their futures revolved around the issue of education. Even when Ebo was on the verge of signing at the Feyenoord academy and everything had been agreed, his mother had some last-minute doubts and needed to be convinced about the level of educational provision at the academy. In Simon's case, education also became a major point of contention both in his joining of a colts team and subsequently in his recruitment to an academy. In Ebo's case, it only became an issue when his relocation to an academy became a realistic option, but for Simon such educational concerns impacted on his football development from a very early stage. As the cases of Ebo and Simon clearly show, when diverging perspectives on football surface, they not only create considerable intra-family tensions but also have significant ramifications for players' football development and their opportunities to join an academy. As in both of the cases presented here, many of the players currently resident in football academies in Ghana have not received the unanimous support of their family.

Conclusion

This chapter had two key objectives. The first was to redress the emphasis on the macro-structural level in analyses of African football migration by detailing the ways in which human agency plays out in the process of migrating (internally) to a football academy. Secondly, it sought to locate family much more centrally in analyses of the mobility of young, talented Ghanaian players by examining the extent to which intergenerational reciprocity is a salient driver in this process. The experiences of Ebo and Simon, recounted in the second half of this chapter, clearly illuminate their agency and resilience as individuals and how they either utilise their family's support to achieve their ambitions or navigate their way through their family's opposition to football. The empirical detail presented here also highlights the variegated involvement of family in supporting or resisting the development of young players and their aspirations to become mobile and migrate to an academy.

What clearly determines the extent to which the family is supportive of or opposed to one of their members investing significant energies in pursuing a football career that may not actually materialise are the differing perspectives on football and football academies that exist in Ghana and the extent to which the prospect of a football career for one sibling might be seen as part of a broader household livelihood strategy. Within the context of the family unit, several competing perspectives are often at play and these were clearly evident in the cases of Simon and Ebo. On the one hand, football or a place at an academy can be considered as wasteful and an undesirable pursuit that detracts from education. On the other, where a family places significant stock in intergenerational reciprocity, pursuing a professional career overseas can be seen as an activity that has the potential to be economically productive for the wider household. These differing perspectives can enable and facilitate players' football-related ambitions when the family is generally supportive, but when there is significant opposition, this can serve to constrain the actions and opportunities of players to pursue football and become mobile. In Ebo's case, the latter perspective was predominant within his family, although not unanimously so. Simon's family had a much less favourable view of football that only improved over time and as a consequence of the persistence and persuasive powers of Simon, his coach and the director of the academy that wanted to recruit him. What this shows is that, for those aspiring to become mobile and embark on a journey that they envisage will proceed from an academy to a professional career overseas, these differing perspectives need to be negotiated and a path through them carefully navigated.

This chapter and the 'thick' ethnographic data that it contains reveal that young Ghanaian football players are not passive actors when it comes to key decisions around how their football careers might develop, and nor are their families' views of football shaped by the 'escape from poverty' discourse that we observe in populist depictions of African football migration. Rather, young players, their parents, older siblings and members of the extended family are active agents whose understandings of football and what it might offer in the future are critical in the process of migrating to a football academy. Acknowledging this and locating the family unit at the centre of analyses of African football migration, whether internally to an academy or transnationally, will allow for a much more nuanced interpretation of this process, one that moves us beyond the macro-structural level.

Notes

1 Interview, Kasao, 21 February 2012.
2 This was confirmed in subsequent informal conversations with Simon in Tema on 6 April 2012 and in Kumasi on 27 April 2012.
3 Interview, Accra, 4 April 2012.
4 Interview, Accra, 4 April 2012.

5 BECE refers to the Basic Education Certificate Examination, while WASSCE relates to the West African Secondary School Certificate Examination.
6 Interview, Kasao, 21 February 2012.
7 Interview, Kumasi, 27 April 2012.
8 Interview, Tamale, 14 March 2012.
9 Usage of this term in the manner described here was confirmed by field observations and casual conversations conducted in Ghana between September 2011 and June 2012.

References

Adegoke, A. (2001) Pubertal Development and Traditional Support Systems in Africa: An Overview. *African Journal of Reproductive Health* 5(1): 20–30.

Adepoju, A. (2000) Issues and Recent Trends in International Migration in Sub-Saharan Africa. *International Social Sciences Journal* 52(165): 383–94.

Akoto, B. (Director) (2010) *Football Fables*. Film, United Kingdom.

Arbena, J. (2003) Dimensions of International Talent Migration in Latin American Sports. In J. Bale and J. Maguire (Eds.) *The Global Sports Arena: Athletic Talent Migration in an Interdependent World*. London and Portland, OR: Frank Cass (99–111).

Bebbington, A. (1999) Capitals and Capabilities: A Framework for Analyzing Peasant Viability, Rural Livelihoods and Poverty. *World Development* 27(12): 2021–44.

Broere, M. and Van der Drift, R. (1997) *Football Africa!* Oxford: Worldview Publishing.

Carter, T. (2007) Family Networks, State Interventions and the Experience of Cuban Transnational Sport Migration. *International Review for the Sociology of Sport* 42(4): 371–89.

Carter, T. (2011) *In Foreign Fields: The Politics and Experiences of Transnational Sport Migration*. London: Pluto Press.

Castles, S. (2010) Understanding Global Migration: A Social Transformation Perspective. *Journal of Ethnic and Migration Studies* 36(10): 1565–86.

Cobblah, T. (2011) *Knee-Jerk Reaction*, 26 August. Ghanaweb.com. Retrieved 22 November 2013 from: http://www.ghanaweb.com/GhanaHomePage/features/artikel.php?ID=217116.

Coe, C. (2011) How Children Feel About Their Parent's Migration: A History of the Reciprocity of Care in Ghana. In C. Coe, R.R. Reynolds, D.A. Boehm, J.M. Hess and H. Rae-Espinoza (Eds.) *Everyday Ruptures: Children, Youth, and Migration in Global Perspective*. Tennessee: Vanderbilt University Press (97–114).

Coe, C. (2012) Growing Up and Going Abroad: How Ghanaian Children Imagine Transnational Migration. *Journal of Ethnic and Migration Studies* 38(6): 913–31.

Darby, P. (2002) *Africa, Football and FIFA: Politics, Colonialism and Resistance*. London: Frank Cass Publishers.

Darby, P. (2010) 'Go Outside': The History, Economics and Geography of Ghanaian Football Labour Migration. *African Historical Review* 42(1): 19–41.

Darby, P., Akindes, G. and Kirwin, M. (2007) Football Academies and the Migration of African Football Labour to Europe. *Journal of Sport and Social Issues* 31(2): 143–61.

De Haan, A. (1997) Migration as Family Strategy: Rural–Urban Labor Migration in India during the Twentieth Century. *History of the Family: An International Quarterly* 2(4): 481–505.

De Haan, A. (1999) Livelihoods and Poverty: The Role of Migration. A Critical Review of the Migration Literature. *Journal of Development Studies* 36(2): 1–47.

De Haan, A., Brock, K. and Coulibaly, N. (2002) Migration, Livelihoods and Institutions: Contrasting Patterns of Migration in Mali. *Journal of Development Studies* 38(5): 37–58.

De Haan, A. and Rogaly, B. (2002) Introduction: Migrant Workers and Their Role in Rural Change. *Journal of Development Studies* 38(5): 1–14.

De Haas, H. (2007) Remittances, Migration and Social Development: A Conceptual Review of the Literature. Social Policy and Development Programme Paper, Number 34, October 2007, United Nations Research Institute for Social Development.

De Haas, H. (2010) Migration and Development: A Theoretical Perspective. *International Migration Review* 44(1): 227–64.

De Jong, G. and Gardner, R. (1981) *Migration Decision Making?: Multidisciplinary Approaches to Microlevel Studies in Developed and Developing Countries?*. New York: Pergamon Press.

Desai, S. (1992) Children at Risk: The Role of Family Structure in Latin America and West Africa. *Population and Development Review* 8(4): 689–717.

De Vasconcellos Ribeiro, C. and Dimeo, P. (2009) The Experience of Migration for Brazilian Football Players. *Sport in Society* 12(6): 725–36.

Esson, J. (2013) A Body and a Dream at a Vital Conjuncture: Ghanaian Youth, Uncertainty and the Allure of Football in Ghana. *Geoforum* 47: 84–92.

Faist, T. (1997) The Crucial Meso-level. In T. Hammar, G. Brochmann, K. Tamas and T. Faist (Eds.) *International Migration, Immobility and Development: Multidisciplinary Perspectives*. Oxford: Berg (187–218).

Fischer, P.A., Martin, R. and Straubhaar, T. (1997) Should I Stay or Should I Go? In T. Hammar, G. Brochmann, K. Tamas and T. Faist (Eds.) *International Migration, Immobility and Development: Multidisciplinary Perspectives*. Oxford: Berg (49–90).

Hammar, T. and Tamas, K. (1997) Why Do People Go or Stay? In T. Hammar, G. Brochmann, K. Tamas and T. Faist (Eds.) *International Migration, Immobility and Development: Multidisciplinary Perspectives*. Oxford: Berg (1–20).

Hashim, I. (2006) The Positives and Negatives of Children's Independent Migration: Assessing the Evidence and Debates. *Working Paper T16: Development Research Centre on Migration, Globalisation and Poverty*. Brighton: University of Sussex.

Huijsmans, R. (2011) Child Migration and Questions of Agency. *Development and Change* 42(5): 1307–21.

Kuhn, R. (2002) The Logic of Letting Go: Family and Individual Migration from Rural Bangladesh. *Working Paper 2002–2004 Population Aging Center*, University of Colorado at Boulder, Institute of Behavioral Science, August 2002: 1–35.

Lamche, P. (Director) (2010) *Black Diamond*. Film, France.

Lanfranchi, P. and Taylor, M. (2001) *Moving with the Ball: The Migration of Professional Footballers*. Oxford: Berg.

Langevang, T. (2008) 'We Are Managing!' Uncertain Paths to Respectable Adulthoods in Accra, Ghana.*Geoforum* 39: 2039–47.

Mabogunje, A.L. (1970) Systems Approach to a Theory of Rural–Urban Migration. *Geographical Review* 2(1): 1–18.

McDougall, D. (2008) The Investigation. *Observer Sport Monthly*, January 2008, 50–5.

McDowell, C. and De Haan, A. (1997) Migration and Sustainable Livelihoods: A Critical Review of the Literature. *IDS Working Paper 65*. Brighton: IDS.

Massey, D.S. (1990) Social Structure, Household Strategies and the Cumulative Causation of Migration. *Population Index* 56(1): 3–26.

Massey, D., Arango, J., Hugo, G., Kouaouci, A., Pellegrino, A. and Taylor, J.E. (1993) Theories of International Migration: A Review and Appraisal. *Population and Development Review* 19(3): 431–66.

Molnar, G. and Maguire, J. (2008) Hungarian Footballers on the Move: Issues of and Observations on the First Migratory Phase. *Sport in Society* 11(1): 74–89.

Poli, R. (2006) Migrations and Trade of African Football Players: Historic, Geographical and Cultural Aspects. *Afrika-Spectrum* 41(3): 393–414.

Poli, R. (2010) Understanding Globalization through Football: The New International Division of Labour, Migratory Channels and Transnational Trade Circuits. *International Review for the Sociology of Sport* 45(4): 1–16.

Porter, G. and Blaufuss, K. (2002) Children, Transport and Traffic in Southern Ghana. Paper presented at the International Workshop on Children and Traffic, Copenhagen, 2–3 May.

Sjanek, R. (1982) The Organization of Households in Adabraka: Toward a Wider Comparative Perspective.*Comparative Studies in Society and History* 24(1): 57–103.

Stark, O. (1991) *The Migration of Labor*. Cambridge: Basil Blackwell.

Stead, D. and Maguire, J. (2000) 'Rite de Passage or Passage to Riches'? The Motivation and Objectives of Nordic/Scandinavian Players in English League Soccer. *Journal of Sport and Social Issues* 24(1): 36–60.

Taylor, J. (1999) The New Economics of Labour Migration and the Role of Remittances in the Migration Process. *International Migration* 37(1): 63–88.

Tiemko, R. (2004) Migration, Return and Socio-economic Change in West Africa: The Role of the Family. *Population, Space and Place* 10: 155–74.

Vanguard Documentaries(2010)*Soccer's Lost Boys*. Season 4, Episode 4. United States.

Whitehead, A., Hashim, I. and Iversen, V. (2007) Child Migration, Child Agency and Inter-generational Relations in Africa and South Asia. *Working Paper T24: Development Research Centre on Migration, Globalisation and Poverty*. Brighton: University of Sussex

Young, L. and Ansell, N. (2003) Fluid Households, Complex Families: The Impacts of Children's Migration as a Response to HIV/AIDS in Southern Africa. *Professional Geographer* 55(4): 464–76.

LIVERPOOL JOHN MOORES UNIVERSITY
LEARNING SERVICES

12 Finding football in the Dominican Republic

Haitian migrants, space, place and notions of exclusion

Nicholas Wise and John Harris

As shown by a number of authors in this collection, football has played an important role in the movement of migrant workers across the world for a number of years. Much of the focus of this book, and indeed the wider published work on football and migration, has been the movement of elite male professional players towards the core football economies. Yet outside of the industry of professional football, millions of other people throughout the world play the game without financial remuneration. The game can play a particularly important role in the lives of people who move between nations and can offer an important site for promoting and reasserting identities. The purpose of this chapter is to look at a micro-locale case study of Haitian migrants in the Dominican Republic. This chapter outlines some of the deeper meanings of sport, especially football, in migrant communities by focusing on notions of belonging and identity. In an analysis informed by geographical research, it looks at sport spaces, sense of place and the gendered dynamics of sport within a particular locale to show the significance and impact football has on the everyday lives of Haitians who now reside in the Dominican Republic. Baseball is the national sport in the Dominican Republic and has been the focus of much academic research (e.g. Klein, 1989, 1991, 2008; Ruck, 1991; Kirch, 2002; Gedda, 2009). However, until recently little work has assessed the significance of football within the country (Wise, 2014).

This work focuses particular attention on a community of Haitians living in Villa Ascension. The Non-Governmental Organisation (NGO) involved in the community designated space for football. This chapter will concentrate on the meanings of the sports space (or landscape) and sense of place from the perspective of Haitian immigrants. Social and cultural geographers recognise that places and landscapes have the power to both unite and divide groups of people (Vertinsky & Bale, 2004; Wylie, 2007). Geographical studies assessing landscapes and identity are concerned with how local participants perceive their sense of place in a community. Additionally, unities and divisions are often structured around issues of race, gender and ethnicity. Therefore, there are multiple senses of place and identity. Within this chapter we show how football plays an important role in the everyday lives of a migrant community and highlight some of the tensions shaping their involvement in the game. Haitian migrants in the

Dominican Republic have a strong social and cultural connection to football. This chapter recognises some of the contestations of identities at play and positions geographical perspectives of place and landscape to support the social contexts. It has been observed that the spaces and places where people participate in sport lend to a greater sense of community identity (Vertinsky & Bale, 2004; Walseth, 2006; Baller, 2007; Gaffney, 2008; Shobe, 2008; Wise, 2011). However, different groups create their own sense of place and divisions are established where dominant ideologies are promoted and celebrated. As research in the sociology of sport has shown, these identities are fluid, contested and often in a state of flux (e.g. MacClancy, 1996; Grainger, 2006; Walseth, 2006; Harris & Parker, 2009). The first two analysis sections will be framed around perspectives of staging and performing identity and sense of place surrounding the sport space in Villa Ascension. Haitians are often excluded and regarded as 'others' in the Dominican Republic, so this work shows how football allows them to integrate, interact and support one another towards establishing a sense of belonging, collectively, and greater links to their home (Haiti). The third analysis section then builds on and contests some of the initial perceptions and understandings which are male-centric, and attempts to (re)frame understandings of inclusion and exclusion based upon contexts of masculinity and how this in some ways contradicts the previous sections concerning the perceived Haitian collectivity.

Further socio-geographical conceptualisations are incorporated to extend the analysis. DeLyser *et al.* (2010) argue that more research is needed to address socio-cultural inquiries focusing on place, landscape, community and identity from a geographical perspective. Ethnographic methods, involving participant observations and semi-structured interviews, were used to conduct the research presented here. Inductive qualitative inquiries attempt to better understand and produce knowledge of individual and group experiences (Watson & Till, 2010; Olwig, 2013). This is especially important in micro-locale case studies where qualitative evidence is administered in the field, discussed and critically reflected upon. The first author spent time in Villa Ascension participating in and observing the daily sports activity within the community. Subsequent conversations with football players occurred before, during and after play, with more formalised discussions with Haitian football players each lasting 30–45 minutes. All interviewees were male and between the ages of 16 and 40 and most participated in football each day; the names used in the chapter are all pseudonyms. Before moving on to the primary research, it is important to briefly outline and note the contested histories between Haitians and Dominicans to frame an understanding of some of the broader factors that shape some of the discussions in the analysis.

Haitians in the Dominican Republic and contested identities

To briefly establish the context for this work, it is important to note the legacy of contestations between the Dominican and Haitian peoples on the island of Hispaniola. The subject of identity, specifically national identity, is important here because historically Dominicans and Haitians have struggled to obtain and administer the island's territory (Augelli, 1980; Howard, 2001; San Miguel, 2005; Goodwin, 2011). The contestations at stake result from Haiti's previous dominance over all of Hispaniola from 1822 to 1844, when the Dominican Republic declared independence from Haiti (Howard, 2001). Moving into the 1930s, amidst global economic recession, many Haitian peoples entered the Dominican Republic and attempted to establish themselves in the border provinces (Goodwin, 2011). Then Dominican President Rafael Trujillo founded a programme known as *Dominicanización* just after the 1936 boundary agreement. What followed were mass killings and expulsions of Haitians and anyone of dark-skin complexion in the established border region (Howard, 2001). Prejudices remained throughout the 1970s and thereafter, as racist sentiment towards Haitians aimed at further combating their immigration into the country (Howard, 2001; San Miguel, 2005). What emerged as a struggle over race and ethnicity threatened the Dominican Republic's "national homogeneity, or national character" (Howard, 2001, p.156). Such results were in defence of civic nationalism, and the Dominican government implemented programmes to halt Haitian movement east into the Dominican Republic (Augelli, 1980).

Goodwin's (2011) country report on the Dominican Republic details that 20,000 Haitians enter the country each year legally and as many as 60,000 illegally. Many Haitians gravitated towards the Dominican Republic to work the sugar-cane fields and refineries (hereby filling undesired labour positions), although much of this industry is dormant today. Many Haitians allowed into the country on temporary working contracts stayed and settled in rural communes across the Dominican Republic (Howard, 2001). Whilst acknowledging the political struggles over civic nationalism, ethnic nationalism also remains contested in regard to language and race, or exactly who is Dominican and who is Haitian (San Miguel, 2005). As denoted by the legacy of the two distinct nations, there is a noticeable sporting disparity between Dominicans, who claim baseball as their national sport, and Haitians, who recognise football as their national sport. MacClancy (1996, p.2) notes that sports "are vehicles of identity, providing people with a sense of difference and a way of classifying themselves and others, whether latitudinally or hierarchically". Therefore, 'difference' complements this imaginary façade of heterogeneous interplays of ethnic nationalism, thereby situating sport as a discourse for accessing socio-cultural semblances of national identity.

Also important to the scope and framework of contested identities is Bairner's (2001) discussion of sport that positions perspectives of ethnic and civic nationalism. Regarding ethnic nationalism, nations are identified through homogeneous ideals (i.e. language or race). In contrast, civic nationalism "celebrates citizenship within particular political entities as opposed to membership in supposedly natural human associations . . . [and therefore] civic nationalism is inclusive" (Bairner, 2001, p.3). Identity, discussed around national identity in this regard, positions how individuals and social actors from a particular nation imprint their unique sense of sporting identity in another country to symbolise their presence. As we reside in an increasingly interdependent world, the movement of people will continue to have an impact on spatial contestations, heterogeneity and local community interactions (Werbner, 1996; Cronin & Mayall, 1998; Edensor, 2002; Yassim, 2013). Furthermore, by recognising the fluidity of national identities (through movement and migration), people will continue to assimilate their ethnic sense of nation(ness) in other countries. Dominicans have long been attempting to defend their sense of civic nationalism, and Haitians, regarded as the 'other', are often unwelcome outsiders who are discriminated against (Howard, 2001). Football's significance to Haitian identity supports Gruffudd's (1999, pp.199–200) observation that identity "is simply an ideological movement . . . [that] can refer to a positive celebration of identity in the face of oppression or marginalization".

Haitians themselves did not bring football to the Dominican Republic. Football first emerged there in the northern coastal cities of Puerto Plata and Sosúa. The game was introduced by Jewish Germans who left Germany prior to the Second World War, and many of whom settled on the country's north coast; it took just under two decades before the Dominican Republic registered with the Fédération Internationale de Football Association (FIFA) in 1959 (FIFA, 2011). Furthermore, what must be acknowledged is that, despite the sport's popularity among Haitians, the sport receives very little recognition because of its stronger presence in more remote areas off the tourist path. Haitian recreational footballers in Villa Ascension express great emotion and passion for the sport that distinguishes their sense of ethnic nationalism.

Integration/interactions around the football field in Villa Ascension

The community of Villa Ascension is predominantly Haitian and is located in a remote area of the province of Puerto Plata. Dominicans also reside in Villa Ascension, but the majority of Dominicans live in the adjacent community of Caraballo. The community of Villa Ascension, constructed between 2003 and 2005, is supported by NGOs. Encouraged by the Haitian majority, the NGO designated a football field in Villa Ascension. In spaces used for sport, observations of the landscape offer insight into how groups act to stage or display symbolisms that aid in connecting people with their collective sense of identity (Edensor, 2002). Whilst identity can be staged, it is also performed, in this case through football practice and matches. It is also important to recognise how people are perceived as being in place or out of place (Cresswell, 2004). This is a common focus when assessing migrant groups because what they often represent is different from the social and cultural ideals of a particular place (Werbner, 1996; Langellier, 2010; Yassim, 2013). Here it is important to situate how and what people do to establish a sense of belonging and perform their identity in a foreign place.

Many Haitians migrate to the Dominican Republic because economic opportunities in Haiti are minimal. This is of course also a factor in the migration of many elite level football players, as identified at numerous points in this collection. Although opportunities for Haitians are sparse in the Dominican Republic, and despite the prejudices and social difficulties they face, they are able to take up undesirable labour positions. The availability of any such job outweighs the poor social conditions faced by Haitians who move to the Dominican Republic. To overcome the challenges associated with social inequality, Haitians often congregate in communities as a way to preserve their sense of cultural identity and to establish a sense of belonging.

Football has become a significant part of everyday life to these migrants in Villa Ascension. Elice stated that "the people here are very interested in football, this field is very important for the community [and] the people enjoy watching and playing on the field". Two other participants added:

> If we didn't have this field here then it would be bad because then I could not play football, there would be no place to play. This field is so important in my life and for the community.
>
> (Thierre)

> The field is important; when I am not working I pass my time playing football. To me the field is like a friend, when I stay at home I feel like I have to go to the field to play football – it is a distraction.
>
> (Brunel)

Brunel offers an alternative and important insight here and evidences how the field as a distraction was addressed and discussed with other participants before and after practice. Several other Haitians reiterated this point because they find it difficult to gain regular employment, so during difficult times (socially and financially) the field did act as a distraction to many.

The sports space in Villa Ascension is somewhat unique. In many other areas where Haitians reside and congregate, they practise football on baseball fields. In Villa Ascension, as noted earlier, the homes of the community were constructed by NGOs. The organisations also designated some vacant space with appropriate perimeters for football as a way of further encouraging community development and the opportunity to practise the sport. Previously, before the field in Villa Ascension existed, Haitians had to use the field in Caraballo to play the game. Dominique noted that "sometimes we could not play in Caraballo when the Dominicans played late". He further added that "when the community organisers saw this they said they would designate a football field for us".

The presence of a football field has not always been well received by Dominicans. It has been argued that some Dominicans regard it as a threat to their national sporting ideals (Wise, 2013). Several Haitian participants, and a representative from one of the local NGOs, spoke about the riots that occurred in Villa Ascension in 2008. Kenel mentioned that many Haitians departed the village during the riots. When they left their homes, some were then occupied by Dominicans. However, many Haitians who left during the riots have since returned, although there is now more of a Dominican presence in the community. Tensions between Haitians and Dominicans have been a fairly common occurrence over time, although these tensions are not truly representative in Villa Ascension as local conflicts/tensions are rare. Often during interviews, participants discussed the community's past to assist with descriptions of the ongoing situation, pertinent to the sharing of a common sports space. When discussing meanings of identity and asking Haitians to reflect on football, Franz noted that:

> Before the riots the Haitians and Dominicans did not have any problems, we still played football and [they played] baseball. When the problems happened we just stopped, and passed [several] months without using [the field], and after that we returned to play in the same [space].

The riots were mentioned by several participants because they are a part of local myth that previously affected everyday sporting affairs, interactions, relationships and acquaintances. To support Franz's statement, Kenel further elaborates on the situation leading to the riots:

> Someone [Dominican] died in the cane fields, they said it was a Haitian that killed that guy, when they said this all the Dominicans were very mad. You know the Dominican people, they have this land. They get power and they say if a Haitian kills a Dominican we will fight with them. So they just come to fight with Haitian people. But the Haitian people don't want to fight with Dominican people. You find many Haitian people lose many things in their house, because when this happened they just entered [Haitian homes]. When the Dominicans found an empty house they just moved into the empty house.

Kenel mentioned that he felt the Dominicans attacked the community football programme during the riots because this was something important and close to the culture and interests of Haitians. The football players kept their equipment (footballs, jerseys, shoes and supplies) in a storage room next to the woodshop. One afternoon someone broke into the storage room, and the team then had to rely on organisations that support families in the community and occasionally brought donated supplies such as shoes and footballs. The riots were rooted in what were referred to as ethnic tensions – with the Haitians immediately blamed for what occurred. Although Haitians fled the community, the football equipment was ransacked as an attempt to remove material elements of Haitian identity.

Despite the contestations of the past, nationally and locally, there have been local shifts in power (or control) associated with the sports spaces in Villa Ascension and Caraballo. As noted, in the past Haitians had to use the baseball field in Caraballo to play football, and it was often at the Dominicans' discretion as to whether they would be able to play on a particular day. When asked about any local problems or contestations between football and baseball players, Alexander responded as follows:

> When we played in Caraballo, the Dominicans did not have a problem with us. They enjoyed playing baseball. Even if their time was up, they would still play baseball. Sometimes the Haitians did not have time to play football because the baseball players would take up all the time.

Now the situation has changed and the Haitians have a space for football and the baseball players no longer use the field in Caraballo, suggesting a change in who controls the sports space locally. Brunel notes:

> This field [in Villa Ascension] is not for baseball, it's for football. When [community organisers] started building this village, [one of the leaders] said he will make a field for us to play football, because the Dominicans have their field over there [in Caraballo], and I will make you one to play football. But, the Dominicans' field has problems. That is why they come here to play baseball.

Pedro, one of the Dominican baseball players, offered his insight into how the football players share the sports space with baseball players:

> This field is for the football. When we come here [to the field in Villa Ascension], we want to play [baseball] all the time, but we have to leave for the team who plays football so they can play football. When we start to play, we want to play in the long-term, but when the Haitians come to play football we just leave [so] they [can] start to play football. We can't play on the field in Caraballo, but we share the field here in Ascension for playing baseball and football.

What can be gleaned from Pedro's statement is that there is not a problem with sharing the field since this field is for football. It also shows the influence of Haitians in the community, and this scenario is the opposite of the past situation in Caraballo, when the baseball players would continue their games into the evening hours and not allow Haitians time to play football.

The Haitians consistently mentioned how grateful they were to have a space to practise football every day, with some participants even referring to the field as a possession. The Haitians would allow the Dominicans ample time to practise their sport as well because baseball is important to the people in the country they now reside in. Heterogeneity is complex, and identities are often contested when migrant groups introduce a foreign sport, but the sports field in Villa Ascension is interpreted as a space involving layers of identity where insider and outsider cultures are performed on one field. Several people stated that there are never any problems over using the field, as evidenced in the following comment from Dominique: "We share the field, the Dominicans come to play at 2:00 or 3:00 until 5:00 or 5:30, and after 5:30 when they finish their play . . . we start to play football without any problem." The problems referred to in the past have for the most part been overcome, and according to Kenel "right now, concerning sports, they practise and play together. Now we have this [one recreational] field (space) and we are playing together football and baseball". Alexandre builds on Kenel's response, mentioning that "in sports there is no difference, you can see that when we play football, some Dominicans just come to watch; when they play baseball some Haitians just come to watch".

These comments show that the Haitians are receptive to the fact that baseball is a sport commonly played in the Dominican Republic.

This section attempted to position the staging and performing of identity in the landscape among Dominicans and baseball; the following parts of the chapter focus particular attention on Haitian identity by exploring sense of place.

Haitian identity, sense of place and the social geographies of sport

The geographical concept of sense of place draws from the literature on community and identity (e.g. Rose, 1995; Edensor, 2002; Cresswell, 2004). Sense of place is defined as (Rose, 1995, p.88):

> the phrase used by many geographers when they want to emphasize that places are significant because they are the focus of personal feelings . . . to refer to the significance of particular places for people. These feelings for place are not seen as trivial; geographers argue that senses of place develop from every aspect of individuals' life experience and the senses of place pervade everyday life and experience.

Wise (2013, p.2) notes that sense of place "suggests belonging, socially and emotionally, through attachment and collective community identity". Anderson (1991, p.7) argues that people are bound together through "horizontal comradeship" – which in contemporary times extends beyond national borders (Carter, 2007). In this sense, sport becomes a performance of national identity and connects people "with their home nation and their current place of residence" (Wise, 2011, p.260).

To transnational migrants, achieving a sense of place abroad can be even more complex. In discussions about the importance of football, the men were asked to describe the relevance of the sport to their community identity. Dominique noted that "football is very important for the community because it brings people together". Two other respondents expanded further on the significance of the game:

> The football field brings the people together, such as Sunday afternoons – you can see many people on the field, you have to push [other people] aside so you can see the football game, they [Haitians] are very interested in these games. When we have a game to play, the game really unites the people.
>
> (Jean)

> Football here is much more important. When I play football I can see all the people come to watch: men and women, children and adults. It is different when they play baseball, there are some fans but not much; but during football there are many, it brings the people together.
>
> (Edgard)

Most participant responses were similar, but it is important to emphasise the above responses show differences of expression regarding community, place and meaning surrounding the influence of football on relations and interactions. Some participants suggested togetherness as collectively binding their ethnic community. Others stressed how football brings people together for a positive cause, despite all the negative connotations Haitians are surrounded with when they leave Villa Ascension. Having a designated field allows Haitians to stage and perform their identity in such a manner that when practice and matches occur, the space is exclusively Haitian. This is more difficult in nearby communities/cities, as was observed when travelling with Haitians to other communities to play football. In Montellano, Sosúa, Cabarete or Puerto Plata it appeared as if more segregation exists. Segregation is common in the Dominican Republic, because of contestations over civic and ethnic senses and emotions of nationalism (Howard, 2001).

Relating to discussions of sharing a single space for two sports, this also suggests the social marginalisation of Haitians in Villa Ascension is not apparent as they have access to, and the opportunity to practise, football on a daily basis. Kenel offered another perspective, suggesting that "when you are using sport . . . sport doesn't mean any nations, like Haitian, Dominican". He explains that sport "is for all" because he views sport simply as a means of recreation and opportunity.

Issues and struggles over nationalism still exist but, as stated earlier, Villa Ascension is somewhat different because Haitians and Dominicans are neighbours who commonly interact with each other. Dominicans encourage Haitians to play baseball, as a way of encouraging them to conform to Dominican sporting ideals. Jose, one of the Dominican baseball players, notes that:

> When we play [baseball] it brings many people together – there is no difference between nations. You can see when we play many just come to watch, so yes it [baseball] does bring many people together. Baseball brings Haitians and Dominicans together. When we play we are looking for Haitians to play with us. When we play we just go out to play and ask some Haitians to play. We look for Haitians that know how to play baseball.

Pierre builds on Jose's comments:

> When we play baseball here in Villa Ascension, you find many Haitians come to watch; you even find Haitians playing. We see it is a kind of sport that brings the Haitians and Dominicans together. When we play, the Haitians, even if they can't play [baseball], we support them. The Haitians give the baseball players more experience by allowing baseball players to use the field.

When the Haitians gather to play football in the evening and during the weekend, they use the football field to create a distinctly Haitian space. Typically the Dominicans leave once the Haitians congregate, take the field and commence playing. At least one night each week the football players educate youths in the community about the game. This was interpreted as a type of passive resistance, or an attempt to preserve their sense of Haitian identity and place amongst the youths in the community. Although the Haitians have migrated to the Dominican Republic, in many cases indefinitely, they still want to preserve their identity despite influences from the local Dominican population.

(Re)framing notions of exclusion: collectively Haitian or distinctly masculine

As addressed above, the presence of Haitians in the Dominican Republic comes with social issues and exclusion. However, another form of exclusion in Villa Ascension also became apparent. Being in another country can be difficult for an immigrant group, but they are brought together through cultural ties and bonds, such as the staging and performance of football as an expression of their collective identity. Women and girls also form part of this collective group of Haitians who have an interest in football, but females are excluded from active participation with the men despite congregating in the evenings and weekends to watch football matches. Therefore, women are also an inherent part of the football atmosphere in Villa Ascension. The following comments by Kenel summarise some of the key points of discussion in this section. He notes that the girls "don't play because they have no equipment to play, no uniforms, shoes, that's why they are not going on the field to play". He adds that the girls "appreciate football and if they find some equipment the team can re-form and they can re-start to play".

Although ethnic heterogeneity adds to the complexity and meaning of the game, the space where football was practised was exclusively masculine. This chapter now focuses attention on and questions some of the notions of togetherness discussed above. Inclusion and exclusion at the national scale are often based on an individual's ethnic, or national, identity. Now that the field and Villa Ascension and football have been determined as an important signifier of Haitian identity, the focus of the chapter narrows to address the context of masculinity around issues of inclusion and exclusion. The field itself, designated for football, has become a distinctly masculine space. The Haitian girls in Villa Ascension often seemed disappointed because they were never included in afternoon sporting activities. When observing afternoon practices during the week, the women did take an interest in football, but once the men arrived to practise at 5 p.m. the girls had to remain along the perimeter of the field and only observe. Most females would meet to watch football, but then often collect a football and play on the corners of the field where space was available. Whilst discussions above emphasised that football brought Haitians together, this semblance of togetherness is observed differently based on sex because each evening the men would actively participate, while the women were kept to the sidelines.

Much academic literature has focused on masculinity and football (e.g. Arbena & LaFrance, 2002; Clayton & Humberstone, 2006; Clayton & Harris, 2008). According to Jean, football is a sport for the boys in the community:

Football is 60 percent for boys and 40 percent for girls. Football is a movement sport, when the girls want to play football, only the boys are more interested in the football than the girls.

Dominique further added that "the girls want to play but the problem is they don't know how to play football. But they are very interested to play and watch football." While Jean's 60/40 figures are fairly accurate based on observations, this interviewee did not take into account who is participating and who is watching, as many of the spectators were female. Many of the men mentioned how football has brought the Haitian community together. However, by visualising the space as inherently (or exclusively) masculine, in some regard this takes away from a collective sense of community. Brunel noted that:

> The boys play football [and] the women watch the boys play football. In the same way the boys like the girls watching them playing football – sometimes if there was a girl here, they will ask her: do you like to watch the boys play football?

Haitians are often regarded as the 'other' in the Dominican Republic, but when narrowing the focus on who actively participates in football here, females represent the 'other'. Some of the male football players mentioned that the girls no longer play because they are now married or have children.

Jean alluded to the fact that females in the community do not participate because girls lack the material requisites: "the girls never play because of uniforms, [they don't have] shirts and t-shirts, shoes and socks – that is why they don't play". Dominique said something similar, that "they [girls] don't have something like uniforms or shoes [so] they are missing some things to play football". Brunel also mentioned that "they don't have uniforms to play". It was confirmed by some of the women in the village that they no longer have uniforms; however, men in the community also lacked materials. The men's team did have one set of uniforms that they would wear at weekends when they would invite another Haitian community to Villa Ascension – but only enough for the team and not everyone else. Moreover, football boots, shin pads and socks were often supplied by organisations who visited the community. One particular organisation relied on the assistance of volunteer community members, and many Haitian men who played football would assist alongside several women. To thank the Haitians who volunteered, they were rewarded with donated football supplies. The men, primarily those who played for the community team, would immediately claim the football supplies.

Brunel mentioned that "there was a team in the past for the girls". However, they had to use the field during the day when the men were not using the field. Jean discussed a time when girls did play, but refers back to the lack of supplies:

> In the past, when we had a girls' team, when we would play the girls play with the boys, sometimes we mixed, and with the boys' team you find some girls side-by-side. Sometimes the girls play with the boys, but when a girls' team existed, we had other teams of girls come here to play with the girls from Sosúa. But when we evaluate them they don't have any shoes. When the other

team comes they have all the things—uniforms and protection. So they stopped playing until they have some things to play with.

(Jean)

Alexander wanted to advise some of the girls to re-form the team and play football "because football is a good thing for the women too". He pointed to the fact that women are interested in football. If the women re-form a team in the future, this could perhaps contribute to the experience of Haitian women who face the same social difficulties as men in the Dominican Republic. During the field research, when another Haitian community visited Villa Ascension, several hundred Haitians (both men and women) would congregate on the field. The scene suggested Haitians had forged a sense of place in the Dominican Republic by playing and watching football, and greater notions of social exclusion amongst the collective group were not an issue during these times. It is important to be critical of local situations and acknowledge the role of women and football, especially since many of the comments made by the male football players reflect socially constructed gendered norms. In terms of being together, collectively, displays of masculinity led to interpretations of an exclusively male space.

Conclusion

This chapter has discussed the role football plays in the everyday lives of people residing in a Haitian migrant community in the Dominican Republic. Whilst much of the published work on football and migration has focused on the lives of elite (male) professional football players, there is more to learn about the ways in which recreational football helps shape the experiences of people who move between nations. In this sense, the chapter has highlighted the importance of sport and recreational spaces in shaping the ways in which the men in Villa Ascension are able to use football as a link to their homeland and to reinforce their cultural ideals and identity. When people relocate to another country, they often stage and perform their cultural ideals and identity as a way to connect themselves to their home. This allows people to better foster a sense of place in their new home. Yet for all the ways in which football is important in reaffirming a national identity and providing participants with a real sense of place, the chapter has also drawn attention to the ways in which this space, or defined place for football, is distinctly male – and so female migrants are excluded in some ways. Moreover, this research shows how there are multiple identities at play here and that inclusion (and exclusion) take on many different forms. It is also important to reaffirm that the research findings presented in this chapter are of the experiences of men in a particular place at a particular time. As noted at various junctures, the experiences of those in Villa Ascension may be quite different from the experiences of Haitians in other parts of the Dominican Republic who do not have such a dedicated space for football. One thing that Haitian communities across the Puerto Plata region did was to organise matches and perform football in a distinctly Haitian atmosphere. To refer back to Anderson (1991, p.7), this displays "horizontal comradeship" and a semblance of identity that binds Haitians together.

References

Anderson, B. (1991) *Imagined Communities* (London: Verso).

Arbena, J. and LaFrance, D. (2002) (Eds.) *Sport in Latin America and the Caribbean.* Wilmington, DE: Scholarly Resources Inc.

Augelli, J. (1980) Nationalization of Dominican Borderlands. *Geographical Review* 70(1): 19–35.

Bairner, A. (2001) *Sport, Nationalism, and Globalization: European and North American Perspectives.* Albany: State University of New York Press.

Baller, S. (2007) Transforming Urban Landscapes: Soccer Fields as Sites of Urban Sociability in the Agglomeration of Dakar. *African Identities* 5(2): 217–30.

Carter, T. (2002) Baseball Arguments: *Aficionismo* and Masculinity at the Core of *Cubanidad.* In J. Mangan and L. DaCosta (Eds.) *Sport in Latin American Society.* London: Frank Cass (117–38).

Carter, T. (2007) Family Networks, State Interventions and the Experience of Cuban Transnational Sport Migration. *International Review for the Sociology of Sport* 42(4): 371–89.

Clayton, B. and Harris, J. (2008) Our Friend Jack: Alcohol, Friendship and Masculinity in University football. *Annals of Leisure Research* 11(3/4): 311–30.

Clayton, B. and Humberstone, B. (2006) Men's Talk: A (Pro)feminist Analysis of Male University Football Players' Discourse. *International Review for the Sociology of Sport* 41(3/4): 295–316.

Cresswell, T. (2004) *Place: A Short Introduction.* Oxford: Blackwell.

Cronin, M. and Mayall, D. (1998) *Sporting Nationalisms: Identity, Ethnicity, Immigration and Assimilation.* London: Frank Cass.

DeLyser, D., Herbert, S., Aitken, S., Crang, M. and McDowell, L. (2010) (Eds.) *The SAGE Handbook of Qualitative Geography.* London: Sage.

Edensor, T. (2002) *National Identity, Popular Culture and Everyday Life.* Oxford: Berg.

FIFA (2011) Dominican Republic on FIFA.com. Retrieved 9 March 2011 from: http://www.fifa.com/associations/association=dom/index.html.

Gaffney, C. (2008) *Temples of the Earthbound Gods: Stadiums in the Cultural Landscapes of Rio de Janeiro and Buenos Aires.* Austin: University of Texas Press.

Gedda, G. (2009) *The Dominican Connection.* New York: Eloquent Books.

Goodwin, P. (2011) (Ed.) *Global Studies: Latin America and the Caribbean, Fourteenth Edition.* New York: McGraw-Hill.

Grainger, A. (2006) From Immigrant to Overstayer: Samoan Identity, Rugby, and Cultural Politics of Race and Nation in Aotearoa/New Zealand. *Journal of Sport & Social Issues* 30(1): 45–61.

Gruffudd, P. (1999) Nationalism. In P. Cloke, P. Crang and M. Goodwin (Eds.) *Introducing Human Geographies.* London: Arnold (199–206).

Harris, J. and Parker, A. (2009) (Eds.) *Sport and Social Identities.* Basingstoke: Palgrave Macmillan.

Howard, D. (2001) *Coloring the Nation: Race and Ethnicity in the Dominican Republic.* Oxford: Signal Books.

Kirch, J. (2002) *El Béisbol: The Pleasures and Passions of the Latin American Game.* Chicago, IL: Ivan R. Dee.

Klein, A. (1989) Baseball as Underdevelopment: The Political-Economy of Sport in the Dominican Republic. *Sociology of Sport Journal* 6(2): 95–112.

Klein, A. (1991) *Sugarball: The American Game the Dominican dream*. New Haven, CT: Yale University Press.

Klein, A. (2008) Progressive Ethnocentrism: Ideology and Understanding in Dominican Baseball. *Journal of Sport & Social Issues* 32(2): 121–38.

Langellier, K. (2010) Performing Somali Identity in the Diaspora. *Cultural Studies* 24(1): 66–94.

MacClancy, J. (1996) (Ed.) *Sport, Identity and Ethnicity*. Oxford: Berg.

Olwig, K. (2013) Notions and Practices of Difference: An Epilogue on the Ethnography of Diversity. *Identities: Global Studies in Culture and Power* 20(4): 471–9.

Rose, G. (1995) Place and Identity: A Sense of Place. In D. Massey and P. Jess (Eds.) *A Place in the World*. Oxford: Oxford University Press (87–132).

Ruck, R. (1991) *The Tropic of Baseball: Baseball in the Dominican Republic*. Westport, CT: Meckler.

San Miguel, P. (2005) *The Imagined Island: History, Identity, & Utopia in Hispaniola*. Chapel Hill: University of North Carolina Press.

Shobe, H. (2008) Football and the Politics of Place: Football Club Barcelona and Catalonia, 1975–2005. *Journal of Cultural Geography* 25(1): 87–105.

Vertinsky, P. and Bale, J. (2004) (Eds.) *Sites of Sport: Space, Place, Experience*. New York: Routledge.

Walseth, K. (2006) Sport and Belonging. *International Review for the Sociology of Sport* 41(3/4): 447–64.

Watson, A. and Till, K. (2010) Ethnography and Participant Observation. In D. DeLyser, S. Herbert, S. Aitken, M. Crang and L. McDowell (Eds.) *The SAGE Handbook of Qualitative Geography*. London: Sage (121–37).

Werbner, P. (1996) Our Blood Is Green: Cricket, Identity and Social Empowerment among British Pakistanis. In J. MacClancy (Ed.) *Sport, Identity and Ethnicity*. Oxford: Berg (87–111).

Wise, N. (2011) Transcending Imaginations through Football Participation and Narratives of the *Other*: Haitian National Identity in the Dominican Republic. *Journal of Sport & Tourism* 16(3): 259–75.

Wise, N. (2013) Maintaining Dominican Identity in the Dominican Republic, Forging a Baseball Landscape in Villa Ascension. *International Review for the Sociology of Sport*. DOI: 10.1177/1012690213478252.

Wise, N. (2014). Belonging, Togetherness and Sense of Place: Identity, Geography and Haitian Footballers in the Dominican Republic. In K. Spraklen, S. Dun and N. Wise (Eds.) *Game Changer: The Transformative Potential of Sport*. Oxford: Interdisciplinary Press.

Wylie, J. (2007) *Landscape*. London: Routledge.

Yassim, M. (2013) Cricket as a Vehicle for Community Cohesion: Building Bridges with British Muslims. *Journal of Islamic Marketing* 4: 218–27.

Conclusion: Playing the long-ball game

Future directions in the study of football and migration

Richard Elliott and John Harris

Football and migration have been entwined since the late nineteenth century. Indeed the development and diffusion of the game beyond British soil occurred as a consequence of the movements of migrant workers. Railwaymen, electrical contractors, sailors and tradesmen were amongst some of the earliest migrants to take the game to others countries and continents. Arguably, most famous amongst this group was Charles Miller, the son of a Scottish railway engineer. Born in São Paulo, Brazil, but educated in Southampton, England, when Charles Miller returned to Brazil in 1894 he took with him two footballs and a copy of the rules of association football. Widely credited as the 'father of football' in Brazil, Miller is also remembered in Southampton. A mural leading to Southampton FC's St Mary's stadium depicts an image of him framed alongside a representation of the statue of Christ the Redeemer in Rio de Janeiro. An inscription reads: "In 1894 Charles Miller took two footballs to Brazil and the rest is history . . ." The images and text underline the ubiquity of migration in the development of the modern game.

Football has changed enormously since Charles Miller left England to return to Brazil. However, some 120 years later, migration continues to influence the development of the game in a range of social and cultural contexts. A growing body of research, framed within the broader study of athletic labour migration and viewed through a variety of sociological, historical, geographical and anthropological lenses, has drawn attention to a range of debates that reflect in the interplay that exists between football and migration. The chapters in this collection have contributed to these debates in a number of ways; they enhance and extend our understanding in some areas, whilst providing new directions for research in others. When considered collectively, a complex, interdependent and disjunctive series of processes emerge.

These processes are complex, because, like many facets of life in a globalised world, the development of association football has not followed an even trajectory over time (Elliott, 2013). For example, whilst some countries, such as those in South and Central Europe and Latin America, largely accepted the diffusion of the game from England at the end of the nineteenth century, others, such as the United States, showed greater resistance. Moreover, whilst those nations situated in the capitalist West have been able to engage with the ongoing processes of commercialisation that have fundamentally changed the nature of professional football in the last four decades or so, those in the communist east bowed to the perceived superior power of their enforced political ideologies (Molnar & Maguire, 2008; Elliott, 2013). As a result of the uneven nature of these global flows, professional football's contemporary political economy must be viewed as a web of interdependent relationships, relationships that are shaped by a dynamic and constantly changing power geometry and fuelled by a range of political, economic, social, historical, cultural and geographical factors.

The authors who have contributed to this collection have ably captured the complexities of many of the migrations being made in football. By drawing on a number of different perspectives, and by using a range of different case studies to do so, the authors have shown just how complex and multifaceted the various processes at work actually are. They have shown, for example, that the movements of workers in the contemporary game can be better explained with reference to a range of transnational networks that have developed, and facilitated, these movements over long periods of time. They have also shown that migration in football (at the professional level at least) often mimics the patterns of movements of workers in other spheres of employment, thus largely from south to north and from east to west. Whilst the specific nuances of professional football's contemporary global employment market must clearly be taken into account, it would seem that there are aspects of these particular migrations that can be explained using some of the theories and perspectives that have been applied to make sense of the movements of other categories of migrants – the highly skilled, for example (see Jonathan Beaverstock's work in this area).

It is perhaps when analysing some of the specific places and contexts in which migration takes place that the particularities of football's contemporary global employment market become most visible. The case studies in this collection have highlighted a range of issues and challenges for a number of specific regions as they adapt to their roles as hosts, donors or, most likely, a combination of both. A range of geopolitical challenges and the legacy of state intervention have been identified as contributing to the movements of workers into and out of some leagues. In other contexts, the cultural similarities and/or differences, the particular working practices and the ambition to create a better future have contributed. In some places, relatively simple economics still seem to largely drive the employment market. What the case studies reinforce is that the movements being made cannot be explained with reference to any single factor. To be truly meaningful, the migrations of football workers should be considered in a multi-processual context. Some of the contributors in this collection have done this by analysing aspects of the macro-level structural environment in which migration occurs. Others have focused on the individual agents and their specific experiences as they traverse the globe in search of employment in the game.

Whilst it is important to examine and make sense of the structures through and in which migration is framed, it is vitally important to remember that migration is a human endeavour comprised of individuals and groups moving into, out of and through a range of socially and culturally distinct spaces. The manner in which each migrant will experience their particular sojourn will depend on a number of factors. For example, the chapters in this collection have shown how a clash of employment cultures in terms of perceived effort and professionalism might influence the ways in which some migrant workers experience their particular relocation. Concomitantly, acceptance of the very specific rituals and practices that accompany employment in professional football and the migrants' capacity to be successfully assimilated into the dressing-room environment would also seem important to the success or failure of a particular migrant player.

For specific types of migrants, the challenges might be different. Migrant youth players have featured in a number of the chapters in this collection and, it would seem, the path to elite athletic employment is one that is fraught with difficulties for these types of 'workers'. For example, the tension that exists between securing a professional contract *or* an education seems problematic for some players. Whilst clubs clearly have an obligation to provide their youth players with an appropriate education (be they migrants or otherwise), the value placed on this education would seem to come second to their development as marketable (playing) commodities who can perform for their own club or be sold on for a profit to another. Such tensions, it would seem, can create uncertain futures for potential migrants who come from families where an emphasis is placed on education first and football second. In these sorts of contexts, the (im)mobility of players must be viewed as being dependent on those individuals and/or groups that mediate the process of migration.

For other migrants, such as those whose interest in and experience of football are situated outside of the professional sphere, the role that it can play takes on an altogether different symbolism. Here, then, it is important to remember the function that the game can play in everyday life as an important social and cultural anchor for specific migrant groups. Whilst much of the research that has sought to make sense of the relationship between football and migration has, to this point, focused almost exclusively on aspects of the men's elite game, for many other migrants football continues to provide meaning in their lives. It has the capacity to bring together migrant communities and to connect people to place through a set of shared values and beliefs.

Wherever the game is played, and whoever plays it, the relationship between football and migration exists on a number of levels and in a multitude of different ways. This relationship is, of course, never going to remain static. It is dynamic and constantly in a state of flux. In this respect, the chapters in this collection should not be viewed as definitive representations in any way. Rather, they should be seen to reflect a series of processes, viewed through a number of competing perspectives, at particular points in time, across and through a range of different spaces. To this end, the authors of the chapters in the collection have posited a number of potentially fruitful suggestions for future research in this area.

For example, questions have been raised over the perceived usefulness of existing theoretical approaches to the study of athletic migration, which perhaps too often focus on trying to explain the macro-level structures in which migration 'occurs' and sometimes miss the most important actors – the migrants themselves

(Carter, 2011). Equally, other studies have been criticised for placing too great an emphasis on the minutiae of the migrants' lived experiences and failing to take fully into account the structures in which their movements are framed and facilitated. Of course, research that seeks to enhance our understanding of the various migrations that are occurring in the game should seek to navigate a path between overly structuralist approaches and those that are deemed to be too agentic (Maguire & Falcous, 2011), one where migrants are not viewed as passive social agents but, rather, as dynamic interlocutors (Carter, 2013) whose movements are framed within the local contexts between which they are situated.

A number of approaches have been applied in this collection and, on the basis of the contributions presented, some future considerations for research tracing the relationship between football and migration can be proposed. These questions should, of course, only be seen as reflecting small, but nonetheless important, steps in the next phase of research in this area. As the game continues to develop, other questions will inevitably emerge in the coming years. For ease of reference, we will list the various questions/areas for analysis that have emerged from the chapters here.

1 Do links exist between migration and an increased sense of politicism for migrant footballers? Some evidence exists to suggest that this may be the case.

2 Do some migrant footballers live their lives in 'bubbles' where they largely reject the values of host cultures or are they more likely to live 'translocal' lives that reflect a mix of realities?

3 How significant are working cultures in the migration process for migrant footballers? How do they differ across social and cultural contexts and how do they influence working relationships if/when they clash? How do migrants act as key agents in processes of cultural transformation in host leagues/nations?

4 What are the experiences of coaches, managers and other associated migrants connected to the game? Up to this point, the majority of studies have examined senior male professional players. These other workers have been mostly overlooked.

5 What is the role of female players? Whilst more research is now beginning to emerge, what else can be learnt about this particular group and how could this understanding inform the development of the women's game?

6 What is the role of semi-core and peripheral regions in the production, export and import of professional footballers? Much of the research on non-core regions/leagues conducted to date has focused on the export of (mostly youth) players from African nations, but what about regions such as North America, Asia, Australasia, Eastern Europe and the Middle East?

7 How symbolic is football for migrants not associated with the professional game? How important is the game as a component of everyday life for amateur/recreational players living as migrants? How does it include/exclude particular groups of migrants in these contexts?

8   How important is the family in mediating the process of migration in different cultural and familial contexts?
9   What rituals are associated with acceptance into professional football cultures? Do these differ for migrant players and do they change in different cultural contexts and regions?
10   Through what sorts of mechanisms are migrations being facilitated? The recruitment of elite athletes is rarely straightforward – it is often complex and multifaceted. Is this the case in professional football?

Research tracing the relationship that exists between football and migration has developed markedly in the last three decades, and we hope that this collection makes some small contribution to a number of ongoing debates across the social sciences. More than that though, the intention of the book was to explore aspects of the relationship between football and migration that have been largely overlooked in research up to this point. In this respect, we hope that this text has the capacity to open up new and previously unconsidered avenues for investigation that will, ultimately, move our understanding of football and migration, and its perspectives, places and players, forward.

References

Carter, T. (2011) *In Foreign Fields: The Politics and Experiences of Transnational Sport Migration*. London: Pluto Press.
Carter, T. (2013) Re-placing Sport Migrants: Moving beyond the Institutional Structures Informing International Sport Migration. *International Review for the Sociology of Sport* 48(1): 66–82.
Elliott, R. (2013) New Europe, New Chances? The Migration of Professional Footballers to Poland's Ekstraklasa. *International Review for the Sociology of Sport* 48(6): 736–50.
Maguire, J. and Falcous, M. (2011) (Eds.) *Sport and Migration: Borders, Boundaries and Crossings*. London: Routledge.
Molnar, G. and Maguire, J. (2008) Hungarian Footballers on the Move: Issues and Observations on the First Migratory Phase. *Sport in Society* 11(1): 74–89.

Index

The word order is letter by letter; locators to plans and tables are in *italics*; the letter 'n' refers to an end note; years when appearing next to locators have been placed in brackets to distinguish them from the page numbers; and numbers in headings have been listed as if they are written (viz. 90-minute rule).